History of the parishes of East and West Ham. Edited and revised by G. Pagenstecher.

Katharine Fry, G. Pagenstecher

July 2014

To Len
Congratulations on your very special day
9th July 1934
Have a really lovely day
Love Marion & George xx

History of the parishes of East and West Ham ... Edited and revised by G. Pagenstecher.
Fry, Katharine
British Library, Historical Print Editions
British Library
Pagenstecher, G.
1888
vi. 285 p. ; 4°.
10352.l.20.

DEO CONFIDIMUS

HISTORY OF THE PARISHES

OF

EAST AND WEST HAM.

of

East and West H

by

KATHARINE FRY.

Edited and revised by G. PAGENSTECHER.

[PRINTED FOR PRIVATE CIRCULATION]

LONDON

1888.

PRINTED BY AUG. SIEGLE, 30, LIME STREET, LONDON, E.C

PREFACE.

THOUGH fully aware that prefaces are seldom read, it would be unpardonable to offer this publication to the subscribers without some introductory remarks. My chief object, however, is to have it fully understood that, in editing Miss Fry's history of the parishes of East and West Ham, I have not been actuated by personal vanity or ambition, but rather by love of the subject and respect for the memory of the authoress—or perhaps still more by the desire, that so valuable a manuscript, which contains a great deal of accurate and solid information as regards this locality, might not remain buried in oblivion. In undertaking this task, I am fully conscious of my own incompetency, and that large allowances must be made for my shortcomings, still I cherish the hope that my humble efforts may be somewhat appreciated, and that this publication may prove not only valuable to the professed antiquary, or to anyone who may hereafter attempt to treat the subject more completely, but also interesting and entertaining to the generality of readers. Since engravings preserve the memory of things and convey a much better idea to the mind, than written descriptions, several woodcuts have been introduced, some of which are made from sketches by the accomplished authoress herself, and I am not without hope, that these embellishments may meet with general approbation.

It may not be out of place to insert here a short biographical sketch of the authoress, whose memory will always be regarded with feelings of respect by all who had the happiness of her personal acquaintance. Miss Katharine Fry was the eldest daughter of Mr. Joseph and the celebrated Mrs. Elizabeth Fry, and passed the greater portion of her days at the little village of Plashet, leading a life of tranquil retirement, yet full of activity. Being devoted to archaeological and topographical researches, and pursuing with great eagerness the traces of ancient times and manners, she used occasionally to write interesting articles on antiquarian subjects, which were published in the "Transactions of the Essex Archaeological Society," of which she was a distinguished member. At the same time she collected with great zeal and industry an immense amount of valuable material of local interest, which by degrees took the shape of an historical account of this neighbourhood. Though highly gifted and accomplished, Miss Fry was most unassuming and modest, and it was very seldom, and then only to her most intimate and congenial friends, that she disclosed the treasures of her richly stored mind.

In the village she was highly respected and beloved by all, and many little traits are remembered both of her kindness and liberality to the poor, and her love for the young. Enjoying a freshness and vigour of body and mind, which only a few weeks before her end were clouded by an apoplectic fit, she peacefully expired at her residence "Plashet Cottage," on the 15th of May, 1886, at the ripe age of 85 years.

In concluding these few remarks, it is my pleasing duty to offer my sincerest thanks to all my kind friends, from whom I have received most valuable assistance and information, as well as great encouragement.

PORTWAY, WEST HAM, 1888.   THE EDITOR.

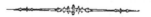

INTRODUCTION.

A S the continual passage of travellers obliterates the foot-
prints of those who have gone the same road before, so
do the successive generations of men destroy in their
onward course the traces of their predecessors in the
localities which they inhabit. The necessities of the present race
sweep away the remains of the former until, especially in suburban
districts, everything becomes so modern and utilitarian, that a
description of the places, as they once were, would sound almost
like a romance. But there are fragments, illustrative of former days,
scattered amongst ancient books, or buried in the Rolls of our Public
Records, which, if collected and arranged in an accessible, simple
form, would assume considerable local interest, especially for the
inhabitants of the district to which they relate.

To do this, as it concerns the parishes of East and West Ham,
is the object of this collection. Though the matter contained in it
may probably be familiar to the professed and learned antiquary,
the general reader will doubtless find in it facts and information both
novel and curious. In combining information of a popular character
with the results of antiquarian research, it has been my endeavour
to maintain strict historical accuracy, and in cases, where the facts
and the evidences respecting them are only fragmentary, no attempt
has been made to embellish them with imaginary incidents, or to
supply suppositious links to a broken chain. To those, therefore,
who seek amusement only, and are accustomed to ancient story as
prepared for them in the lighter literature of the day, this collection
will, it is feared, prove somewhat dry. The historical notices are

obviously rather disjointed, as is generally the case in topographical histories, since the circumscribed space of a parish, or even of a town, rarely is the theatre of historical events or romantic incidents. However, it is hoped, that to the residents in the parishes of East and West Ham the information collected in the following pages may not be without interest.

PLASHET COTTAGE.   KATHARINE FRY.

History of the Parishes

OF

✦ EAST ✦ AND ✦ WEST ✦ HAM. ✦

CHAPTER I.

(CONTENTS).

ROMAN, SAXON, AND DANISH PERIOD.
NORMAN CONQUEST.

HE parishes of East and West Ham occupy the south-west corner of the county of Essex between the confluences of the River Lea and Roding with the Thames, which river forms their southern boundary, whilst on the north they extend to Epping Forest. There is no doubt, that the surface of the whole upland in this part of the county was originally covered with primaeval forest and that this only ceased where the morass, formed by the great estuary of the Thames, forbade the growth of trees. HOLINSHED in his "Chronicles" published in 1577, says of it: "I find also by good record, that all Essex hathe in time past wholie been forest ground, save one (Cantred or) Hundred; but how long it is since it lost the said domination, in good sooth, I do not read."

That this district was occupied by the Romans is proved by the discovery of a Roman Cemetery near East Ham Church, during the

B

construction of the great High Level Sewer, in November 1863. "In the process of excavation the workmen came unexpectedly on a large stone sarcophagus within which were two skeletons lying at opposite ends, one larger and more entire than the other. A skull was at each end and in one the teeth were nearly complete, the entire skeleton, indeed, being very perfect. When first found one of the skeletons was

Roman Sarcophagus and Leaden Coffins, in the entrance to East Ham Church, discovered in a field near. Nov. 1863.

entire and but little decayed. Two leaden coffins were also discovered, and close to them many bones and cinerary urns. Persons skilled in such matters pronounced both the stone and leaden coffins to be un-questionably Roman, although no date whatever could be traced." The Rev. EDWARD F. BOYLE, then Vicar of East Ham, to whom we are indebted for this interesting description, was very active in his exertions for the preservation of these remains of antiquity, which must be at least one thousand four hundred years old, and permitted them to be placed under the tower of the Church, used as a porch. After they had been open to public inspection for about six weeks, the leaden coffins were taken away to be deposited in the British Museum.

Roman remains may also be seen at Barking, where Roman material is worked into mediaeval walls; and at Uphall Farm, which is about a quarter of a mile north of that town, there are still visible the remains of a considerable ancient entrenchment, more than a mile in circumference. Mr. LETHIEULLIER, a late lord of the manor, in his unpublished history of Barking, thinks "that this entrenchment was too large for a camp;" his opinion therefore, is, that it was the site of a Roman town, but he confessses that no traces of buildings have been found on the spot, and accounts for it on the supposition, that the materials were used for building Barking Abbey, and for repairing it after it was burnt down by the Danes. As a confirmation of this opinion he relates that, upon viewing the ruins of the Abbey in 1750, he found the foundations of one of the great pillars composed of Roman bricks.

At Stratford-le-Bow, scarcely four miles distant from East Ham, sepulchral remains were found in considerable quantities, and in the year 1844 a leaden coffin. CAMDEN, a learned antiquarian who, in 1586, published his Britannia, states "that urns and other antiquities were found at Leyton, by the site of the old road from Essex through Old Ford to London, now called Blind Lane." It has also been conjectured, that the road leading from West Ham to Plashet, called "Portway," derived its name from its Roman origin; this road led to North End in East Ham, and thence down Jews Farm by the ferry over the river Roding to the earthworks at Uphall. We may, therefore, fairly assume, though we have no authentic record of it, that this part of Essex was at one time occupied by the Romans.

Meagre and scanty as the annals of the period are, which followed the departure of the Romans from Great Britain, A.D. 432, we possess authentic evidence that the marshes, bordering on the Thames, in what is now called the parish of East Ham, were available property at the time of the Saxon Heptarchy; for it is recorded that King Offa [1] endowed the monastery of St. Peter's, Westminster, with two hides of land in "Hamme." This gift was subsequently confirmed by King Edgar, and afterwards also by King Edward the Confessor, in a charter, dated January, 1066, wherein amongst other grants made to Westminster Abbey by the kings, his predecessors, two hides of land in "Hamme" are recited. In Domesday-Book [2] the estate, owned by St. Peter's in "Hamme," is called "a Manor and two hides of land, containing always one carucate (or plough-gang) of arable, worth in Saxon times twenty shillings, but in Norman sixty shillings, then three bordars, afterwards five, and woodland to find pannage for eight hogs." In 1542, this property of the Dean and Chapter of Westminster was described as "a farm in the marshes of East Ham, near Barking." Part of this estate was sold by the Dean and Chapter, and afterwards converted into the North Woolwich public gardens on the bank of the Thames— alienated, after a possession of over twelve hundred years, by a corporation of clergymen, to become a tea-garden!

In Saxon, if not in Roman times, the great highway leading from London into the Eastern Counties passed along the northern extremity of these parishes, crossing the river Lea at Old Ford, and the river Rheding or Roding [3] at Ilford.

It is considered, that the earliest mention of this road, which is now called the Romford Road, is on the occasion of the death of

---

[1] Dart in his history of Westminster Abbey calls Offa, the great King of Mercia, but bearing in mind that Westminster Abbey was founded by the Saxon King Sebert, it is more probable that it was Offa, King of the East Saxons, whose family held large possessions in this neighbourhood. Moreover, Speed in his history of Great Britain says: "This King Offa, the son of Sighere and Queen Oswith his wife, was a man noted for his comely feature and sweet countenance. He both enlarged with buildings and enriched with lands the goodly and beautiful church of Westminster."

[2] Domesday — the name is probably derived from "Domus dei" as the treasury, in which it was kept at Winchester, was named. In an appendix to the work itself it is called "Liber de Wintonia," or the Winchester book from its first place of custody.

[3] Rheding or Roding from the primaeval root "rhe" to "flow" and "ing" a "plain or meadow."

St. Erkenwald at Barking Abbey,[1] in the year 685, when on a visit to his sister, St. Ethelburga, the first Abbess. It is said of him that he discharged his episcopal functions in a missionary spirit amongst a semi-barbarous people, and even when aged and infirm his pious labours did not cease, as he was carried throughout his diocese in a litter constantly teaching and preaching to his flock. In a work entitled "The Golden Legend," printed by WYNKYN DE WORDE, in 1527, the following description is given of the circumstances attending the removal of his corpse from Barking Abbey to St. Paul's, London, through Ilford and Stratford:

"Whan this blyssed saynt Erkenwolde, as God wold, came to Berkyng, he fell into a grete sekeness, in whiche he ended his temporal lyf, and for so moche as he knewe it before, he sent for his servauntes and such as were drawynge to hym and gave to them holsome and swete lessons, and blyssed them with grete devocyon and amonge them he yelded up his spiryte to Almyghty God; in whose passyng was felt a mervaylous swete odour, as the hous had been full of swete baume. And whan the high Chanons of Saynt Poules at London herde this and the Monkes of Chirchesey also, anone they came to this holy body for to have it. And the Nonnes sayd, they ought to have the body bycause he dyed there, and also bycause he was theyr founder. And the Monkes sayd, they ought rather to have hym, bycause he was bothe theyr Abbot and founder. Than the Chapytre of Poules and the people sayd, that they strove in vayne, for he sholde be brought to London into his own chirche.

---

[1] Barking Abbey, one of the richest and oldest Abbeys in England and dedicated to the Virgin Mary, is said to have been the first convent for women in this kingdom. It was founded about 670 for Benedictine nuns by St. Erkenwald, Bishop of London, who was closely allied to the Saxon monarchs, in compliance with the earnest desire of his sister Ethelburga, who was appointed the first Abbess. The Abbey was destroyed in the year 870 by the Danes, but rebuilt in the tenth century; there is scarcely a vestige now remaining of the once magnificent Abbey. It was surrendered to King Henry VIII. who granted a pension of 200 marks to Dorothy Barley, the last Abbess, and various pensions to the nuns who were then 30 in number.

Barking or Berkyng probably derived from " beorc "—a birch tree, and "ing"—a plain or meadow.

"Thus there was grete stryfe, and at the last they of London toke up the body and bore it towarde London and as they went, there fell a grete tempest, and so moche water[1] that they myght not passe, but were constrayned to set downe the corpse, and in all the storme the tapers that were about the body were alwaye bryght brennynge. And than the Nonnes sayd, that God shewed well, that they of London ought not to have hym, bycause of the tempest. And at the last after many wordes, there was a Clerke, whiche had ben longynge to St. Erkenwolde and sawe this stryfe and strode up and commanded scylence, and tolde the people a grete commendacyon of the vertuous lyf of this holy Saynt and sayd, that it was not honest ne accordynge to mysentreate the holy body by vyolent hands, but let us beseche Almyghty God with good devocyon and meekness of herte for to shewe to us some token by revelacyon, in what place this holy body shall rest. And all the people consented thereto and kneled downe and prayed devoutly, and as they were in prayer they sawe the water divided lyke as it did to Moyses in the Reed See, and to the children of Israel goynge through into the deserte. In lyke wyse God gave a drye path to the people of London for to convey this holy body through the water to the Cytei and anone they toke up the body with grete honour and reverence and by one assent they bare it through the path, the water standyng up on every syde; and the people not wetyng theyr feet and so they came to Stratforde and set down the bere in a fayre mede full of floures. And anone after the weder began to wexe fayre and clere after the tempest, and the tapers were made to brenne without puttynge to fyre of any mannes hande. And thus it pleased our Lorde for to multyplye myracles to the honour and worshyp of this holy Saynt."

Picturesque as this legend is, it must not be accepted as contemporary authority, but as this event occurred about the year 685—two hundred and fifty years after the Romans left Britain—it goes far to prove, that the road between London and Barking passed through the sites of the present towns of Ilford and Stratford, and that along the line of the present highway a road did exist in Saxon or even Roman times.

---

[1] In the Antwerp Edition of the Acta Sanctorum (1645 — 1794) the name of this water is called "Yleford."

For two hundred years after the death of St. Erkenwald no particular circumstance is mentioned affecting the district of Ham. It was included in the territory called East Anglia, which was ceded by King Alfred to Guthrum the Dane, in 878. In this treaty, which is still extant, the boundaries are defined; one of these was the River Lea.

It was on occasion of a terrible invasion of the Danes, in 895, that Alfred the Great undertook a work, which has proved of essential benefit to this district. The Danes had drawn their ships up the River Lea to a place about twenty miles above London—either Ware or Hertford— where they constructed a fortress, and wintered. The citizens of London and others, who attacked them, were repulsed by them with great loss. During the following harvest, however, Alfred with his army encamped in the neighbourhood of the City, to protect the inhabitants whilst they reaped their corn. Riding one day by the banks of the Lea he conceived the idea of altering the channel of that river, so as to cut off the retreat of the enemy.

HENRY HUNTINGDON, to whose opinion SIR HENRY SPELMAN inclines, says "that he caused the mouth of the Lea to be opened and divided into three parts, there being, it seems, some straitness before towards the mouth which kept up the waters above, and at low water made a great descent of the current, as we may perceive by the Danes toughing (towing?) of their ships up against it. The mouth being opened into three several branches, it laid the stream so low as moored (stranded?) their ships, so as they could not at their pleasure have them forth again." It is SPELMAN's opinion "that this might be the first winning of that great level of rich meadow and pasture from Hertford to Bow, which divers ways now beneficial, through the fertility thereof both to the City and the towns adjoining, is likely enough to have been formerly only fens and waters, and to have had the improvement of it first occasioned by that act of the king's."

The numerous water-courses connected with several mills of more modern date render it difficult of clear elucidation, yet the name of the Channelsea river, given to one of the branches of the Lea, seems to point to this origin.

During the following reigns the terrible wars, that raged between the Anglo-Saxon and Danish races, also swept occasionally over this district, but we are left to infer, that events recorded in history must have had great influence on its local condition, until the time of King Edward the Confessor.

Of the owners of the land, its extent, and population at that period, undoubted information is given in Domesday-Book. From this indisputable authority we learn that, in the reign of Edward the Confessor, two Saxon freemen, Alestan and Leured, held each a manor of considerable extent in Hamme, that the Abbey of St. Peter's, Westminster, held a third but much smaller estate, and that Edwin, a free Priest, possessed a small estate, adjacent to that of Leured, consisting of three virgates of land, containing one carucate of arable, nine acres of meadow, and forest sufficient to afford pannage for ten hogs; to this little estate two bordars (cottagers) were attached. A socman [1] also held thirty acres of land close to the manor of Leured. For " Edwin the Priest " there was doubtless a presbytery, and probably a church. The silence of " Domesday " by no means proves that a church did not exist. The architecture of East Ham Church permits the idea, that part of that most curious edifice may even have existed at this date.

A manor (manerium) was originally so called from being the residence of the owner, surrounded by an estate, part of which, called demesne (*Lat.* dominium, *Norm.* de mayne, de mansio), he retained in his own hands for the use of the family; another part was divided amongst the tenants, and the remainder served as common pasture for himself and his tenants.

The manor of Leured seems to have been to the East and North side of Ham, in what is now East Ham, and about Forest Gate. It comprised from 800 to 1000 acres of arable, 50 acres of meadow, and woodland sufficient to afford " pannage " from the acorns and beech mast for 700 hogs. There were 34 villains, 3 boors, and 19 serfs on the estate, 8 head of cattle and 20 hogs; the annual value was £10.

The manor belonging to Alestan was worth £16 per annum. It contained about 1,040 acres of arable, 60 acres of meadow, and woodland enough for only 100 hogs. To this manor were attached 32 villains,

---

[1] Socmen were inferior landowners, who had land in the " soc " or franchise of a great baron on some fixed and determined rent service.

16 boors and 3 serfs: 1 cow, 6 sheep and 5 hogs. There were also 9 mills. These 9 mills indicate the position of this estate to have occupied the Western side of Ham, where the Lea and its various cuts afforded them water power.

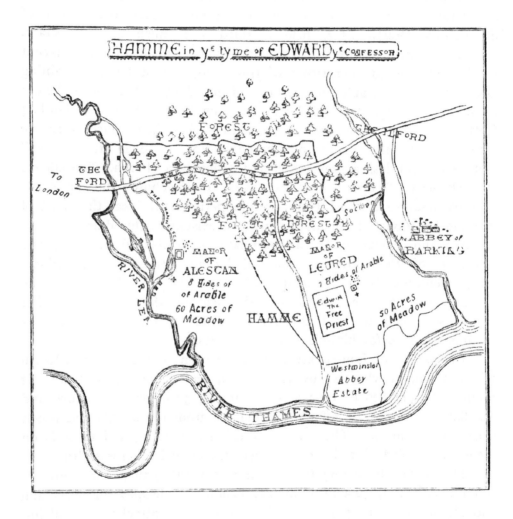

This map, though not correct as to detail, has been inserted here to show the relative positions of the manors of Alestan and Leured, and also the probable site of the old Roman road by the "Ford."

It may be interesting to many of our readers here to insert the following extracts from "Domesday"—being the entries which relate to what are now the Parishes of East and West Ham—with a literal translation. Liber Domesday, vol. II., fol. 64 et 72.

Terra Roberti Gregonis, Hund. de Beuentree.

Hame tenet Robertus in dominio, quod tenuit Alestanus, liber homo, T.R.E. (tempore Regis Edwardi) pro manerio et pro VIII hidis[1] et XXX acris. Et hoc manerium Willielmus Rex dedit Ranulfo Piperello et Roberto Gregoni. Tunc V carucatae in dominio, modo IV. Tunc VIII carucatae hominum, modo XII.

Tunc XXXII villani, modo XLVIII. Tunc XVI bordarii, modo LXXX—I minus. Semper III servi. Silva C porcis. LX acrae prati. IX molini, modo VIII.

The land of Robert Gernon in Beacontree Hundred.

Ham is held by Robert in demesne; it was held by Alestan, a free man, in the time of King Edward, for a manor and for 8 hides[1] and 30 acres. And this manor King William gave to Ralph Peverell and Robert Gernon. Then there were 5 carucates in the demesne, now 4. Then 8 carucates of the vassals, now 12.

Then 32 villains, now 48. Then 16 bordars, now 80 less one. Always 3 serfs. Pannage for 100 hogs. 60 acres of meadow land. 9 mills, now 8.

---

[1] A HIDE OF LAND; derivation, exact meaning and extent of the hide have all been sharply contested and are by no means settled yet. Perhaps it orginally meant as much as would maintain a family. Familia in Bede is translated "Hide land" by Alfred and the derivation is probably "Hyd" a habitation. Spelman thinks it 100 acres. In Essex the Inquisitors considered it theoretically as consisting of 4 virgates or 120 acres.

A CARUCATE. No expression has given rise to more discussion. Caruca means a team, not simply existing but actually employed on the land. The quantity of land therefore, that was actually cultivated by a team, including such part as in the course of husbandry would be lying fallow for the year, but exclusive of meadow or pasture held with it. In the time of Richard I. a carucate was 60 acres of 26 feet to the perch. The quantity varied in different counties and also according to the mode of tillage—probably from 60 to 80 acres.

The hide was the measure of land in the Confessor's time, the carucate that, to which it was reduced by the Conqueror's new Standard.

Tunc valuit XVI libris et quando receperunt XII libris, modo valet XXIV libris. Et de hoc manerio habet Ranulfus Piperellus medietatem. Et in dominio Roberti recepit Ranulfus I runcinum et modo similiter ibi est. Tunc I vacca, modo IX animalia. Tunc VI oves, modo XII. Tunc V porci, modo XI.

De hoc manerio tenet Osbernus de Roberto XXX acras et dimidium carucatae et valuit X solidis in eodem pretio.

Hame tenet Robertus in dominio quod tenuit Leuridus, liber homo[1] T.R.E. pro manerio et pro VII hidis. Semper III carucatae in dominio. Tunc VII carucatae hominum,[2] modo XIII.

Tunc XXXIV villani[3], modo XXXVIII. Tunc III bordarii[4],

It was then worth £16 and when they got possession £12, and it is now worth £24. And of this manor Ralph Peverell has the half. And in the demesne of Robert, Ralph received 1 horse and now there is in it the same number. Then 1 cow, now 9 beasts. Then 6 sheep, now 12. Then 5 hogs, now 11.

Of this manor Osbern holds of Robert 30 acres with half a carucate, and this was worth 10 shillings of the above named value.

Ham is held by Robert in demesne; it was held by Leured, a freeman[1] in the time of King Edward for a manor and for 7 hides. Always 3 carucates in the demesne. Then 7 carucates of the vassals,[2] now 13.

Then 34 villains,[3] now 38. Then 3 bordars,[4] now 26. Then

---

[1] HOMINES LIBERI — freemen — were freeholders, holding on some fixed and determined rent-service.

[2] HOMINES — homagers, vassals — so frequently mentioned in Domesday-Book included all sorts of feudatory tenants, they owed the duty of submission and professed dependence to their lord.

[3] VILLANI — villains, villeins — either from the word "vilis" or else villa, because they lived chiefly in villages—occupied small portions of land, but were not allowed by law to acquire any land. They were burdened with stated services due from themselves to their lord.

[4] BORDARII—bordars or cottagers, from "bord" a cottage — were a little inferior to the villains, but still vastly superior to the serfs, subject no doubt to services more onerous and servile than the villains.

modo XXVI. Tunc XIX servi[1], modo III. Silva DCC porcis, L acrae prati. Tunc VIII animalia, modo XV. Tunc XX porci, modo XXXIV. Modo CC oves XX minus. Modo IV runcini et III vasa apium.

Et huic terrae additae sunt III virgatae tempore regis Willielmi, quas tenuit Edwinus, liber presbiter T.R.E.

Tunc I carucata, modo dimidium. Modo II bordarii. Silva X porcis, IX acrae prati.

Et hoc manerium valuit T.R.E. X libris, et quando recepit VII libris, modo XVIII libris. Et huic manerio adjacent XXX acrae, quas tennit I sochemannus.

De hoc manerio tenet Ilgerus XL acras et II bordarios et I carucatam et valuit XV solidis in eodem pretio.

19 serfs,[5] now 3. Pannage for 700 hogs, 50 acres of meadow land. Then 8 beasts now 15. Then 20 hogs, now 34. Now 200 sheep less 20. Now 4 horses and 3 hives of bees.

And to this estate belong 3 virgates in the time of King William, which were held by Edwin, a free priest in the time of King Edward.

It then contained 1 carucate, now a half. Now 2 bordars. Pannage for 10 pigs, 9 acres of meadow.

And this manor was worth in the time of King Edward £10, and when he got possession £7, now £18. And to this manor belong 30 acres, which are held by 1 socman.

Of this manor Ilger holds 40 acres, and 2 bordars and 1 carucate, the value of which is 15 shillings of the above-named sum.

Domesday-Book, vol. II., fol. 72.

Hund. de Beuentreu.

Terra Ranulfi Piperelli.

Hame tenet Ranulfus in dominio, quod tenuit Alestanus, liber homo T. R. E. pro manerio et pro VIII hidis et XXX acris.

Hundred of Beacontree.

The land of Ralph Peverell.

Hame is held by Ralph in demesne, which was held by Alestan, a free man in the time of King Edward for a manor and for 8 hides and 30 acres.

---

[1] SERVI — serfs — were subject to the absolute dominion, very nearly to the absolute caprice of their master, their lives and limbs only being under the protection of the law.

Et hoc manerium dedit Willielmus Rex Ranulfo Piperello et Roberto Grenoni &c. &c.

And King William gave this estate to Ralph Peverell and to Robert Gernon &c. &c.

The remainder of this entry is identical with that already given respecting the estate of Robert Gernon, formerly belonging to Alestan the Saxon, except that it concludes with these words:

Et de hoc manerio habet R. Grenon medietatem.

And of this estate R. Gernon has a half.

In Ham, therefore, at this date we find that the two Saxon proprietors, Alestan and Leured, had been succeeded by two Normans whose names were Robert Gernon and Ralph Peverell. Alestan is recorded in "Domesday" to have possessed other smaller manors and portions of land in Essex, while the name of Leured appears only in this instance. The presence of Edwin, the free priest, affords presumptive evidence that he had a church or chapel to serve. Churches were not always recorded in "Domesday," even in cases where from other authorities they are known to have existed.

It is quite possible that the chancel of the present church of East Ham—not the Norman apse—is of Saxon construction, and may have been served by Edwin the priest.

From these entries in Domesday-Book we may form an approximate estimate of the population of the district, now divided into the parishes of East and West Ham. At the time of the conquest, there were besides the proprietors—or more properly speaking the two feudal lords, their families and households including 22 serfs—19 little farmers or bordars, and 66 villains or husbandmen. Since then both bordars and villains had considerably increased in number, and as they probably were all heads of families, we may fairly presume that in 1086 there would be an agricultural population of no less than three or four hundred persons in this district, there being about 14,500 persons registered in Domesday-Book for the whole county of Essex.[1]

[1] We have in Domesday-Book what was intended as a complete list of all holding or attached to lands actually registered by the Inquisitors, but there is no doubt, that a large number of Saxons, who either were unattached to land before the Conquest or dis-severed from it by that event, would scarcely figure in a Record like that.

We have no knowledge who the Saxon proprietors Alestan, Leured, and Edwin, the free priest, were, or what became of them. They disappeared amidst the convulsions which attended the conquest of England by the Normans, an event which reduced the Saxons to complete subjection and poverty; their goods, their revenues, their lands and their homes were seized by the Normans, life alone being left them, which their conquerors considered a sufficient boon.

The meanest Norman rose to wealth and power, even the poorest soldier of fortune found his part in the spoil, and became master in the house of the vanquished Saxon. "Ignoble camp followers"— exclaims the indignant chronicler ORDERICUS VITALIS—"and infamous rascals (sales vauriens) disposed at their fancy of the most noble maidens. Uncontrolled dependents wondered in their unworthy pride, whence such power could come to them, and imagined that they were permitted to do whatever they fancied agreeable to themselves. They shed blood at random, they snatched the morsel of bread from the mouth of the wretched inhabitant. He who had passed the channel with nothing but the quilted casque and wooden bow of an archer, now rode on a war horse girded with the baldrick of a knight. He who came a landless adventurer now raised his banner and led a troop, whose war cry was his name."

It is very probable that William the Conqueror, soon after his arrival in England, retired to Barking Abbey,[1] and continued there till the fortress he had begun in London was completed. The old Saxon Abbey might have afforded him sufficient accommodation, while the Roman earthworks at Uphall served as the camping ground of his army.

The direct and only road from Barking to London was through Ilford and Hamme to Old Forde, bordered on the southern side of the way by fertile fields, and on the northern by the forest with its hunting grounds, which temptingly lay in the sight of the many suitors, who resorted to the Norman Court and naturally looked for a share of the spoil for having aided the Conqueror in the subjugation of the land.

---

[1] Some historians affirm, that Berkhamstead was the place of the King's abode, but the proximity of Barking to London certainly rendered that place a more convenient station for the new monarch.

To Robert Gernon, one of the most powerful and influential barons, who had come over from Normandy with William the Conqueror, he gave the whole of Leured's manor in Hamme, to which was afterwards added the little estate of Edwin the free priest, and a moiety of the estate which had belonged to the Saxon Alestan. This afterwards formed the great Lordship of Montfichet in East and West Ham, whose chief seat was eventually fixed at Stanstead-Montfichet. Little is known of Robert Gernon's personal history and ancestry; he was of Norman lineage, probably from the parts about Bayeux. He seems to have held some official authority, for it is recorded in " Domesday " that, after the king's arrival in this country, he took a swineherd, belonging to the Royal Manor of Writtle, and made him a forester in the king's forest.

The other moiety of Alestan's manor became the share of Ralph Peverel. Some obscurity rests upon its history. It seems to have fallen to the Crown with the rest of the Honor of Peverel in the reign of Henry I., and in part to have been settled as appanage on two Royal princes, by whom and their feudatories under the name of Sudbery in West Ham it was eventually given to the Abbey, the Crown reserving to itself an annual rent of £31 12s for which the Abbots of Stratford regularly accounted to the Exchequer. It is probable that Queen Maude appropriated another portion of Peverel's moiety to the endowment of her bridges and causeway.

Progress was not the ordinary result of the first Norman occupation in this part of England, but we find it recorded in " Domesday," that during the twenty years between the conquest (1066) and the time when that marvellous Inquisition was made (1080-1086), Ham had greatly increased both in value and population. Eleven more carucates of land had been brought under cultivation, which it is a moderate calculation to estimate at nearly a thousand acres. To till this land we find eighty-six villains instead of sixty-six, while the bordars had increased from nineteen to one hundred and eight, and the annual value from £19 to £42. Live stock had also multiplied; the nine heads of cattle had become twenty-four, the six sheep were multiplied to nearly two hundred and the twenty-five hogs to forty-five; to this increase four farm horses and three hives of bees were added.

The estate belonging to Westminster Abbey was also improved, but not in the same proportion; from twenty shillings it had risen to sixty, and there were now five bordars settled upon it.

It will have been observed, that in the estate of Alestan nine mills, then eight, are recorded. Sir Henry Ellis states in his interesting introduction to Domesday-Book, that "where a mill is mentioned in that record, it almost invariably occurs that a mill still exists on the same spot." The water power for these mills would be found then, as now, in the various branches of the River Lea. Thus we are enabled with confidence to fix the position of Alestan's estate in the district of Hamme, now known as West Ham, and it may be assumed that his manor house and the hovels of the villains formed the nucleus of the village of West Ham.

Such was Hamme under its first Norman Lords twenty years after the Conquest (1086). Even in its then improved condition how great is the difference compared with the present state of the district! How small were the flocks and herds that grazed upon the widespread pastures, extending from the river Lea to the river Roding! Four farm horses then sufficed for the tillage of the district, while now (1850) we see long strings of loaded waggons nightly pursue their way to the London markets. Yet, small as the improvement was, it was considerably greater than that recorded of the surrounding places, and induces the conjecture that Ham was the chief residence of Robert Gernon in Essex. He had here two tenants, Osbern and Ilger by name, holding their land of him by that feudal tenure which was established in this country by the great Conqueror, and it is from such families as these, and the socmen before mentioned, that the important races of our country gentlemen and yeoman are derived. With these exceptions the lordship of Ham was in the possession of Gernon and Peverel, the latter of whom seems to have had his chief seat at Hatfield Peverel, in this county.

It was not until the beginning of the twelfth century that William de Montfichet, a successor of Gernon, built the castle of Stanstead, and as he also about the same time (1135) built the Abbey of Stratford, and endowed it with his demesne in West Ham and "the place of the said Abbot," it is very probable that he then abandoned the ancient Saxon manor and established himself in the Castle of Stanstead which now became the head of the great barony

of Montfichet. Moreover, the fact that at the period of the
" Domesday Survey" the Lordship of Ham was of greater extent,
and also more populous than that of Stanstead, seems to confirm
this supposition.

Beyond the undoubted information derived from the above entries
in Domesday-Book concerning the condition of these parishes in the
year 1086, no record exists relating to Ham until the early part of
the twelfth century, when two circumstances occurred which have
probably affected its subsequent condition more than any event, the
knowledge of which has come down to us. The first of these in date
and importance was the erection of Bow and Channelsea Bridges,
with the construction of the raised causeway between them by
Matilda, Queen of Henry I., better known as Queen Maude; the other
was the foundation of the Abbey of Stratford Langthorn by William
Montfichet, one of the successors of Robert Gernon. These will be
treated in the next chapter.

CHAPTER II.

(Contents).

Division of the parishes of East and West Ham. Construction of Bow and Channelsea Bridges and Causeway. Endowment of the same by Queen Maude. Wygan's Mill. Repairs of the Bridges. Litigation about repairs. Tolls on Bow Bridge. Chapel on Bow Bridge. The Mills and Water Courses.

THE HIGHWAY, BRIDGES AND CAUSEWAY.

N the documents already quoted respecting Hamme we have not found any distinction made between the present parishes of East and West Ham. That the distinction did exist is probable, since the division of land into parishes is mentioned in the laws of King Edgar about the year 790. JUDGE BLACKSTONE in his "Commentaries" says: "It seems pretty clear and certain that the boundaries of parishes were originally ascertained by those of a manor or manors. The Lords—he adds—as Christianity spread itself, began to build churches on their own demesnes or wastes, and obliged their tenants to appropriate their tithes to the maintenance of the officiating minister." We may therefore fairly presume that the estates of Alestan and Leured, the Saxons, are locally defined by the boundaries of the present parishes of East and West Ham, although the exact date of their distinct appellation is not known. That the distinction was made before the year 1186 is proved by a charter of King Henry II. to the Monks of Stratford, confirming the gift made (1135) by William de Montfichet of the "place of the said Abbot, which is called Stratford in West Ham." This charter, as is commonly found in such ancient Norman documents, has no date, but amongst other witnesses whose names are appended, is that of "G" my son—which probably means "Geoffrey," son of King Henry II., who was killed (1186) at a tournament in Paris, being trampled under foot by the horses. This fixes the date of the charter he witnessed as anterior to that event.

The old Roman road from London into Essex passed about a mile to the north of the present highway through a tidal river —the Lea—across the often flooded and impracticable marshes. It is related by the old historians, that about the beginning of the twelfth century "the good Queen Maude[1] with her attendants when crossing on horseback into Essex by the "Old Ford," was well washed in the water and not without danger of drowning."

Stow records this event in his annals, and it is here transcribed in the language of the curious old antiquary's work: "Matilda, when she saw the way to bee dangerous to them that travelled by the Old Foord over the river of Lue (Lea)—for she herself had beene well washed in the water—caused two stone bridges to be builded in

---

[1] Queen Maude was the eldest daughter of Malcolm Canmore, King of Scotland, and Margaret, sister of Edgar Atheling, the legal heir to the English crown. She was sent by her father to be educated at the Monastery of Wilton, where she took the veil and was with difficulty prevailed on to relinquish it for a throne, but she declared to Anselm, Archbishop of Canterbury, that she had only worn it when forced by her aunt, Princess Christina. Many ladies did at that time embrace the monastic life as a security from the ferocious Normans of that barbarous age, their rank being no protection to them. She was a pious, amiable princess, a lover and promoter of learning, passionately fond of music, of which she was a liberal patroness; yet such was her humility that when her brother David, King of Scotland, came to visit her, he found her engaged in washing the feet of some lepers; her piety was so great, that it was her custom to walk every day in lent barefooted to church, wearing a garment of hair. She founded the priory of Holy Trinity, Aldgate, London, and the Hospital of St. Giles in the Fields for leprous maidens, and had Barking Abbey for some time under her governance. She died on the first of May 1118 and was buried at Westminster.

a place one mile distant from the Old Foord, of the which one was situated over Lue at the head of the towne of Stratford, now called Bow, a rare piece of work, for before the time the like had never beene seene in England. The other over the little brooke comonly called Channelsebridge. Shee made the King's high-way of gravell between the two bridges."

It is true, that in an official account, given about two hundred years after the death of Queen Maude (1118), it is stated, that "she heard, the ways were dangerous," — yet it appears highly probable that she had personal experience of the state of the road and its inconveniences, when it is remembered that this was the direct road both to the Royal Hunting Palace of Havering Bower, which was the dower of the English Queens, and to Barking, whose Abbey of Nuns of Saxon foundation was not only under her special patronage, but also her occasional residence. At any rate the passage of the river Lea by means of a ferry at Old Ford being difficult and dangerous, and many persons losing their lives, Queen Maude caused two bridges to be made, of which the one over the river Lea was situate at one end of the town of Stratford, now called Bow, and the other at Ham Stratford.

Tradition has constantly affirmed that the bridge at Bow was the first bridge built with a stone arch in England, and that the name "Boghe or Bow" originated in this circumstance. STOW speaks of it "as arched like a Bowe—a rare piece of work, for the like had never been seen in England." It certainly was erected nearly sixty years before the first stone bridge over the Thames in London was commenced by Peter, the Chaplain of Colechurch, about the year 1176; whereas Queen Maude died as before stated in 1118. King Henry I. was a great patron of architecture, and in particular of Gundulph, Bishop of Rochester, who was highly distinguished in this beautiful art, and who has erected or rebuilt some of our finest ancient buildings such as Windsor Castle, the Castle and also the Cathedral of Rochester. It is possible, therefore, that Bow Bridge may have been designed by him, who was the great architect of his age.

That the bridge was originally built of stone can need no further confirmation, but the number of arches it consisted of originally must remain a matter of uncertainty. It is evident that the pointed arches, as shown in the accompanying picture, formed no part of the original construction of the bridge, as no other but a circular arch would have been used at that time. The original arches,

therefore, appear to have been removed and may probably have given place to several forms of construction, each partaking of the fashion prevalent at the time of their erection.

The other bridge was over a channel of the river Lea, called Channelsea, upon which the Abbey Mills are situated at about half a mile below the bridge; but whether it was originally also of stone and arched like Bow Bridge, has not been stated. The similarity of the architecture leads to the supposition that it was so.

Queen Maude turned the old Roman road with a considerable curve to the southward from the "Old Ford" to where it now is, and raised the causeway between the two bridges, "so that persons passing by, well and securely might pass." Nor is this supposed to have been the only highway improved by her bounty, for during the

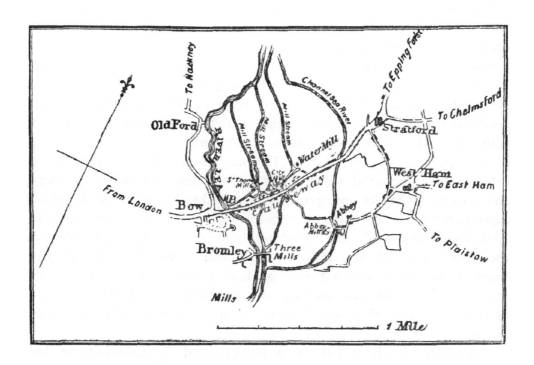

period of her regency, when her husband King Henry I. was absent in Normandy, she had the power to execute such works, and we are told "that she directed her attention to the important object of making new roads and repairing the ancient highways that had fallen into decay during the stormy years, which had succeeded the peaceful and prosperous reign of her great-uncle Edward the Confessor. By this means travellers and itinerant merchants were greatly facilitated in their journeys through the then wild and perilous country which, with the exception of the four great Roman ways, was only intersected with a few scattered cart tracks through desolate moors, heaths and uncultivated wastes and woodlands."

Two hamlets both called Stratford[1] now sprang into existence, namely "Stratford-atte-Boghe or Bow" at the Middlesex end of the causeway, which, though originally a hamlet of Stepney, is now a distinct parish, and "Stratford Langthorne or Ham Stratford" on the Essex side, forming part of West Ham. The description of the neighbourhood of London, given by FITZ-STEPHEN between the years 1170 and 1181 may properly find a place here. He calls it the northern side, but we know that it must have applied with equal correctness to the north-eastern. "Adjoining the buildings all round lie the gardens of the citizens, who dwell in the suburbs, which are well furnished with trees, are spacious and beautiful. In the north are cornfields, pastures and delightful meadows intermixed with pleasant streams, on which stands many a mill, whose clack is so grateful to the ear. Beyond these an immense forest extends itself, beautiful with woods and groves, and full of the lairs and coverts of beasts and game, stags, bucks, boars and wild bulls." Aged persons can still remember cornfields and pastures between Mile End and Bow, while the meadows, streams and clacking mills on the Essex side of the bridge are hidden from the view of the traveller by the continuous row of houses now bordering the road, and further on wild recesses may still be found among the remnants of the vast forest of Essex, though no longer infested with wild bulls and boars.

Stratford-le-Bow has been immortalised by CHAUCER in his "Prologue to the Canterbury Tales," in terms which seem to imply, that five centuries ago it was a well-known place of education for young ladies. Most of our readers will remember the comely prioress, how in the words of the poet

> "French she spoke full fayre and fetisly
> After the scole of Stratford-atte-Bowe,
> For French of Paris was to hire unknowe.'

It must be remembered that in the adjoining parish of Bromley within a mile of the bridge stood the Convent of St. Leonard's,

---

[1] Stratford, from " Strata sci. via," Saxon " Straet," Street or Road by the Ford.

usually called the "Priory in Stratford," and it is very probable, that the Nuns of that religious house taught the French language among other accomplishments to the young ladies of that favourite suburb.

Good Queen Maude did not leave her charitable work incomplete, for she not only built the above named two bridges and improved the causeway, but also endowed them. For this purpose she bought certain manors and a water mill, called "Wiggen's Mill or Wiggemulne" for their perpetual maintenance and repair. Wiggen's Mill, now called the Abbey Mills, eventually became one of the entrances to the precincts of the Abbey of Stratford, latterly more familiarly known by the name of "West Ham Abbey." In 1768 these mills were repaired, when on taking up the "mudsel" there was found a piece of timber with the following inscription:

We are indebted for this information to a manuscript book by a Mr. JAMES of Stratford, which formerly was in the possession of the "Abbey Land Commissioners." Mr. JAMES considers it to mean the date of the first laying down the timber in the year 1064 and the name of the owner of the mill.[1]

Having thus endowed the bridges and the causeway between them, Queen Maude entrusted the care of them to the Abbess and convent of Barking, as being at that time the nearest religious house. She feared that, if the endowment were consigned to secular persons, the trustees or their heirs might prove unfaithful to their trust. Whether this agreement was ratified by a charter or other written deed, does not appear; no mention is made of any such

---

[1] As to the name of the owner he is probably right, but in respect to the date he must be incorrect, since Arabic numerals were not used in England at so early a date. It was not until the year 1290, that Arabic numerals are found at all in England, and then in astronomical treatises only. They became not uncommon after 1320 in M.S.S. The mixture of Roman and Arabic is very improbable.

document in the official enquiries respecting the bridges. The Abbess of Barking did not long retain this charge, for as soon as the Abbey of Stratford was founded (1135) by William de Montfichet, she transferred it together with the lands, rents, meadow and mill attached to it, to the Abbot of Stratford, "who was desirous to purchase the same, because they were near his Abbey and lying commodiously for his house."

The Abbot undertook to repair the bridges and the causeway, and to pay the Abbess of Barking a yearly rent of four marks, equal to £2 13s 4d of our money.

For some length of time the Abbot of Stratford continued to fulfil these conditions, but from a number of curious and interesting documents referring to law proceedings, occasioned by the refusal of the Abbot of Stratford to repair the bridge, this great work of the pious Queen Maude — which were brought to light at an inquisition held at Stratford-le-Bow in the year 1302, before Robert le Brabazon and Stephen de Gravesende, the King's Justices, by twelve jurors of the county of Essex and twelve jurors of the county of Middlesex, to ascertain who ought to repair the bridges and causeway between Stratford-atte-Bowe and Hamme Stratford—it appears that the Abbot delegated the charge to a bridge master, one called Godfrey Pratt, for whom he built a certain house upon the causeway. He also delivered to him his horses and carts and granted him by deed a daily allowance of bread from the Abbey. Godfrey Pratt did the repairs for a long time, occasionally asking and receiving alms from the passengers for this purpose, whereupon the Abbot, perceiving that an income might be raised this way, told Godfrey that he was able to do the repairs without any aid or gift from the Abbey, and totally withdrew the allowance.

It was also ascertained that in the reign of King John an inquisition had been held before Robert de Retford and Henry Springurnall, the King's Justices, and that after the allowance from the Abbey had been withdrawn, Hugh Pratt, a kinsman of Godfrey Pratt, who was living near the road and the bridges, did of his own authority beg the aid of passengers to keep them in repair. He had staples and bars placed upon the bridge and refused to permit carts or horsemen to pass until they had paid the passage,

E

unless indeed they were of the class of nobles whom, through fear, he permitted to pass. After the death of Hugh Pratt, his son William did the same until, through the influence of Passelewe, the King's Justice, he obtained a regular toll which enabled him to put up a bar with locks on a certain bridge, called "Lockbridge," from which circumstance he changed his name from Pratt to "Bridgewryght." For every cart carrying corn, wood, coal, etc., he received one penny, for one carrying tasel[1] two pence, and for every dead Jew eight pence.

This infringement upon the right of free passage did not remain long unchallenged. The Abbot of Waltham and Philip Basset, whose waggons were thus impeded in passing along the road, broke down the barriers. William Pratt being no longer able to levy his tolls, the bridge and causeway fell out of repair and it was left to the Charity of Eleanor, Queen of the reigning monarch Henry III. to do that, which it was the duty of the Abbot to have done. She ordered the needful repairs, committing the execution of them to the care of William de Capella, keeper of her chapel, after which William de Carleton (Charlton) kept them up with the effects of Bartholomew de Castello, deceased.

From this it would seem, as if Queen Maude's trust and confidence in Churchmen had been misplaced.

In the 35th year of the reign of King Henry III. (1250) information was obtained by another inquisition, held by the Sheriff of Essex, that the Abbot and his tenants were bound to repair the bridge on the confines of Essex and Middlesex. Two years later the King having found, when on a journey to Stratford, that the part of the bridge of Stratford towards Middlesex was out of repair, instructions were given to the Sheriff of Middlesex to distrain one mark of gold from the men of his bailiwick, and to pay the same to the Sheriff of Essex, who was appointed to see that the bridge was with all convenient speed placed in the hands

---

[1] Tasel or Teasel (dipsacus), the Fuller's thistle, the dried heads of which were no doubt largely used at the Fuller's Mill, close to the bridge, called "Spileman's Mill," formerly belonging to the Bridge House Estate."

of a man of his bailiwick for repairs. The question seems again to have been agitated in the 46th year (1261) of the same reign.

Notwithstanding the inquisition made in 1302, the Abbot continued to evade the performance of the ancient compact with the Abbess of Barking, whereupon legal proceedings were again taken in 1312 by John de Norton, the King's Attorney-General, in which reference was made to the inquisition held before the King's Justices in the year 1302. In the pleadings of 1312 the Abbot of Stratford, the Keeper of London Bridge and the Master of the Hospital of St. Thomas of Acre (de Acon) were charged with the repairs of the several bridges and causeway at Stratford, the latter two as holding certain mills, and the Abbot as holding other property, originally given by Queen Maude to the Abbess of Barking for their support and maintenance. It appeared that two of these three mills,[1] situate on the northern side of the causeway, belonged to the Keeper of London Bridge, and the third to the Hospital of St. Thomas of Acre, and that the wooden bridges over the three trenches, made for three courses of water to run for the use of these mills and intersecting the causeway, were in a ruinous condition. It was decided that the repairs of the wooden bridges devolved upon the owners of the mills, and that the Abbess of Barking and the Abbot of Stratford were responsible for the maintenance of the other two bridges and the causeway between them.

In the year 1315 another inquisition was held, when after many years spent in litigation the Abbot of Stratford at last acknowleged his liability. He appeared in Court and entered into a formal "agreement made between the said Abbot and Abbess, whereby in consideration of two hundred pounds in silver paid to him by the Abbess of Barking he acknowledged his liability, and bound himself and his successors in spiritualities and in temporalities, to repair and maintain the Bow and Channelsea bridges and the causeway between them," which was accordingly executed with the convent

---

[1] These three mills must not be confounded with what is now known as the "Three Mills" on the southern side of the causeway near Bromley.

seals appended — William the Prior, John the Procurator, Stephen the Cellarer, and other brethren of the house of Stratford consenting to the same — at Westminster, in the presence of Humphrey de Bohun, Earl of Hereford and Essex, John de Sandale, the Chancellor of England, and other high official dignitaries.

However, in the latter part of King Edward III.'s reign (1366), the bridge called Stratford-atte-Bowe was so cut up and broken by the constant traffic "that the King granted a toll for three years to be levied by William Buntanesdale and William del Clay or their deputy, the receipts arising from which were to be placed at the disposition of John de Hynstoke for the repair and reconstuction of the aforesaid bridge."

The tolls thus granted are as follows:

Every cart laden with coal or other merchandise going to market	½ penny
Every horse for sale worth twenty shillings or more ...	1 ,,
Every horse below the value of twenty shillings ...	½ ,,
Every ox or cow for sale	½ ,,
Every four pigs for sale	½ ,,
Every score of sheep for sale	1 ,,
Half a score	½ ,,
Five	1 farthing
And for anything going to market not specified over or under the said bridge exceeding the value of twenty shillings	1 penny
Of the value of ten shillings	½ ,,
Of five shillings	1 farthing

These prolonged litigations now ceased and from this period until the suppression of the Abbey by King Henry VIII. in the year 1539 we do not find that any attempt was made to throw off the responsibility. The bridges were, no doubt, during that period properly taken care of, and for some time after they had fallen into the hands of the Crown required but little repair, as we do not hear of any complaint being made.

King Henry VIII. granted the lands and site of the Abbey to Sir Peter Meautis, who at the time was ambassador from Henry to the Court of France. His heirs sold them to various persons, chiefly to Sir John Nulls. In a manuscript, which was in the possession of the late clerk of the Abbey land commissioners, it is among other things stated "that old Meautis told old Buckeridge, that Mr. John Nulls would not forget what was allowed him in the purchase for the repair of the highway."

In 1628 a rate of £50 per annum was levied on all the manors and lands formerly belonging to "Stratford, *i.e.* West Ham Abbey" in whatever part of the country, for the purpose of keeping the bridges and causeway in repair. However, we find that in 1643 the Abbey landowners, trying to play the same game as the Abbot had formerly done, by repudiating the charge, were indited for the dilapidated condition into which the bridges and causeway had fallen. The question was tried in King's Bench, when the defence was set up by the defendants, that the Abbot's lands had been discharged from the obligation by reason of their transition into and union with the Crown at the dissolution—but the Court found a verdict for the King.

The question was again agitated in the year 1663, but was not carried into Court, the parties being informed that they could make no defence, as appears by a document formerly in the possession of the Abbey land commissioners, of which the following is an extract: "So the Counsel told us, that they could not give us any other counsel, than to tell us we should be overthrown in all our defences and suits, and be at last compelled to repair, after we had spent all our time and money and travel, and if the repairs were not performed, great fines could be levied upon those who were indited now in the Crown office this Easter term 15 Charles II."

At this date the real rental of the Abbey lands had increased to £15,100, but the bridge rate appears to have been levied according to the old rental of £652 3s 1½d. Although so many attempts had been made to throw off this burden with the like unsuccessful result, we again find the question tried in the year 1691, when an information was brought in the King's Bench against Buckeridge and others for not repairing a highway in their tenure between Stratford and Bow. "The Court was of opinion, that all the lands of the Abbot were liable to repair this way, and directed the jury accordingly, who found for the plaintiff, and the possessors of the Abbey lands were ordered to abide by the tenure."

From that period, the landowners profiting by the experience of the past, and not forgetting the wholesome advice of the honest lawyer of 1663, contented themselves to abide by the exertions of their predecessors, and continued the charge of the bridges and causeway at Stratford for the free and uninterrupted use of the public, as was originally intended by the royal founder.

That a wide and properly constructed road should be considered of the first importance to the public is not surprising, and with a view to make the road as perfect as any of its kind, many great improvements were made from time to time. In the year 1741 the bridges of Queen Maude were found much too narrow for so great a thoroughfare and to occasion considerable inconvenience and sometimes danger in passing them. The width of the roadway across the bridges, which was originally only 13 feet wide between the parapets, was increased to 21 feet and angular recesses were placed in intervals, in which foot passengers took refuge from the passing carriage or horseman. In still later times, when more vehicles rendered these primitive refuges insufficient for safety, a wooden foot-bridge was appended to the ancient structure which, however, soon fell into decay.

In the year 1832 there was a trial on this subject between the "Trustees of the Middlesex and Essex turnpike roads," and "the Abbey landowners." It was contended, that by an act passed in the fourth year of George IV., the Abbey landowners were by reason of their respective tenures bound to support, maintain and repair both the bridges and the causeway between them. The Abbey landowners refused to do so, on the plea that the wooden foot-bridge formed no part of the original structure or of the intention of Queen Maude, the founder. The verdict was given against the counties.

The bridge itself, however, had now become quite inadequate to the necessities of the time. Railroads had not yet diverted any portion of the traffic, the number of travellers had considerably increased, moreover several "fast coaches" from the Eastern Counties had been started in addition to the local omnibuses, besides private conveyances of all sorts. To estimate the number of the latter it must be borne in mind, that the neighbouring parishes as well as

East and West Ham were full of the residences of merchants and bankers, who went daily to the city, and whose various conveyances were continually crossing Bow Bridge. Accidents were very frequent, and the people used to say, that the apothecary's shop at Bow, near the bridge, derived its principal support from them. The ascent also was so steep, that occasionally the horses dropped in drawing their heavy loads up the bridge.

In 1835 it was discovered that the bridge was in such a dilapidated state, that it became necessary to remove the ancient stone bridge altogether. In the course of the endeavours of the "Trustees of the turnpike roads" many difficulties presented themselves, but they were at length overcome, and an act of Parliment was obtained empowering them to rebuild Bow Bridge and to improve the others. During this operation the architects found that of the original structure of Bow bridge but little remained, and from the numerous additions the elevation presented a very patched appearance, nor was there any means of ascertaining the number of arches of which it originally consisted. This venerable and time-worn structure had during the lapse of centuries no doubt undergone many alterations, and since the pointed arches could have formed no part of the original structure — circular arches only being used in those days — the piers and abutments were probably the only remaining portions of Queen Maude's bridge.

We quote from REDMAN's account in the transactions of the institution of Civil Engineers : " The covering was removed and the old roadway laid bare; the track of horses and cattle was clearly defined by a hollow, worn into the arch stones, and on each side of it were deep wheel cuts, on an average six to eight inches deep and nine inches wide, and distant from each other from centre to centre about four. feet six inches, worn in places within three or four inches of the soffit. The wheel tracks had nearly worn the stones through and the bridge had been strengthened by pieces of stone underneath the arch."

The late John Gibson Esq., of Stratford, had these ancient stones carefully preserved and the bridge partly re-erected in his garden, where they were seen by many persons still living. (1880).

The old bridge has given place to a handsome bridge of one oblate arch, the first stone of which was laid by Lady Pelly, wife of

Sir Henry Pelly, of Upton, in the year 1835, and the bridge was completed in 1839 at the cost of £11,000.

The Abbey land commissioners, who had been empowered to make an assessment on the Abbey lands for defraying the expenses of keeping the bridges and causeway in repair, eventually made a composition in money with the Trustees of the Essex and Middlesex turnpike roads, amounting to £300 annually in full discharge of their liabilities in respect of the said bridges and causeway. In 1866 the Trustees of the turnpike roads ceased to exist, and by Act of Parliament the management of the roads and bridges became vested in the newly constituted Local Board of West Ham. The Abbey land commissioners were then empowered by another act, to make a composition in money with the said Local Board towards the maintenance of the aforesaid bridges and causeway, and finally by a subsequent Act of 1876, on the payment of £1,000 to the Local Board of West Ham, they were relieved from all obligations to maintain the bridges and causeway, whereupon the Abbey land rate ceased to be raised. In the year 1886 West Ham was made a municipal borough and the management of the bridges and causeway have since become vested in the Corporation, to whom the Bridge House Estate still pay their quota towards the maintenance of the causeway.

Before leaving the subject of Bow Bridge it is worth mentioning that a chapel, dedicated to St. Katharine, is said to have stood upon it ; by whom it was built or when taken down is not known. It was the custom of our pious forefathers to erect religious houses upon bridges, which were generally dedicated to the Saint, who was supposed to have under his protection those who navigated the river over which the bridge was built. That a chapel was attached to Bow Bridge in former ages is more than probable, especially when we consider the period of its erection and the circumstances which led to its foundation.

Moreover, SIR WILLIAM DUGDALE in his work on " Embanking and Draining" states, "that in the 33rd year of King Henry VI. (1454) a commission was appointed to view and repair the banks of the river betwixt St. Katherine's Chapel upon Bow Bridge, in the parish of West Ham, unto East Tilbury," and again in the first year of Edward IV. (1460) another view was ordered from the mill called " Tempyl Mylle" to the chapel of St. Katherine upon Bow Bridge. Of the former existence of such a chapel there can therefore be no doubt.

Nor must the three mills, already referred to in what is called " High Mead," to the north of the causeway, and whose watercourses intersect the same, be left unnoticed, since they have seriously affected it and its interests. Two of these mills are the property of London Bridge, or what is now called the " Bridge House Estate ;" by whom and when the gift was made is not known, but it was certainly made before the inquisition in 1303, at which date they were — as has already been stated — in the possession of the " Master of London

F

Bridge." One of these mills was a water-mill, called Sayen's Mill,[1] with several acres of meadow land belonging to the same and planted round with willows, for which an annual rent of £1 17s was paid to the heirs of Sir Richard Plaiz, Knt., presumably a feudal fee reserved to the lord of the manor. The other mill, nearer to Stratford, called Spileman's Mill, was formerly a Fuller's Mill, and had four acres of meadow land attached to it.

The Bridge House Estate is also still charged with the support of St. "Michael's"[2] and "Peg's Hole"[3] Bridges, which now supply those wooden bridges, whose ruinous condition was one of the causes of the official enquiries above referred to. This ancient Estate in Stratford produced in 1827 a rental of £409 4s and has since the year 1724 expended the sum of £2467 8s 11d on those two bridges, besides a yearly composition in money for repairing the causeway between them.

The third mill, called "St Thomas' Mill"[4] together with the meadow and appurtanances adjoining, was originally a gift made by John Rickman to the Hospital of St. Thomas de Acon. This Hospital was a branch of the Templars, and was founded by Thomas Fitz Theobald de Helles and Agnes his wife, sister to the Archbishop Thomas à Becket,[5] to whom it was dedicated. It was situate in Cheapside and belonged originally to Gilbert à Becket, father of the Archbishop, who was born within its walls. At the period of the dissolution of the Abbeys the property of this Hospital was purchased by the Mercers' Company, who converted the house into their Hall and sold the mill at Stratford.

---

[1] Sayen's Mill is now called the "City Mills" and in the occupation of Messrs. Howard, who are in posession of deeds confirming this statement.

[2] St. Michael's Bridge is now called "Harrow Bridge."

[3] Peg's Hole Bridge is a small bridge adjoining the premises of Mr. Maw. There is a tradition, that it derived its name from a noted woman, named "Peg," being found drowned there.

[4] St. Thomas' Mill is in Marshgate Lane and now in the possession of Messrs. Du Barry & Co.

[5] One of the legendary tales of its dedication says, that he was the son of Gilbert à Becket, citizen of London, and a pagan princess. Gilbert travelled into

These three mills must have brought a certain number of people to both sides of the causeway even at an early period. On the south side, however, there were but few buildings, for the old topographers tell us, that after passing Bow Bridge the meadows and the Abbey came immediately in sight. CAMDEN who wrote about 1586, after relating the foundation of Bow Bridge, describes the Lea at Stratford "as divided into three streams, it washes the green meadows and makes them look very charming. In these we meet with the ruins of a little monastery, built by William de Montfichet, a great Norman lord, who lived in 1140. Then the Lea presently uniting its streams runs with a gentle current into the Thames, whence the place is called Lea mouth."

WEEVER, who commenced his researches in Essex by the same road, informs us in his "Funeral monuments," published in 1631, that going over the bridge at Stratford towards West Ham he saw "the remains of a monastery pleasantly watered about with several streams, and the meadows near the mills planted round with willows." ·

Having brought down the history of the high road to comparatively modern times, we must return to the age of antiquity and give an account of the feudal lords of East and West Ham and the origin of the manors.

---

the holy land, where he was taken prisoner and escaped by the assistance of Matilda. A short time after, the lady following her lover to England, they were married at London, where their son Thomas was born, and upon the site of his father's house this Hospital was built.

CHAPTER III.

(CONTENTS).

The Feudal Lords of East and West Ham and Origin of the Manors. Ralph Peverel's Moiety of a Manor of Suthbiri or Sudbury. William Plantagenet. Leonard de Venois. The great Barony of Montfichet. Manor of West Ham.

THE FEUDAL LORDS AND ORIGIN OF THE MANORS.

HE feudal system, which was introduced into England by William the Conqueror, appears to have been fully recognised at the period of the Domesday Survey. What that system was, it is needless here to explain beyond the fact that it completely changed the tenure, by which the land was held over the whole country. While the Saxon had considered himself the proprietor of the soil, the Norman was only the tenant of the King, holding his land subject to certain obligations. The great nobles, who had aided in the subjugation of the land and naturally looked for a share of the spoil, had vast estates bestowed upon them, while they, in like manner, had to provide for their followers by a subdivision of the estates conferred upon them by the Crown. Hence the distinction of tenants in chief and under-tenants; the former held their lands immediately of the King, the latter of the tenants in chief. Although their possessions were bestowed upon them for past services, they were nevertheless subject to certain obligations to the lord paramount of whom they held; to the King, in the case of the tenant in chief, and to the tenant in chief, in that of an under-tenant. Thus, every noble or baron, who owned a great extent of land, was obliged to serve the King in time of war and for a certain period in the year with as many knights under him, as there were knights' fees upon his estates. And as the large holdings were divided by their owners into smaller sub-tenancies, the sub-tenants were bound by the same condition to their lord. "Hear, my lord" swore the feudal dependent, "I become liege man of yours for life and limb and earthly regard, and I will keep faith and loyalty to you for life and death, God help me." By a usage peculiar to England each sub-tenant, in addition to his oath of fealty to his lord, swore fealty directly to the Crown. Hence we see, that the essence of the feudal system was fidelity in time of peace, and active assistance in time of war, a system admirably adapted to the state of society then in existence.

In process of time this at first simple military tenure drew after it other feudal obligations, which were enforced with remarkable strictness. The first of these was called an "aid," which the tenant was bound to pay in money to his lord, to ransom his person from captivity, to knight his eldest son or to marry his eldest daughter. The second was a fine or "relief," paid when the heir of the tenant came into possession of his estate. If the estate devolved upon an heiress, her hand was at the King's disposal and was frequently sold to the highest bidder. Widows also paid fines either for exemption from forced marriage or for having contracted one without the permission of the sovereign. The third was the "wardship" of the heir, when a minor; all profits from his estate went for a time to the King. We shall see in the account of the feudal lords in Hamme, that these rights and dues owing from their estates were frequently enforced.

It has already been stated in a former chapter, that with the exception of the small estate belonging to the Abbey of Westminster, "Hamme" was given by William the Conqueror to Ralph Peverel and Robert Gernon. Ralph possessed one moiety of Alestan's manor, while Robert held the other moiety together with the whole of Leured's manor. In the present chapter we will endeavour to trace the descent of these estates and their ultimate division into the manors of the present day. The smaller portion, which was allowed to Ralph Peverel, shall be considered first.

PEVEREL'S MOIETY OF A MANOR.

Respecting this portion of Hamme little but presumptive evidence can be offered, but there is sufficient proof that the greater part of it, if not the whole, became the property of the Crown, as forming part of the "Honor of Peverel of London," and thence passed to the Abbey of Stratford Langthorne.

In the reign of King Henry I. (1100—1135) William Peverel of Essex and Maude his sister, the grandchildren of Ralph above named, having settled certain lordships in Devonshire on the Peverels of Sandford in that county, resigned the entire remainder of their barony to the King. This was called the "Honor of Peverel of London," and there is no doubt, that their estate in Ham belonged to it. It is, therefore, highly probable, that Wigan's Mill and the land in Ham, appropriated by Queen Maude to the maintenance of her bridges and causeway, were part of the property thus ceded by the Peverels to the King, her husband.

Besides the land thus given to endow the bridges, there was an estate or manor in West Ham called "la Sudbirie," which belonged successively to two royal princes, whose possession of it can in no way be more satisfactorily accounted for than by supposing that, having become the property of the Crown, as part of the " Honor of Peverel," it had been settled as appanage upon them. These princes were William Plantagenet, brother of King Henry II., and John, afterwards King of England, who was endowed by his father with considerable portions of the "Honor of Peverel of London." From a charter signed by King Richard Coeur-de-lion we learn, that his uncle Plantagenet in conjunction with Alan de Faloise, his feudal vassal, gave some land called "Sudbirie" to the Abbey of Stratford. William Plantagenet dying without issue in the year 1163—4, a certain Leonard de Venois, of Norman origin, and deriving his name from the lordship of Venois, near Caen, appears to have been the mesne lord or feudal tenant in another part of this estate or manor, for we are told, that he accounted to the Crown for land in Ham, worth 48 marks. This estate is called "Sudbirie" in two charters, which are still extant and now preserved in the Public Record Office.

In the year 1167 John, son of Leonard de Venois, rendered

account of ten marks for this knight's fee, paying five marks at a time, besides 300 marks for his relief[1] on succeeding to his father's lands, and he was also bound to make a yearly present to the king, when the king pleased to take it. Of the identity of the property with that for which his father Leonard accounted to the Crown in 1166, the year of King John's birth, there can be no doubt. Eventually John de Venois gave his estate of Sudbirie to the monks of Stratford, reserving to himself an annual rent of £31 and twelve pence. It will be found in the history of the Abbey of Stratford, that the Abbots long continued to account to the royal exchequer for this annual rent of £31 and twelve pence due from the Manor of Sudbirie or Sudbury in West Ham. Sometimes it was advanced to pay the expences of Ambassadors sent by the King, sometimes it was settled on some one as an allowance. Thus, in the year 1218, during the minority of King Henry III., the Regent Pembroke; in the name of his royal ward, granted to William de Casingham £20 to be paid him annually out of the £31 owed by the Abbot to the exchequer, while the remaining £11 was assigned to Robert de Dene, a priest, until he was otherwise provided for. In this simple way were the scanty revenues of the Crown eked out.

In the eleventh year of the reign of King Edward I. (1282) certain knights' fees of the Honor of Peverel were assigned to Queen Eleanor, in compensation for fees taken from the Honor of Richmond, belonging to her; among those fees, thus assigned, is "one fee in Stratford by the Abbot of the same place." There is no doubt that this referred to the manor of Sudbury, now forming part of the dower of a Queen, as it had already been the appanage of a Royal Prince.

To this latter purpose it was again applied, when in 1320 King Edward II. settled upon his brother Edmund, Earl of Kent, 2000 marks annually from lands and manors, amongst the items of which

[1] On succeeding to a fief at the death of the possessor the heir was required to pay a certain sum to the lord, of whom he held. This was called a relief and originally consisted of horses, hauberks, helmet, lance etc., but which was afterwards commuted into a pecuniary fine.

allowance was £22 2s, which the Abbot and Convent of Stratford paid annually into the exchequer for the manor of "Sudbury at Hamme, in the county of Essex." On the death of Edmund of Woodstock, Earl of Kent, who was beheaded in 1330, it was found that he and Margaret, his wife, were possessed of £11 12s rent from the Abbot of Stratford for the manor of "Suthbiri at Hamme in Essex." It continued for some time in the possession of the heirs of Edmund of Woodstock, Earl of Kent, until his granddaughter, Joan Plantagenet, better known as "the fair maid of Kent,"[1] on the death of her husband, Thomas Holland, (1360), became sole heiress. Joan, whose last husband was the famous "Black Prince," left the estates to her eldest son, Thomas Holland, on whose death (1397) the manor seems to have passed from the Holland family.

Besides the manor of Sudbury, in West Ham, there remains a trace of some other property, which was probably also part of Peverel's estate. Ingelrica, wife of Ralph Peverel, founded the Priory of Hatfield Peverel, which was afterwards (1100) enlarged by their son William. This Priory was possessed of forty shillings "tythes" and ten shillings rent in West Ham, and at the dissolution we find, that property in Stratford Langthorne and West Ham is included in the estates belonging to that house.

There is also the "Manor of Bretts," whose origin has not yet been satisfactorily traced, and which further researches may perhaps show to have likewise been derived from Peverel's moiety.

Thus, we venture to think, "a moiety of the manor in Hamme," recorded in Domesday-Book as possessed by Ralph Peverel, may be accounted for, not with certainty, it is true, but with great probability, especially in the absence of any evidence to the contrary.

---

[1] Joan Plantagenet, "the fair maid of Kent," was first married to the Earl of Salisbury and from him divorced; she was then remarried to Sir Thomas Holland, one of the founders of the Order of the Garter, who commanded the van of the English army at Crecy, and was created Earl of Kent, by right of his wife, who was granddaughter of Edward I. This great soldier died in 1360 and his son, the second Earl of Kent was the ancestor of the ducal families of Norfolk and Beaumont, as well as of those of Hamilton and Abercorn. And lastly she was married to Edward Woodstock, the Black Prince, and by him the mother of the unhappy Prince, known in our history as King Richard II.

We now proceed to consider the other and larger share, which was given to Robert Gernon, and from whom it passed to the Baronial house of Montfichet.

THE MONTFICHET'S LORDSHIP IN HAM.

We have already stated, that the Conqueror's gift to Robert Gernon in Hamme consisted of one moiety of the estate of Alestan, the Saxon, (the other moiety having been given to Ralph Peverel), and the whole of the property of Leured. It comprised the entire parish of East Ham, with the small exception of the Westminster Abbey Estate, together with that part of West Ham, which extends over the present manors of West Ham, East West Ham, Plaiz and West Ham Burnels, also a part, if not the whole of Woodgrange, otherwise called "Ham Frith." For some period after the Norman Conquest all this property formed one great lordship, attached to the barony of Montfichet, of which Stanstead became the chief seat or as the lawyers call it "caput Baroniae," when William de Montfichet built the castle there and made it his principal residence.

This same William founded the Abbey of West Ham, more generally designated in ancient documents as that of Stratford Langthorne, in the year 1134 or 1135. By the wish of Margaret, his wife, and with the consent of his sons he endowed the same with the whole of his demesne land, eleven acres, two mills, his wood of Buckhurst, sometimes called Monk's-hill in Woodford, and the tythe of the pannage of his hogs. The word "dominium," used in the Charter, may be translated either lordship or demesne; in this instance it clearly means demesne, and can only refer to such lands as were next to the lord's mansion, and which he retained in his own hands for the use of his household and for hospitality, since his heirs continued in possession of the larger portions of the lordship of Montfichet in Ham for centuries after the foundation of the Abbey. He did not, therefore, give to the monks the whole of his lordship in Ham, but the whole of his demesne only. "The place of the said Abbot, which is called Stratford in West Ham and the whole demesne of the said town," is the description of this gift in the Charter of King Henry II., confirming the same. This gift, which appears to have been the first dismemberment from the

G

great lordship of Montfichet in Ham, became the Abbey demesne and now constitutes the Manor of West Ham.

There could within the precincts of the Abbey thirty years since still be traced a square moat, enclosing about an acre of ground, where formerly stood a house, called in the time of the later Abbots "the Moated House or Lodge." It is probable that this was the site of William de Montfichet's manor place, perhaps vacated by him when his castle at Stanstead was completed—or it may even have been the habitation of Leured, the Saxon.

At this period William had also a vassal here, whose name was Gerard de Hamme, with whom he had exchanged eleven acres of meadow for fourteen acres of land in the marsh, to add to his demesne. By a charter, still extant, he also confirmed the gift of a meadow which Gerard de Hamme, with the consent of his son Martin and his other sons, bestowed upon the Abbot and Convent, and likewise consented to Roger, his chaplain, giving the "tythes of the demesne;" both are transactions of a feudal lord, exercising his prerogative.

The next lord of these manors, the evidence of whose possession we find recorded, is Gilbert de Montfichet, son of William, who, before the year 1181 confirmed his father's gifts to the Abbey, by a charter which is lost but mentioned in King Henry II.'s Confirmation Charter, and himself gave to the Monks of Stratford the Churches of West Ham and Leyton. The same document also mentions the land "they have in the same town of the gift of Luke, the son of Martin," probably Martin, the son of the above mentioned Gerard de Hamme.

The name of Baalun may, with great probability, be added to the feudatories holding land at this date in Ham, for we find that a certain Walter de Baalun gave to the Abbey some land in Ham; besides, among the local witnesses to the charter of the afore-mentioned John de Venois appear the names of Alan and Gilbert Baalun.

Gilbert de Montfichet was succeeded in the barony of Stanstead by his son Richard, after whose death Milicent, his widow, in the year 1204, paid 400 marks to the king for liberty to marry William de Warren, Lord of Wormegay in Norfolk, who shortly afterwards paid 100 marks to the king on her behalf, that she might have her reasonable dower as widow of Richard de Montfichet.

Richard de Montfichet was succeeded by his son, also named Richard. Both father and son served as Sheriffs of Essex, and it was during his period of office that one of them raised a gallows, held a view of frank-pledge[1] in East and West Ham, and took the assize of bread and beer.[2] To regulate the prices of bread and beer, as well as the measures, were common manorial rights, while that of erecting a gallows belonged to the higher jurisdictions and may have been connected with the Shrievalty. The name of "Gallows' Green," which was anciently given to Stratford Green would, we presume, indicate that such an erection had once stood there.

The next proof of the dominion of the Montfichet family in these parishes is a charter, given by King Henry III., in the thirty-seventh year of his reign (1253), whereby he granted to Richard de Montfichet "a fair and market" in West Ham, of which the following is a translation :

We grant and by this our Charter confirm to the same Richard de Montfichet for us and our heirs, that he and his heirs for ever shall have a market at West Ham every week on Wednesday. And that they may have in the same place a fair every year for four days' duration, viz : the vigil and the day of the feast of St. Margaret, the Virgin, and on the two following days, with all liberties, etc. etc.

These are the witnesses, etc. etc.

---

[1] The view of frank-pledge (or Court-Leet) was a Court of record, held once in the year within a particular hundred, lordship or manor before the Steward of the leet, to view the frank-pledges, that is the freemen within the liberty, who according to the Saxon form were mutually pledges for the good behaviour of each other and the preservation of the public peace. They were divided into tithings (decenna), so called, because each group usually consisted of ten householders ; hence it became customary for the sheriffs of every county court (leet) from time to time to take the oaths of young persons, as they grew up to fourteen years of age and to see, that they were settled in one group or another, whereby this branch of the sheriff's authority was called " view of frank-pledge."

[2] By ancient statute, bakers who broke the assize, were to stand in the pillory, and brewers, in the tumbrel or dung-cart.

In times, when commerce was in its infancy and the means of conveyance uncertain and hazardous, fairs and markets were of great consequence. Traders travelled with their wares from one place to another and supplied the scattered population, who were assembled on those occasions, with the necessaries of life as well as with luxuries.

Richard de Montfichet, second of the name, baron of Stanstead, the last of his family in the direct line, died without issue in the year 1267, possessed besides other estates of the manors of East and West Ham in Essex.

His barony now became divided and subdivided among the heirs and descendants of his three sisters and coheiresses, viz: Margaret, wife of Hugh de Bolbec, Aveline, wife of William de Fortibus, Earl of Albemarle, and Philippa, wife of Hugh de Plaiz.

On the death of Jacosa his widow, in 1274, her dower consisting, besides other portions, of the manor of West Ham, the woods of East and West Ham, and £21 11s 3d rents in West Ham, was shared by the four granddaughters of Margaret de Bolbec, as coheirs of one third part of the barony of Richard de Montfichet.

Two hundred years had now elapsed since Robert Gernon the Norman, was enfeoffed by the Conqueror in the lordship of Hamme in Essex, and during the whole of that period it remained in the possession of his successors the Montfichets, as the capital tenants, with the exception of the demesne land in West Ham with which William de Montfichet had endowed the Abbey of Stratford Langthorne in the year 1135.

The particulars of the dismemberment of the barony among the coheirs of the last baron will be treated in the next chapter.

CHAPTER IV.

(CONTENTS).

DISMEMBERMENT OF THE LORDSHIP OF MONTFICHET AND ORIGIN OF THE SUCCEEDING MANORS.

ICHARD DE MONTFICHET having died without issue, and his three sisters Margaret, Aveline and Philippa being also deceased, the barony of Montfichet was divided among their descendants, which necessarily caused its dismemberment.

Margaret, Richard's eldest sister, wife of Hugh de Bolbec, was represented in her third part by her four granddaughters, the children and coheirs of her son Hugh de Bolbec, viz:

> Philippa, wife of Roger de Lancaster.
> Margaret, married first to Nicholas Corbet, and
> secondly to Ralph de Grimsthorpe.
> Alice, wife of Walter de Huntercombe.
> Matilda, wife of Hugh de la Val or de Laval.

Aveline, the second sister of Richard, wife of William de Fortibus, Earl of Albemarle, was represented in her third part of the barony of Montfichet by her granddaughter and sole heiress Aveline, wife of Edmund, son of King Henry III. As she died without issue (1275) her inheritance and share in the lordship of Ham, consisting of the Manor of East Ham, as well as of several knights' fees in East Ham and other places, which formed part of the barony of Stanstead Montfichet, seems to have reverted to the heirs of Richard's eldest sister, Margaret de Bolbec.

Philippa de Plaiz, the third and youngest sister of Richard, was succeeded in her third part by her son Richard, whose share continued in the possession of his descendants of the same name for several generations.

While in possession of these heirs of Montfichet the manorial rights of the various holders appear to have extended indefinitely over portions of both parishes.

By a deed dated 1269, two years after the death of Richard de Montfichet, we find that Richard de Plaiz, being his kinsman and coheir and paying his relief according for one third part of the barony of Montfichet, had that portion in Ham assigned to him, which has since been known as the Manor of Plaiz, and includes the township of Plaistow.[1]

A second deed proceeds to divide and assign amongst the four granddaughters of Margaret de Bolbec and their husbands a third part of the knights' fees of the barony of Montfichet, amongst which a fourth part of a knight's fee, held by the heirs of Richard in West Ham, is assigned to Hugh de la Val and Matilda his wife.

A third deed provides that the woods of East and West Ham, which had been excepted from the above assignment out of the dower of Jacosa, the widow of Richard, should pass to the other heirs, and it appears, that in the year 1290 these woods were in the possession of Giles, grandson of the above named Richard de Plaiz.

The manor of West Ham is thus accounted for, first as the dower of Jacosa, and afterwards as partitioned among the granddaughters and coheirs of Richard de Montfichet's eldest sister Margaret.

Soon after the partition of the lordship of Montfichet, East Ham Manor became divided. In 1286 Ralph de Grimsthorpe and Margaret, his wife, who was the granddaughter of Margaret de Bolbec, sold their manor in East Ham, with other property of their inheritance, to Robert Burnels, Bishop of Bath and Wells, and it is believed that another moiety belonging to another sister, Alice de Huntercombe, was added

---

[1] Plaistow — "tow" being the Saxon name for place or seat, means the seat of Plaiz.

to it. The two manors, therefore, now known as East and West Ham Burnels, were thus dismembered from the great lordship of Montfichet. These two manors have always gone together and as the account of them extends to modern times, they will be more appropriately treated in a future chapter.

Matilda de la Val, who had inherited the manors of East and West Ham, died in the year 1288 without issue, and it appears that her manor of East Ham passed to her elder sister Philippa de Lancaster. But the reader will have already perceived, that it is difficult to identify the portions of land which were assigned to the various coheirs at this period.

Philippa de Lancaster died in the year 1294, possessed of the whole manor of East Ham, with the exception of that portion, which had been sold to Robert Burnels, Bishop of Bath and Wells.

John de Lancaster having inherited the manor of East Ham and other lands of his mother Philippa and of his aunt Maude de la Val, obtained in the year 1307 the King's licence to give two acres of land in East Ham to the Abbot and convent of Stratford, together with the advowson of the church of that parish, to which he afterwards added forty acres of land in East Ham. In the original document the Abbey is designated as of "Stratford-atte-Boghe," a mistake which is occasionally made both in ancient and more modern times.

He afterwards granted, in conjunction with his wife Annora, to the same house the reversion of his manor of East Ham, reserving to himself and his wife a life interest in the same, for which purpose he obtained a licence from the Crown. Dying without issue in the year 1334, his cousin Richard de Plaiz, who was the husband of his sister Margaret, became his heir. Annora, his widow, survived him a few years, but died before the year 1339; on her death the Abbot and Convent became possessed of the manor of East Ham, probably including that portion which is now known by the name of East-West Ham, and held it until the dissolution of the monastic houses in the year 1539.

Having given an account of the portions of the manorial property inherited by the two eldest sisters of Richard de Montfichet, Margaret de Bolbec and Aveline, Countess of Albemarle, it remains for us to account for the third part, the share of his youngest sister, Philippa de Plaiz.

We have already stated that in 1269 Richard de Plaiz had the manor of Plaistow assigned to him, and that Giles de Plaiz, great grandson of Philippa de Montfichet, inherited the woods of East and West Ham in the forest,[1] out of the dower of Jacosa de Montfichet. At the death of Giles in the year 1303, the manor of West Ham and rent from thirty tenements in East Ham, amounting to £8 3s 4d, besides, a wood of six acres and the view of frank-pledge devolved to his son Richard, husband of Margaret, the sister of his cousin John de Lancaster. After his decease the whole remnant of the barony de Montfichet centred in his descendants.

His son, also named Richard, gave in the year 1254 to the monks of Stratford his manors of East and West Ham and all his tenements there that he had or might have, and £8 3s 4d rent from the same, with the accustomed services, view of frank-pledge etc., also ten acres of wood and twelve acres of heath in Ham Frith. In this as in the preceeding documents it appears, that all the heirs of Montfichet possessed manorial rights extending indefinitely into both parishes.

DEED OF GIFT BY RICHARD DE PLAIZ, KNT., CLOSE ROLLS 27 EDWARD III.

Translation:

Know ye present and future that I, Richard de Plaiz, Knight, give, concede and by this my present charter confirm to God and the Church of Mary of Stratford, the Abbot and Convent of the same place, and their successors in pure and perpetual alms, all my tenements with all my lordship and its appurtenances, which I have or may have in the towns of East and West Ham in the county of Essex, and all services, suit and custom, as well from my freemen as from the villains, their chattels and services and right of enfranchisement together with cottages, houses, gardens and yards. Also ten acres of heath lying in the place, called Ham Frith, £8 3s 4d rent of assize yearly from the aforesaid tenants and their tenements and right of entry thereon, and all

---

[1] It must be borne in mind, that as late as 1622 all the land north of the high road between Stratford and Ilford was in the forest.

sorts of reversions of lands and tenements with their appurtenances, in whatever way they belong to the said lordship in the aforesaid towns, and other liberties whatsoever, as fealty, homage, wardship, marriage, rents, services, heriots, reliefs, escheats, lands, mills, woods, meadows, panage and pastures, marshes, moors, turbaries, waters, fisheries, streams, ponds, rivers, dikes, ditches, roads, footpaths, vagabonds and suit of Court, with view of frank-pledge, and all other and singular liberties and appurtenances of this tenement and lordship in whatever manner it may appear. To have and to hold all the aforesaid tenements, lordship, services, rents, woods, lands and reversions aforesaid, with all and every their liberties, rights and appurtenances aforesaid by the said Abbot and Convent and their successors, freely, quietly, wholly, well and peaceably in pure and perpetual alms of the capital lord of the fee, by the services therefrom due and by right of the occasional custom. And I, the aforesaid Richard and my heirs, all the aforesaid tenements with the lordship and its appurtenances, services, rents, suits and customs, whether of the freemen or villains, etc. ctc., will warrant the said Abbot and Convent and their successors against all persons, etc. In testimony whereof to this present charter I have set my seal.

These are the witnesses:

JOHN DE STAUNTON.

HUMFREY DE WALEDEN, (WALDON).

JOHN DE HAVERING.

JOHN DE GOLDINGHAM.

THOMAS PASSELOW.   KNIGHTS.

With this last gift to the monks of Stratford the interest of the family of de Plaiz and of the heirs of Montfichet ceased in these parishes. With the exception therefore of that dismemberment which was caused by the sale of land to Robert Burnel, Bishop of Bath and Wells, in 1286, the whole lordship of "Hamme," granted by

H

William the Conqueror to Robert Gernon, was now absorbed by the Abbey, and contained the following manors:

MANOR OF EAST HAM OR EAST HAM HALL.

This manor extends over all that part of East Ham which is not included in East Ham Burnels. East Ham Hall, now a farm-house, is situate near the church. This manor had been successively the possession of Aveline de Fortibus, Countess of Albemarle, of Matilda de Laval, of Philippa de Lancaster, and finally, of her son John de Lancaster, who gave it to the Abbey.

THE MANOR OF EAST-WEST-HAM.

This manor in West Ham, and adjacent to East Ham, was included in John de Lancaster's gift to the Abbey. In 1337 a jury was summoned respecting the state of the marsh lands, when it was stated by the jury that this manor was in or belonged to the lordship or manor of Lancaster in West Ham and had long existed, as well as those of Burnels and Plaiz.

THE MANOR OF PLAIZ.

This manor took its name from Hugh de Plaiz, whose descendant, Sir Richard, gave it to the Abbot and Convent in the year 1353. *(See page 48, line 11 — read 1353 instead of 1254).*

THE MANOR OF WEST HAM.

This manor includes the original endowment of the Abbey by the gift of William de Montfichet.

THE MANOR OF WOODGRANGE OR HAM FRITH.

This manor was given to the Abbot and Convent by the Montfichets and others in various parcels, which it is impossible to define.

These five great capital manors remained in the possession of the Abbot and Convent until the dissolution by Henry VIII., by whom they were granted to various persons. With his reign, therefore, a new era in their history commences, which will more properly find its place after that of the Abbey, and will bring it down to our own time.

Besides these five great manors we find in West Ham parish some smaller or subordinate manors. These, of course, took their rise before the year 1290, when the statute of "Quia Emptores" was passed to check the further sub-division and sub-enfeoffment of manorial property. There were four in number, namely "Sudbury," which we have already discussed, "Coverlee's Fee," "Bretts" and "Chobhams."

COVERLEE'S FEE.

This manor has entirely disappeared. It was one of those small sub-infeudations which the statute "Quia Emptores" was intended to check. It came out in evidence, in 1337, before Henry Gernet and his fellow justices, who were assigned for the view of the repair of the banks of the river Thames in this county, that in the time of King Henry III., one John de Coverlee held of the Fee of Montfichet in the marsh of West Ham fifty acres of land, together with a bank called Coverlee's Wall, and a certain piece of pasture reported to be sufficient for the pasturage of six kine, called "Le Hope," lying near the said bank without the precinct of the said marsh, namely, between the bank and the course of the river Thames.

John de Coverlee alienated the Bank and Hope to Robert le Ku, to hold of him and his heirs for the repair of the said bank or wall. And afterwards, long before the statute "Quia Emptores" was enacted, John de Coverlee sold his land by parcels to divers tenants and their heirs, to hold of him and his heirs for a yearly rent and suit of Court. Lastly, he sold the whole demesne, rents and service to one Simon de Paslewe, who again sold them to Cecilie de Lancaster. The latter granted the whole lordship and manor to the Prioress and Nuns of St. Leonard's-at-Bow.

At the date of this enquiry (1337), this manor was held by Sir John de Handlo, as heir to Robert Burnel, over and above the services due to him as chief lord of the fee, while to the Prioress of St. Leonard's was left only a rent of fourteen shillings.

MANOR OF BRETTS.

Of the early history of Bretts or of its dismemberment from the greater lordships there has as yet not been any satisfactory account.

MORANT informs us, "that of this manor nothing is heard before the reign of Edward IV., when John Ferrers, who died in 1478, held the manor of Brettys in East Ham." The boundary-line of East and West Ham was clearly in those days very different from what it now is; thus Brett's manor was promiscuously placed in both parishes. The next possessor was Edward, Earl of Warwick, son of George Plantagenet, late Duke of Clarence; but the said Edward being afterwards executed for treason (1499), all his estates became forfeited to the Crown. In 1519 this manor was settled by King Henry VIII. on his Queen, Catherine of Arragon. In 1576 Queen Elizabeth granted it in fee to Sir Thomas Heneage, who in 1583 alienated it to Roger Townsend. By him it was conveyed to Edward de Vere, Earl of Oxford, whose widow, in order to re-purchase Hedingham Castle, the ancient seat of the de Vere family, obtained in 1609 an Act of Parliament to sell this manor of Bretts and a farm at Plaistow to Henry Wollaston, who died 1619 possessed of it, leaving Henry his son and heir. Probably, the younger Wollaston alienated it to Sir William Courteen, whose son William sold it to Jacob Garrard in the year 1637 for the sum of £3100. Sir Francis Bickley who had married Alithea, daughter and coheiress of another Jacob Garrard, who was the son and heir apparent of Sir Thomas Garrard, became in her right possessed of this manor and sold it in 1711 to Peter Courtney, who in 1719 bequeathed it to his sister Elizabeth, wife of William Beauchamp, from whom it descended to Joseph Beauchamp. It eventually became the property of Henry Hinde Pelly, Esq., whose grandson, Sir Henry Pelly, disposed of it for building purposes some thirty years ago. In ancient times this manor appears to have included the greater part of the villages of Upton and Plaistow.

There was in former years a capital messuage called "the Manor House of Bretts" which, from a rude sketch accompanying the deed now in possession of the present baronet, Sir Harold Pelly, appears to have been what is called a "Gate House." It may be worth mentioning here that St. Mary's Church at Plaistow, and the schools attached to it, stand on the site of the old manor house, and it is very probable that "Chapel Fields" derives its name from the old manorial Chapel.

Manor of Chobhams or Chobham.

The mansion stands or rather stood on the left of the road leading from Stratford to Low Leyton. It is understood to have been taken from several other manors, and was in the year 1417 in the possession of Sir William Franceys, who held it of Hugh Burnel and of the Abbot of Stratford. Agnes, wife of Sir William Porter, and Elizabeth, wife of Thomas Charleton were his daughters and coheiresses. Agnes left Sir Thomas Charleton, her sister Elizabeth's son, her heir, and on his death the manor passed to his son Sir Richard Charleton, who was attainted of high treason for being of the party of King Richard III.; his forfeited estates were granted in 1487 by King Henry VII. to Sir John Rysley. He dying without issue in 1512, they again passed to the Crown. In 1513 they were granted to Sir William Compton who, dying in 1528, left his son Peter Compton, only seven years old, his heir. In 1589 the notorious Tipper and Dawe procured a grant of this and other lands, but in 1596 the manor was granted by Queen Elizabeth to Thomas Spencer and Robert Atkinson, who in the following year conveyed it to Richard Wiseman, whose heirs sold it to the Hyet family. It finally became the property of Sir John Henniker, who was created Lord Henniker in 1800 and had a seat in Stratford, called "Stratford House," where he died in the year 1803. His father was an eminent merchant in London and, dying in 1749, was buried in the church yard at West Ham. The manor of Chobhams is now extinct, and the land which belonged to it has been acquired by the Great Eastern Railway Company for their railways and extensive works.

Thus we have endeavoured to trace the dismemberments of the ancient Anglo-Norman lordship of Montfichet in the parishes of East and West Ham. They afford a good example of that sub-division of manors and consequently of the feudal services attached to them which resulted in the well known statute of "Quia Emptores." In fact, it had now become almost impossible for the feudal system of personal service, a knight for a knight's fee, to be carried out through all these partitions and complications of tenure.

CHAPTER V.

(Contents).

GENEALOGY OF THE FAMILIES OF MONTFICHET.

MONG the greater of the Essex barons in the time of our Anglo-Norman kings were the Montfichets, the chief seat of whose barony was at Stanstead, on the western borders of the county, which from them took its distinctive appellation of Stanstead-Montfichet. In this barony the Montfichets were preceded by Robert Gernon, to whom it was allotted in the general distribution of land that took place after the Norman Conquest.

In Domesday-Book Robert Gernon is recorded to have possessed in Essex forty-four manors, twelve of which he held in demesne, that is, in his own hands. They comprised fifty-three hides and eighty-one acres of land, the total yearly value of which amounted to £50 in Edward the Confessor's time, but had at the date of the "Survey" — deducting the moiety of the manor of West Ham which he shared with Ralph Peverel — increased to £78. Of these twelve lordships, four were very considerable, namely, Oakley, which contained ten hides, West Ham eight hides, East Ham seven hides, and Stanstead six hides.

Of the ancestry or personal history of Robert Gernon little or nothing is known; his birth-place and descent are alike involved in obscurity.

MORANT, in his "History of Essex," asserts Robert Gernon, upon whom the Conqueror bestowed the great lordship of Hamme, to have been the ancestor of the Montfichets of Stanstead, but he appears to have been unconscious of their connexion with the Sires de Montfichet in Normandy, or of the existence of the place of that name, since he imagined that the name was derived from the artificial mound, on which their castle at Stanstead was built. In one place he states, that Robert Gernon descended from the house of Boulogne, while in another he says "we have reason to suppose, that he was descended from the same family as the fourth Earl of Chester." For the first of these assertions there appears to be no foundation ; the second is probably derived from a coincidence in name, Ranulph de Meschines, fourth Earl of Chester, being surnamed Gernon from his birth place, the castle of Gernon in Normandy.

DUGDALE in his "Baronage" makes no mention of Robert Gernon in his account of the Montfichet family, nor of the source whence they derived their estates in England, but he knew of their connexion with Normandy and of the existence of William de Montfichet, lord of the castle of Montfichet in the Cotentin, who was a benefactor to the Abbey of Cerisy, before the year 1087.

Genealogists assert that he accompanied the Norman army into England, and received his large grant of land in reward for his services. He has been considered by MORANT and others to have had two sons, William de Montfichet, the elder, and Robert Gernon, the younger. The posterity of the latter retained the surname of Gernon for some centuries in the counties of Norfolk, Suffolk, Essex and Derbyshire. Although so often asserted and extremely probable, no absolute proof of the affiliation of these families with Robert Gernon, the capital tenant of the "Domesday Survey," has yet been afforded, whilst it is certain that the entire barony of which he was possessed passed to the Montfichets as early as the reign of Henry I., perhaps earlier.

Before dismissing the subject of Robert Gernon, we ought to mention that one branch of the Gernons was seated at Moore Hall and Bakewell in Derbyshire, as early as the time of Edward I. William Gernon was Lord of Bakewell in that county in 1286. The daughters and coheiresses of John Gernon of that place, who died in 1383, married into the families of Peyton and Botetot, whose heirs sold Bakewell to the Vernons in 1502.

Another branch settled in Suffolk. Roger Gernon, of Gunston Hall, who died 1324, married the daughter and heiress of John Patten, Lord of Cavendish; the sons of this marriage are said to have assumed the surname of Cavendish.

A third branch remained in Essex, where they held small portions of land under the Montfichets, as well as estates of their own. At Birch they had a castle which, tradition says, was fortified by Ralph Gernon against Henry III.

The existence of these families of the name of Gernon precludes, therefore, the idea that Robert Gernon was a childless member of the Montfichet family, whose possessions reverted to the house of Montfichet.

The first person of the name of Montfichet, mentioned by DUGDALE, is Gilbert, whom he calls a Roman by birth and a kinsman to the Conqueror, adding that he accompanied him to England, bringing "a great strength, and fighting stoutly in his cause in the field of Hastings, for which he received large possessions." Unfortunately for this account, the name of Montfichet does not occur in "Domesday Survey," and all the estates afterwards possessed by the Montfichet family were at that time, as far as we are able to trace them, the property of Robert Gernon, with the exception of the Montfichet tower in London, concerning which there is no record in "Domesday." DUGDALE appears to have been led into these mistakes, respecting this family, by an ancient M.S. called "Origo Baronum de Montfichet," the object of which M.S. is to prove the descent of the de Veres from the Montfichets and their consequent right to the patronage of Thremhall Priory. Any one, who will take the trouble to compare it with the genealogy of Montfichet in DUGDALE's Baronage, will perceive the similarity; although DUGDALE rejected part, he accepted the remainder.

The value of this paper as an authority is, however, very doubtful. MORANT speaks of it as erroneous and having led SIR WILLIAM DUGDALE into some mistakes. The date of it cannot be earlier than 1429, when John de Vere, twelfth Earl of Oxford, married an heiress of the Howard family, whose grandmother was one of the heiresses of

Sir Richard de Montfichet, the last baron of that name, who died in 1267. In this lapse of time, after so varied a descent, the history of the Montfichets must have become only a tradition with the de Veres, to be received by us with caution and not to be put in competition with contemporary evidence.

The Family of Montfichet.

Having ventured to discard the former accounts of this family, it remains for us to prove, what appears to be the true history of this ancient Anglo-Norman race, and in this endeavour we are greatly aided by the access to Norman documents, which we possess in the present day.

Not far from Bayeux in the department of La Manche are the ruins of an ancient Abbey, founded in 1032, by Robert, duke of Normandy, at a place called Cerisy, which now gives its name to the surrounding forest, of which the Lords of Montfichet once were the hereditary foresters. Near by is the present village of Montfiquet, which was of great consequence in ancient times and had a very strong castle, the ruins of which are still to be seen on the road from Bayeux to St. Lo. According to tradition, a flourishing town once existed under the protection of its walls. Towards the middle of the fourteenth century this town was besieged by the enemies of its lord, who with his vassals retreated within the castle; the besiegers, unable to reduce it by force, burnt it together with the town.

This place is considered by the Norman antiquaries to be the cradle of the family of Montfichet, afterwards seated in Essex, and whose barony comprised the manors of East and West Ham. The old Norman writers spell the name Montfichet, the modern spelling is Montfiquet, but as the letter C is pronounced hard in Norman-French, the sound of both is the same.

During the time England and Normandy were under one sovereign, the Seigneurs de Montfichet had interest on either side of the Channel, but when Normandy was lost by King John, we find that Richard de Montfichet, then a minor, remained in England until his death in the year 1267, when his English inheritance was divided amongst the heirs of his three sisters.

Whether seated in France or in England, this family is mentioned

I

as of high antiquity and consequence. DUGDALE imagines them to have been related to the Conqueror himself; CAMDEN says "They were reckoned amongst the chief of our nobility," and WEEVER'S expression is "They were reputed men of very great nobilitie."

The earliest individual notice we have seen of a member of this family is between 1082 and 1087, when William de Montfichet, a contemporary of Robert Gernon, with the consent of William de Tancarville, Chamberlain of Normandy, bestowed on the monks of Cerisy the Church of St. Marculf and its tithes. We also find among the Norman leaders, whom ROBERT WACE enumerates in his "Roman de Rou," the Sire de Montfichet among those present at the battle of Hastings, and it is not unreasonable to suppose, that William, the benefactor to the Abbey of Cerisy, is the Sire de Montfichet, from whom Montfichet's tower in London took its name, notwithstanding that at the time of the "Survey" he held no land in capite in England. This tower de Montfichet was one of two, placed at the western extremity of the wall of the City of London, the other being under the charge of Ralph Baynard. STOW, after describing Castle Baynard, adds "that the next tower or castle, banking also on the Thames was, as is afore-showed, called "Montfiquet's Castle," belonging to a nobleman, baron of Montfichet, the first builder thereof, who came in with William the Conqueror and was surnamed le Sire Montfichet. This castle he builded in a place, not far distant from Baynard's castle towards the west."

By some historians a Roman origin is attributed to this tower, but this is improbable; the frequent tradition of Roman builders ascribed to ruins, unquestionably Norman, leads to the opinion, that the Normans availed themselves of the well chosen sites and enduring remains of that people.

FITZ-STEPHEN, who described London in 1190, says that "on the East stands the Palatine tower, a fortresse both large and strong, the walls and body of which were erected on deep foundations and built with a cement, tempered with the blood of beasts. On the West are two castles, well fortified, and the city wall is both high and thick."

Richard de Montfichet, baron of Stanstead, was in possession of this tower at the time of his death 1267. It was probably dismantled during his banishment, for we are told, that it was old and demolished in the year 1276. By gift of King Edward I., the materials of this tower were used for building the great house of "Blackfriars or Dominicans," which stood within the walls, opposite to Bridewell, and was founded by the interest and exhortations of Robert Kilwarby, Archbishop of Canterbury.

It is true the name of Montfichet does not occur in Domesday-Book, and DUGDALE states, that Gilbert, who was contemporary with that record, died at Rome, yet we think it clearly proved that the family of Montfichet, which settled at Stanstead and other places in Essex, is of Norman origin and name, and that a member of it accompanied the Conqueror in his invasion of England, although authorities differ about his christian name, whether Gilbert or William. Moreover, when it is shown, that besides adopting or retaining the surname of Montfichet, the successors of Robert Gernon had an interest in Montfichet's tower in London, no reasonable doubt can exist of the identity of race, though the exact application may not, in every instance, have been hitherto discovered.

MONTFICHET IN ENGLAND.

We have above stated that William de Montfichet, the benefactor to Cerisy, is presumably identical with the Sire de Monfichet, who was Châtelain of Montfichet's tower in London. His name does not occur in Domesday-Book, nor does he appear to have held any land of the Crown at the time of the "Survey," yet we find that all the ninety-one lordships or manors recorded in "Domesday" as in possession of Robert Gernon, were in the next generation in the possession of the barons of Montfichet.

In the absence of all other known cause, the transfer of the barony, held by Robert Gernon to William de Montfichet, has been ascribed to inheritance, possibly by marriage with an heiress, or it may have been a fresh gift from the Crown. MORANT positively asserts that the eldest son of Robert Gernon took the name of Montfichet, while the younger sons retained that of Gernon. Such, however, is clearly not the case.

Having no authentic evidence respecting Robert Gernon, there is nothing but conjecture to offer. The most probable is, that William de

Montfichet or his son may have married the heiress of Robert Gernon, or that Robert Gernon may have been a member of the Montfichet family, who for some personal reason was surnamed Gernon. Such changes were not uncommon among the Norman baronage, rendering their genealogies at times almost inexplicable. Some tie, either of feudality or blood, seems to have united the names, but what that tie was, or the cause of the succession of the English barony, remains unexplained. Here, therefore, we must leave the account of Robert Gernon imperfect, and proceed to the more complete history of the successors in his English barony, the family of Montfichet, of whom was William de Montfichet, castellan of the tower, called after his name, in London, and to whom we will give the designation of William de Montfichet the first.

WILLIAM DE MONTFICHET I.

Although not a capital tenant, we have presumptive evidence that he was a feudatory of Robert Gernon's, in Hertfordshire. Of the thirteen manors recorded as belonging to Robert in that county, ten were held of him by "Willielmus." Among these were Letchworth (there spelt Leceworth) and Wallington. In the reign of King Henry I., William de Montfichet, in conjunction with Rohais, his wife, and William their son, gave the Church of Letchworth, with its appurtenances, and twelve acres of land in the village of Letchworth, to the Abbey of St. Albans. This gift was confirmed by Henry II. in a charter sans date, which, from the witnesses, must have been executed between 1173 and 1182. CHAUNCEY, in his "History of Hertfordshire," considers William, the son, to have been the founder of Stratford Abbey, and the husband of Margaret de Clare.

WILLIAM DE MONTFICHET II.

He was the son of William and Rohais and married Margaret, daughter of Gilbert Fitz Richard, Earl of Clare. Ignorant of the date at which William de Montfichet I. died, it is impossible to identify the individuals and to distinguish the father from the son in the following instances.

William de Montfichet is described by the bard, GEOFFRY GAIMAR, as being among the hunters in the New Forest on the day that

William Rufus was shot by an arrow. Again, William de Montfichet was one of the witnesses to a charter of privileges, granted by King Henry I. to the City of London. Thirdly, in the returns made into the exchequer by the sheriffs of the various counties in 1131, we find that William de Montfichet was excused from makiug various payments, due to the revenue, especially for Danegelt.[1]

There certainly appears to have been some confusion in the minds of genealogists about these Williams de Montfichet, the successors of Robert Gernon, as to whether two or three persons bearing that name are intended. Although in Normandy Robert Gernon may have had a contemporary William de Montfichet by name, who was the Conqueror's companion, his successors were first, William, the husband of Rohais, secondly William, son of the above, who married Margaret de Clare. This William de Montfichet II. was in all probability the son William, named in the deeds of gift to St. Albans by William de Montfichet, lord of the manor of Letchworth, and his wife Rohais. At this date, 1134, William II. was capital lord of Hamme, another of Robert Gernon's great lordships, and there he established the Abbey, afterwards known as Stratford Langthorne, endowing it with the whole of his demesne in Hamme, and two mills near the Stratford causeway, his wood of Bockurst in Woodford, and the tithe of his pannage. This charter is witnessed by Margaret his wife, William de Montfichet his nephew, Mathew Gernon and others. A second charter, confirming this gift, is also witnessed by Margaret his wife, and in both these documents he addresses himself, according to the grand old baronial form, then in use, to all his servants, bailiffs and tenants, whether French or English greeting.

He is also suppposed to have built the castle at Stanstead, making it the head of his barony, which previously Hamme had been. To it was attached a park with hereditary park-keepers, whose

---

[1] The ancient tax for Danegelt was revived by the Conqueror in 1086 to defray the expences of guarding the Eastern coasts from a threatened invasion of the Danes, but was levied by his successors long after all cause for fear on this account had subsided. The Danegelt for Essex was £252 6s.

family name was Parker. The lordship of Stanstead is nearly forty miles round and the castle was, like all Norman castles, erected on a mound, from which circumstance some have erroneously imagined that the name of Montfichet was derived. Such may have been the case in Normandy, but certainly not at Stanstead Montfichet, in Essex.

Margaret, the wife of this baron, was of the family of Clare, being a granddaughter of Richard, son of Count Gilbert, a Norman of great renown and an offspring of the ducal house. Her brother Richard, who died in 1136, was the first Earl of Hertford; another brother was Gilbert de Clare, created first Earl of Pembroke in 1138, and father of the celebrated Richard Strongbow, conqueror of Ireland. From this period the names of Gilbert and Richard were introduced into the Montfichet family, in lieu of the old name of William.

According to a custom of that period with respect to armorial bearings in families nearly allied, we find the houses of Clare and Montfichet bearing variations of the same arms, and the Abbey of Stratford adopting those of its founder, with the significant addition of the crosier.

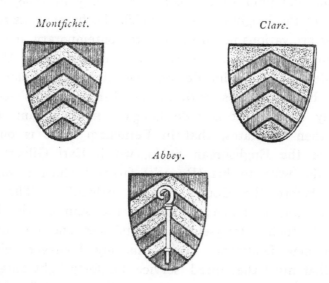

Montfichet.

Clare.

Abbey.

The "Abbey Arms Inn" at Plaistow, in the parish of West Ham, formerly had the arms of the Abbey painted on its sign.

Of the Lady Margaret little is known. One of the manors that belonged to the barony of Stanstead, appears to owe its present appellation of "Margaret-ing" to having been held by her in dower. In "Domesday" it is called Ginges, and Robert Gernon held part of it as demesne. Ginges is now divided into two parishes, Margareting and Friaring; the latter, now called Fryerning, is that portion of the estate, which was given by Gilbert de Montfichet to the Knights Hospitallers of St. John of Jerusalem.

WILLIAM DE MONTFICHET III.

The names of the sons of William and Margaret are not given in their father's charter to the Abbey of Hamme, but there exists documentary evidence that they were William and Gilbert. The distinction between this William III. and his predecessors has hitherto escaped notice, although it rests upon conclusive authority no less than on that of the man himself, that he was a minor during the civil wars of Stephen, which raged from 1138 to 1153. The proof is this; when Henry II. levied a feudal aid from his barons on the marriage of his daughter to the Duke of Saxony in 1168, each baron sent a return of the knights' fees for which the barony was responsible. These returns are various in form, but are contemporary and authentic. That for the barony of Stanstead is headed "Carta Willelmi de Montefichet de feodis Willelmi de Montefichet." Then follows a list of the names of his feudatories, with the number of knights' fees held by each. Lastly on the list is " de Ginga 1 militis quam mater mea tenet," and then he states, that in Ferneham there is one knights' fee that Roger the Englishman holds, which Earl Gilbert de Clare gave during the wars to his (Roger's) father "whilst I was a minor, and is now before the Courts on my behalf." The document concludes with this sentence: "This is the sum of the knights of William de Montfichet, forty-eight knights' fees and one-fifth part of the old and new feoffment. And this my homagers give me to understand, that my father owed service for forty-eight knights' fees."

Here we have documentary evidence, that in 1168 a William de Montfichet was the lord in possession of the barony of Stanstead, that his father had preceded him in the same, that his mother was living and holding a knight's fee in Ginges, and that he himself was a minor during the wars of Stephen, when Earl Gilbert de Clare had power over his estates. The inference is obvious, that his mother's brother was the guardian of the minor. Of the further history of this William de Montfichet III. nothing is known. That he died without issue is certain, since the next baron was Gilbert, son of William II. and Margaret de Clare, who must have been the younger brother of William III.

GILBERT DE MONTFICHET.

Gilbert de Montfichet, obviously so called after his maternal grandfather, the illustrious Gilbert de Clare, succeeded William III. in the barony of Stanstead and was most probably his brother. Of him we read, that in the third year of the reign of Henry II. (1157), he stood indebted to the king in the sum of two hundred marks of silver for two hawks and two gir falcons. This occurred some years before he became head of the family, and denotes the extravagant habits of a gay young courtier. The silver or Danish mark was twenty shillings or one hundred Saxon pennies; the sum, therefore, he paid was £200, an enormous sum if the comparative value of money in those times be considered. The passion of our ancestors for hawking is well known; the birds were protected by penal enactment and their value was almost equal to a modern race-horse.

After his succession to the barony Gilbert became a warm friend to monks. He confirmed his father's gift to the monks of Stratford, adding on his own account the Churches of West Ham and Leyton. This charter is probably lost, but in another charter of King Richard I. there is a confirmation to the Abbey of the Church of "All Souls, (Saints?) in West Ham, and the whole land which they have in the same town of the fee of Gilbert de Montfichet." Nor did he confine his bounty to the monks of Stratford, for he was also a liberal patron of other religious houses. The priory of Thremhall in Stanstead, is believed to owe its foundation to him, and at Wyrardisbury, in Bucks, a manor, which had descended to his ancestors from Robert Gernon, he and Aveline his wife founded a small Benedictine nunnery on the banks of the Thames, called Ankerwycke. An impression of the conventual seal of Ankerwick, which still remains, is very curious; it is a rude representation of a half-timbered hall or house, of the period of the foundation and may, perhaps, be considered as a portrait of the home bestowed on the nuns by Gilbert. The louvre for the escape of smoke from the roof of the Hall and the round-headed arch of the doorway are clearly portrayed.

There is also another relic of this period in the Ankerwycke grounds, near Runnymede, between Staines and Windsor, a yew tree,[1] in the vicinity of which those brave barons compelled King John to sign the Great Charter. The trunk of this grand old tree, which was most probably included in Gilbert's original gift to the Priory, measured at three feet above the ground twenty-seven feet in girth, and at eight feet, thirty-two feet and five inches.

On the Knight's Hospitallers of St. John of Jerusalem Gilbert bestowed half his manor of Ginges, except the outer wood called Westfrid, which he reserved to himself and heirs. This became eventually a parish by the name of Friaring, or friars pasture. The church there still retains some remains of the original Norman structure, to which period the font may be referred.

In 1183 he converted the chapel, belonging to the castle of Montfichet into the parochial church, dedicating it to Thomas à Becket. His name also occurs in a confirmation charter granted by Henry II., King of England and Duke of Normandy, to the Abbey of Longues, as holding a fief at Creully, near Bayeux.

Respecting the wife of Gilbert de Montfichet there arises

---

[1] This yew tree is supposed to have flourished 1000 years. Tradition says that Henry VIII. occasionally met Ann Boleyn under the lugubrious shade of its spreading branches at such times as she was placed in the neighbourhood of Staines, in order to be near at Windsor, whither the king used to love to repair from the cares of the state. Ill omened as was the place of meeting under such circumstances, it afforded but too apt an emblem of the result of that arbitrary passion which, overlooking every obstacle in its progress, was destined finally to hurry its victim to an untimely grave. It is more pleasing to view the tree as a silent witness of the conference of those barons, who afterwards compelled King John to sign the Magna Charta in its immediate vicinity, between Runnymede and Ankerwyke House, than as the involuntary confidences of love so unhallowed and so unblest as that of King Henry and Ann Boleyn. (Strutt's Silva Britannica).

K

one of those difficulties, which not unfrequently obscure ancient genealogies. Dugdale does not name the wife of this baron in his "Baronage," but in Henry II.'s charter to Ankerwycke she is named Aveline, and the name of Aveline was retained in the family and borne by a granddaughter and great-granddaughter of Gilbert's. After the death of Gilbert de Montfichet, his wife is recorded as Ancelina de Lucy, who in the year 1206 went to law with the Abbot of Stratford, respecting the right to the advowson of the Church of Leyton, which she claimed as her dower, given her by her late husband Gilbert de Montfichet. Two years later when Richard, the grandson of Gilbert, was a minor in the guardianship of the Constable of Chester, is an order, registered in the Close Rolls, by which R. de Cornhull "is commanded to take into the king's hands the lands of Aveline de Montfichet and, if possible, ascertain which of them were of the inheritance of Richard de Montfichet, and that such of them as belonged to him by right of inheritance should be given over to the Constable of Chester, who has the custody of all the lands of the said Richard." But only four months later the same record contains a precept to the Sheriff of Essex, commanding him "to cause the Constable of Chester to have the land which Ancelina de Lucy held at her death, which the said Constable says is, by right and inheritance, the inheritance of Richard de Montfichet, at that time his ward, and which Rohais de Dover says is her's by right of inheritance."

Rose or Rohais de Dover was the granddaughter of the eminent judge Richard de Lucy, lord of the honor of Ongar, at which place he built a castle on an artificial mound, surrounded by intrenchments, like that of his neighbour and contemporary Gilbert de Montfichet at Stanstead. Rohais was heir to her brothers Geoffry and Herbert de Lucy, and this same year, 1208, paid her relief for the whole barony of Lucy. It is clear, that the families of Montfichet and Lucy had a disputed interest in some of the land held by Ancelina de Lucy, and that she had been the wife of Gilbert de Montfichet. It is equally certain, that his wife is called in other instances Aveline. Whether the variation is simply the result of a clerical error, writing n for u or v, or that Gilbert de Montfichet had two wives, must be left to future research.

RICHARD DE MONTFICHET I.

The year of Gilbert de Montfichet's death is not known, but he was succeeded by his son Richard, as baron of Stanstead, in the latter part of the reign of Henry II., who confirmed him in the office of forester of Essex and the custody of the palace at Havering, by a charter which is still extant. The form of "Sciatis me" proves this charter to be antecedent to King Richard I. who commenced the use of "Sciatis nos." Of this document the following is a literal translation:

Henry, by the grace of God, King of England, etc.

Know ye, that I have granted and conceded, and by this my charter have confirmed to Richard de Montfichet and his heirs the custody of all my forest at Essex and of my houses at Havering and whatever other houses I may have in the said forest, together with all my parks and all the appurtenances belonging to the said charge. To have and to hold the same hereditarily from me and my heirs, as his ancestors more completely and securely held the same in time of peace of my predecessors.

Likewise with this condition, that no servant shall reside in the said forest, unless appointed by the said Richard for the custody of the same, except those who hold in my demesne manors by a certain service. Nevertheless these feudatories shall be wholly subject to the said Richard and in all that relates to their Bailiwicks, shall be responsible to him and his heirs as my Chief Forester of Essex.

These are the witnesses, etc.

Shortly after the accession of King Richard I., surnamed Coeur de Lion, we find Richard de Montfichet with the Court at Westminster. On the return of the king from his captivity in Germany he accompanied him on a warlike expedition into Normandy, for which service he, with other barons, was excused the payment of the scutage.[1] After this,

---

[1] Scutage—or shield money—was a money composition for military service, and was levied by assessment at a certain rate for every knight's fee.

the health of Richard de Montfichet became infirm and he was in consequence unable to attend the Michaelmas assizes at Hertford in 1198, nor had he sufficiently recovered to appear in May 1199 at Canterbury, on business connected with a plea against the Jews, for service due to "Our Lord the Duke," for we find his name amongst the essoigns.[1] The recorded date is May 9th 1199, during the interregnum, for thus that period is styled, which elapsed between the death of King Richard I. on the 6th of April, and the coronation of John on the 27th of May. In Normandy John was girt with the sword of the Duchy on the 25th of April, and is consequently styled in the above record "Our Lord the Duke," while in England the nobility hesitated in acknowledging the title of John, whom they knew and hated.

In 1202 Richard de Montfichet was sheriff of Essex and Herts, and keeper of the castle of Hertford. He also paid in that year 100 marks to the king, to be confirmed in the forestership of Essex. He died in the year 1202, leaving by Milicent his wife, whose family name is not known, four children, one son and three daughters:

Richard, the son and heir.
Margaret, wife of Hugh de Bolbec.
Aveline, wife of William de Fortibus, Earl of Albemarle.
Philippa, wife of Hugh de Plaiz, lord of Weeting in Norfolk.

RICHARD DE MONTFICHET II.

He proved a turbulent and warlike man, and may be considered the more historical personage of his family. Left a minor at the death of his father, the wardship both of his person and lands, as a "Capital Tenant," belonged to the Crown, and was sold by King John to Roger de Lacy, Constable of Chester, for 1000 marks; on the death of de Lacy in 1211, King John again sold his wardship for 1100 marks to Milicent, the mother of the minor. It is probable that he was approaching the age to be married, which would greatly

---

[1] Essoign—denotes a lawful excuse for him that is summoned to appear and answer to an action, or to perform suit to a court baron by reason of sickness, infirmity or other just cause of absence.

enhance the value of the remnant of his minority. The right of ward-ship was originally intended to secure to the feudal lord the military service due from the fee, during the nonage of the hereditary tenant. However it degenerated into a great hardship, the estate of the minor being too often wasted by the guardian, to repay himself the sums he had paid for the privilege. The whole system became a simple matter of bargain and sale, including the person of the heir, who was sold in marriage, or as it was softened in expression, "whose marriage was sold," without the slightest reference to the wishes of the persons concerned. The sale of a marriage of an heir, whether male or female, was a most valuable privilege or perquisite; the price was regulated by the bargains of the contracting parties *i.e.*, the king or his grantee, who sold the bride or bridegroom, and the parent who bought the match for the benefit of his offspring. It is hard to conceive a more general and cruel grievance than this shameful market, which so universally outraged the most sacred relations among mankind.

This abuse of wardship was one of the many complaints of the discontented barons, and was reformed in Magna Charta, being the second right conceded by King John to his lay subjects. It has already been observed in the incidents of Montfichet family, that heavy fines and reliefs were paid by them to John at this period, to obtain their reasonable rights; presuming, therefore, every family in the kingdom to have been similarly circumstanced, we can fully understand the national discontent which existed at that time of our history.

The exact date when Richard de Montfichet came of age is not known, but he appears immediately after to have joined the ranks of the rebellious barons, among whom were already enlisted John de Lacy, the son of his former guardian, William de Fortibus, Earl of Albemarle, and Hugh de Plaiz, his brothers-in-law, and his cousin Richard de Clare. MAITLAND, in his history of London, asserts that Richard was expelled the kingdom by King John in the year 1213, when Montfichet's tower in London was dismantled. The account of him given in the paper called "Origo Baronum de Montfichet," written by the monks of Thremhall, may be considered a family tradition relating to the baron, but that document is so vague as to persons, and so incorrect as to the dates respecting these early generations, that its evidence is rendered of little value. It is there stated, that Richard de Montfichet I. died on pilgrimage at Rome, and that when his son Richard attained to man's estate he went to Rome; "being a person of extraordinary strength, he obtained much fame in casting a stone, no man being able to do the like. In memory whereof certain pillars of brass were set up to show the distance." To this is added, that during his absence from England "all his castles were destroyed and devastated in the wars of the barons." This assertion is indirectly confirmed by the fact, that in 1276 Montfichet's tower in London was "old and demolished." The appearance of the site of the castle and its earthworks at Stanstead would also lead to the conclusion that it had been destroyed by violence. If this story be correct, the young Montfichet must have returned home burning with indignation, and eager to throw himself into the heat of the civil war, in which he soon distinguished himself by his prowess. WEEVER says: "Richard de Montfichet was in the raignes of King John and Henry III. famous for his prowesse and chivalrie," and STOW remarks: "Three most forcible and valiable knights of England were Robert Fitz-Walter, Robert Fitz-Roger and Richard Mountfichet." It is a proof of remarkable hardihood and valour to be thus distinguished amongst the whole chivalry of England as one of three, among whom figured no less a person than Robert Fitz-Walter, lord of Dunmow, the leader of the host of the confederated barons.

Richard who was one of the twenty-five barons chosen at Runnymede in 1215, to enforce the observance of Magna Charta, could at this time not have been more than twenty-five years old, probably less, as he was a minor in 1211, when Milicent his mother gave 1100 marks for the guardianship of the remainder of his minority. He may have owed this distinction not only to his being the lord of Wyrardesbury, in which parish the islet in the Thames, still bearing the name of "Magna Charta Island," is situate, but also to the fact, that a manor house in the adjoining parish of Langley, which belonged to him and appears to have been second only to Stanstead in importance, was his occasional residence. It is true that neither tradition nor history allude to it, in connexion with Magna Charta, but it seems highly probable, that the hall with its ancient walls was at that important period the resident of its lord. Six days after the royal signature had been affixed to the Great Charter of our national liberties, Richard de Montfichet obtained the restoration of the forestership of Essex, by an order from King John, dated from Runnymede on the 21st of June 1215 and addressed to Hugh de Neville, warden and chief justice of all the king's forests..

Richard de Montfichet had enjoyed his hereditary office only a short time, when he lost it again on the renewal of the civil war, which recommenced in all its fury the following October, in consequence of the Pope having presumed to annul the Charter of liberties, and to denounce excommunication against the barons. Exasperated by the perfidy of John, the barons at length invoked the aid of the French king, offering the crown of England to his son Lewis. On this occasion Robert Fitz-Walter was sent as ambassador to France, accompanied by Richard de Montfichet, the whole of whose lands were now seized by John, who ordered the sheriffs of Essex, Bucks, Kent, Norfolk, Suffolk and Herts to give immediate possession of them to Ralph de Toney.

Montfichet remained in arms against King John during the short remainder of his reign, and continued to espouse the cause of Lewis, the French prince, even after the accession of King Henry III. The battle of Lincoln, in which the French or Barons' party was completely defeated, was fought on the 19th May, 1217, and amongst the prisoners taken on that hard fought field were Richard and his old companion in arms, Robert Fitz-Walter. It is needless to remind the reader that King Henry III. was at that time only a child of ten years old, under the guardianship of the regent William le Mareschal, Earl of Pembroke. This nobleman, steadfast in his loyalty to his royal ward, but also able to understand and sympathize in the grievances of his fellow subjects, devoted himself to settle the distracted affairs of the kingdom and to conciliate his peers. Accordingly, in the month of October, following the battle of Lincoln, he restored many of the forfeited estates, in which number those of Richard de Montfichet were included, who now was also reinstated in the forestership of Essex.

One of the subjects to which the regent Pembroke directed his attention, was the relaxation of the forest laws which were most oppressive and in some respects very cruel, especially what was called the "Lawing of dogs," which consisted in cutting off three claws of the fore-feet, close to the ball of the foot, to prevent their chasing the deer.

For some time we find Richard almost exclusively devoted to the multifarious duties of his office as forester; the powers and privileges connected with that office must have been eminently congenial to the sporting tastes of an Anglo-Norman. Not only did the forests yield largely to the royal revenue, but their productions were also in other respects useful and available property to the Crown. The entries in the "Close Rolls" and other public records afford curious illustrations of the uses to which they were applied, and also show the customs of that period and the powers which were vested in the foresters. Some of these are too curious to be passed over.

It was the duty of the forester to preserve the boundaries of the forest intact, and to permit no encroachments within them. Should a neighbouring landowner desire to free his woods from the view of the foresters and regarders, to cultivate a portion of them, or to enclose a park and kill the game on his own manors, he had to obtain the royal permission, and an official writ was addressed to the forester on the subject. Such a writ, on behalf of the Abbey of St. Edmund's Bury, was despatched from Oxford to Richard de Montfichet on the 20th July, 1216, whereby he was informed that a charter had been given to the abbot and monks there serving God, granting that their woods at Harlow, Stapleford and Werketon should be for ever free from regard,[1] waste[2] and view of the foresters and regarders, and that the abbot and monks should have use of the same woods at their own will, except always driving forth the game.

And on the same day, under another writ to Richard de Montfichet, free warren was granted for ever to the Bishop of London and his

---

[1] The duties of the Regarder are to go through the whole forest to view and inspect the same, and to report to the Eyre—general sessions of the forest, or justice seat—held every third year. (Blount).

[2] Waste of the forest is where a man cuts down his own woods within a forest, without licence of the King or Lord Chief Justice in Eyre. (Blount).

successors, in his manor of Clackington, and that of Walton-cum-Thorpe, which is the manor of the chapter of St. Paul's, London. Also, that the said bishop and his successors for ever had full liberty to take stags and hinds, and all sorts of wild animals within the limits of the said manors. The forester was also commanded to permit Richard de Rivers to make two deer leaps in his great park at Ongar, as he had right and custom to have.

About the same time Mabilia de Boseham, Abbess of Barking, seems to have had some cause of complaint against the foresters for questioning her right to cut wood in her forest of Hainault, and to keep dogs to hunt hares and foxes. The following royal mandate was accordingly addressed to Richard de Montfichet: "We command you to allow the Abbess of Barking her reasonable Estovers[1] in her wood of Hainault for her firing, her cooking, and her brewing, if she has been accustomed so to do in the time of our Lord King John our father; also to permit the same abbess to have her dogs to chase hares and foxes within the Bailiwick, if she was accustomed to have them in the time of our aforesaid father." That the right of this wealthy spiritual abbess, to cut wood or disport herself in the chase in her own vast domain, should require royal confirmation, affords a curious proof how jealously and strictly the old forest laws were enforced. Either the consumption of the abbess was esteemed unreasonable, or the strictness of the foresters was excessive, for two years later Richard de Montfichet was again commanded to allow her reasonable Estovers for her fires, out of her woods within his jurisdiction. The right of Estovers was the right of use or sustenance out of an estate, or the wood that might be cut in forests for domestic or agricultural purposes.

---

[1] Estovers—is an ancient law term; the word is derived from the French "estoffer," to supply the material for any kind of work—hence the English word stuff as used by carpenters. From the same derivation is the old expression "to stove trees," which means to lop off the branches, leaving the stem bare, just the contrary of pollarding, which is cutting off the top. In this part of Essex there are too many trees in the hedgerows that have been stoved, to require any further explanation of the term.

L

The King made also numerous gifts of timber and firewood out of the forest for which writs were issued to the forester of Essex. For instance, he was ordered to give Rose de Sculiz, a nun of Barking, "an oak out of the forest of Essex, to repair her chamber in the said Abbey, taken where it would least injure the said forest." Again he was informed, that the king had given to the Brethren of the Hospital at Ilford three dry trunks of oak for their fires, out of the forest of Havering, which they were to have without delay. This must have been an acceptable gift to the poor lepers in the little Hospital of St. Mary, at Ilford, where to the present day dwell six poor men, their representatives, in the low-browed brick almshouses by the roadside, but there is no longer a forest of Havering to supply even a handful of sticks.

Numerous orders for timber, charcoal and other products of the forests, were issued for the use of the royal household or the repair of the buildings. These were all addressed to Richard de Montfichet and were doubtless executed by his deputies. The conveyance of these by water to London is occasionally mentioned; for instance, it was ordered that in the wood nearest and most accessible to the Thames, close by Barking, he was to cause two vessels to be loaded with brushwood, and to have twelve cart-loads of charcoal made. One shipload of wood and the charcoal were to be sent to Westminster, and the other of wood to the New Temple in London. The charges for the same were to be repaid. From the New Temple, where the court seems occasionally to have resided, he received commands to send without delay to the Constable of the Tower of London, three shiploads of brushwood, where he could obtain it nearest to the Thames; also six cartloads of charcoal to dry the king's crossbows there. Richard de Montfichet was also directed to send the best and most suitable timber, that he could find in the park at Havering, to finish the stockades round the Tower of London, also timber for flooring the same. This order is obviously connected with the repair of that fortress for the reception of the king, who was thence re-crowned shortly afterwards.

The Castle of Dover, as well as the Tower of London, had been greatly damaged in the wars of the late reign, and was also thoroughly repaired about this time. For the works there Richard de Montfichet sent to the Constable of Dover as many timber trees as would make a hundred joists; they were to be taken, wherever the verderers and foresters find the most suitable in the wood of "Cestrewald" or elsewhere, and whatever material these timber trees should yield, was to be also applied to the king's service.

No apology is offered for dwelling so long on the subject of the Vert and its value in the forest of Essex. Great changes have taken place since those times. Barges no longer come up Barking Creek to receive loads of firewood, and the fires of charcoal burners no longer glow in the silvan recesses of Chigwell or Barking-side. The woodlands of Hainault—with the exception of a small and very pretty wood by Lambourne—have been destroyed and converted into open fields and farmsteads, and the forest glades which, peopled with herds of deer, once surrounded on every side the ancient Fairlop Oak,[1] the thousand years old monarch of the forest, have completely disappeared.

Nor were the duties of the forester confined to the Vert; he had also charge of the venison, and there are many official orders

---

[1] Fairlop Oak—was of such great age that, as Mr. Gilpin says, "the traditions of the country trace it half way up the Christian era." The trunk measured 36 feet in girth, and the branches spread over an area 300 feet in circumference. Under this oak a fair was long annually held on the first Friday in July; it was founded by one Daniel Day, a block and pump maker of Wapping, who died on the 19th of July, 1767, aged 84. About 150 years ago he commenced the practice of dining with his friends annually beneath the shade of this monarch of the forest on beans and bacon. For several years before the death of the benevolent, though eccentric founder of this fair and public bean-feast, the pump and block makers of Wapping, to the number of 30 or 40 went annually to the fair in a boat, made like an Indian canoe of one piece of timber. In the course of time other parties were formed in London and suttling booths were erected for their accommodation; these continued to increase till in 1725 the place assumed the appearance of a regular fair. Great care was taken to preserve this venerable oak, but in 1805 it was accidently set on fire, the trunk was considerably injured and most of the principal branches wholly destroyed. The work of decay went gradually on, until the grand old oak was blown down in a violent gale in 1820. But although the oak was gone the fair continued to be held there, and indeed, down to within the last few years, the East Londoners used to flock there in crowds for their annual outing, on the first Friday in July.

addressed to the forester for venison, either given by or used for the king. When Ralph de Nevill was to be consecrated Bishop of Chichester, the king gave him six deer for the inauguration feast, from the forest of Essex. At a much later period of this king's (Henry III.) reign, when Eleanor of Castile came over as the bride of Edward, the king's eldest son, she was preceded by ambassadors, who were entertained in the New Temple in London, and among other things provided for their use were ten bucks, which Richard de Montfichet was desired to send without delay from the forest of Essex.

Occasionally live deer were given to stock parks, for we find that in 1223 Richard was commanded to give to Robert Fitz-Walter ten live deer to stock his park at Roydon, and to Henry Fitz-Archer likewise ten, to stock his park at Epping; another time Geoffery, Bishop of Ely, was to have ten does and two stags out of the king's forest in the parts about Colchester.

At this date the parks within the bounds of the forest were not properly fenced in. During Henry III.'s residence at the Tower of London in 1221, the owners of these parks were informed through the forester that, if parks, not enclosed with a hedge and ditch, were not with all speed so enclosed before the Michaelmas next following, they would be thrown into the forest, if not restored to ancient parks by being so enclosed.

Another duty of the forester was to accompany, either by person or by deputy, those who had a right to kill deer or other game in the royal forest. By the first charter of Henry III. it was granted that "whatever archbishop, bishop, earl or baron shall be passing through our forests, it shall be lawful for them to take one or two deer, by the view of the forester if he shall be present, but if not, he shall cause a horn to be sounded lest it should seem a theft." Besides these occasions, when the tedium of a journey on horseback was relieved by killing a buck in the forest by right, there were others when it was specially granted, apparently to persons returning home from Court. Thus letters were dispatched to Richard de Montfichet, to permit Richard de Rivers, who had a castle at Ongar, to take three deer in the forest.

The office of forester of Essex was not a sinecure. The timber, the burning of charcoal, the game harboured in its recesses, and the parks within its boundaries were under his care and control, indeed no part of the produce seems to have been neglected, as we find accounts for the proceeds of the sale of grass, for the grazing of cattle, as well as for brushwood (faggots) and charcoal, sent in shiploads to the Tower of London and the New Temple.

Having given an account of some of the forest laws and of the duties devolving upon the royal forester, and having noticed the great care exercised over the various products of the forest, whether "Vert or Venison," as well as the different uses to which they were applied, we return to the more personal history of Richard de Montfichet, as baron of Stanstead and feudal lord of East and West Ham.

His warlike propensities induced him, in 1223, to take part in the famous tournament at Blygh in Notts, held in defiance of the express command of the young king and his advisers, who feared such an assemblage of discontented barons. Indeed this tournament was known for its political character rather than as the scene of chivalric spirit, and was so displeasing to the king's councillors, that they declared the estates of those who tourneyed there to be forfeited, and they were seized by the Crown accordingly, although restored the following year.

A year or two later Richard de Montfichet was present at the parliament, or great national council, held at Westminster, when King Henry III. demanded a supply to enable him to defend the English possessions in France from the encroachments of King Louis VIII. This was granted upon condition that the king confirmed the liberties required by his subjects; and in February 1224 the third Great Charter of Henry III. was witnessed by all the barons, whether spiritual or temporal, of which number was Richard de Montfichet, who gave the king in return a fifteenth of all their moveables.

Notwithstanding the nominal restoration of his estates after the tournament at Blygh, the great barony of the Montfichets, as now possessed by Richard, was at this date reduced to little more than half its original extent. The civil wars, two forfeitures, and large endowments of religious houses, as well as the various amounts of feudal aids tended the same way. In 1236 when Isabella, youngest daughter of King John was married to Frederick II., Emperor of Germany, a feudal aid was levied, the account of which has been preserved in the record called "Testa de Nevill," by which we see that Richard was rated at £19 6s 8d for the twenty-four knights' fees held by him, whereas his predecessor William, when he paid his aid in 1166, returned his knights' fees at upwards of forty-eight.

While Richard de Montfichet was sheriff of Essex and governor of Hertford Castle, from 1242 to 1246, he together with fifty other knights and barons received the following circular from the king:

Translation.

The King to Richard de Montfichet, greeting.

Whereas the King of France by doing us grievous injury has relieved us from the obligation of keeping the truce, made with him, and provoked us to recommence the war (which had happened quite unexpectedly while we were crossing the channel), and inasmuch as we are not adequately supplied with foot soldiers and especially deficient in Englishmen, in whom we always place the most confidence, for carrying on the war against him, we hereby command you by these presents, as you value our honor, to join us with as little delay as possible, equipped with horse and harness, so that by your aid and that of other faithful retainers, to whom we have likewise addressed these instructions, we may have the pleasure of recovering our honor, and placing ourselves at the same time under a perpetual obligation of gratitude to yourself, being well assured that without your aid and that of other faithful followers we should meet with heavy discomfiture and defeat, incur eternal obloquy and, which heaven avert, irrevocable derision.

Witness ourself at Xanten, June 15, 1242.

The courteous tone of entreaty for assistance marks the power and independence of those to whom it was addressed.

In 1253 Richard was summoned to attend the king at Chester to oppose the hostilities of the Welsh, and again in 1260 to meet the king and the army at Salisbury, with his horses, arms, and retainers to go against the Welsh, who were at this period particularly irritable, and had also compelled Prince Edward to retreat before them three years previously.

We have seen that, in the earlier part of his career, Richard de Montfichet was both turbulent and warlike; distinguished as one of the great warriors of the age, he seems to have been foremost in every scene of strife. In the latter years of his life we trace indications of care to improve his impoverished and diminished estate. He obtained a grant of free warren[1] in all his demesne lands in Kent, Hertfordshire and Buckinghamshire, also a market and fair in his manors of Acle and West Ham, and by another charter he was permitted to enclose his wood of Theydon and Ruhedon.

Nor must it be left unnoticed that Richard was also a great benefactor to the Church. To the Priory of Thremhall, in the parish of Stanstead, he granted a charter in which he styles himself "Richard, son of Richard de Montfichet," and confirms to the monks there his father's gift of thirty acres of land, and also gave them on his own account eighty acres of land, lying between his park at Stanstead and the lands of Walter de Hatfield, in Birchanger. He also granted the monks permission to turn all their cattle into his park at Stanstead, including pannage for twenty hogs, fuel for their baking and brewing by view and liberty of his servants and park-keepers, and likewise free ingress and egress to and from their yard (curia) in his park.

He was also a benefactor to the University of Cambridge, and in 1243 he gave to the monks of St. John's, Colchester, land near the old Hythe; but there is no record of any gift bestowed by him on the Abbey of Stratford.

The last notice of Richard de Montfichet, is his summons to parliament in 1261. HOLINSHED says with reference to this parliament that "after Christmas, the king coming into the Tower of London fortified it greatly, and caused the gates of the city to be warded,

---

[1] The right of free warren could only be conferred by royal grant or prescription, which implied a grant and vested in the owner of the franchise a property in the game, and excluded all other persons from hunting or taking it.

sending forth commandments to the lords, that they should come to the tower, there to hold a parliament; but they flatly denied to do so, sending him word that, if it pleased him, they would come to Westminster, where usually the parliament had been kept and not to any other place. Whereupon there arose great discussions between him and his barons." The same year he received the following summons "to attend the king in London on the morrow of the feast of the Apostles Simon and Jude, without delay with horse and harness, accompanied as well by all your own vassals, as many as are due to us from your fee, as those you are able to raise by the assistance of friendly disposed persons, on account of certain grave and pressing affairs, specially affecting the welfare of Crown and Person. And that you will in no wise neglect, we confidently expect from your loyalty and affection."

The name of the wife of Richard de Montfichet was Jacosa. She is described as a lady eminent for beauty, virtue and piety, "but alas"—exclaims the writer of the Origo Baronum de Montfichet— " childless." Jacosa survived Richard and enjoyed for her dower the park and capital messuage of Hoylands, in Essex, also the manor of West Ham and woods in East and West Ham. After her decease, in the year 1274, her dower property reverted to the heirs of Montfichet, among whom it was divided.

The varied career of this baron closed in 1267. It is probable that he was buried in St. Paul's Cathedral, as the Baudekin or Pall of " purple with a beautiful border and knots, and birds between the knots, used at the funeral of the Lord Richard de Montfichet " was preserved there for many years. He left no issue, and being the last male heir of the family de Montfichet, in the direct line, the barony of Montfichet became extinct, although several individuals bearing the name of Montfichet existed, whose connexion, however, with the baronial house has not been traced. On his decease the whole lordship became dismembered and was divided among the descendants and coheirs of his three sisters who had predeceased him.

CHAPTER VI.

(Contents).

CO-HEIRS OF THE BARONY OF MONTFICHET
IN EAST AND WEST HAM.

ARGARET, the eldest sister and one of the coheirs of
Richard de Montfichet married, as has already been
stated, Hugh de Bolbec, whose family derived its name
from a small town in Normandy, not far from the mouth
of the river Seine. Their son Hugh was sheriff of Northumberland
in the fourth year of King Henry III.'s reign, and died in 1261 leaving
four daughters, viz: Philippa, Margaret, Alice, and Mathilda, who
inherited from their father the barony of Bolbec, and from their
grandmother Margaret, her third part of the barony of Montfichet.

Philippa, the eldest of these four daughters, became the wife
of Roger de Lancaster, of Barton and Patterdale in Westmoreland,
of which county he was made sheriff in the year 1255. The castle
of Stanstead, which had been assigned to Philippa, seems to have
been their residence, for we find that Roger de Lancaster, who died
in 1290, was buried in Stanstead Church, where his effigy still
remains. His wife, who survived him four years, died possessed of
the manors of Stanstead-Montfichet, Great Hoylands, and East Ham,
of the inheritance of the Montfichets, and of a fourth part of the
inheritance of Bolbec, in Northumberland.

John de Lancaster, their son and heir, inherited the castle of
Stanstead with the rest of his mother's inheritance. He gave, as has
already been mentioned, in the year 1307 to the Abbot and Convent of

M

Stratford Langthorne the Church of East Ham with two acres of land, to which he subsequently (1317) added forty acres of land, and finally also in conjunction with Annora, his wife, the reversion of their manor of East Ham, after their decease. Dying without issue in 1334, his nephew Richard de Plaiz, then twelve years old, became his heir in the barony of Stanstead-Montfichet.

Margaret de Bolbec, the second daughter of Hugh de Bolbec, was first married to Nicholas Corbet, and afterwards to Ralph, Lord of Grimsthorpe, who paid 100 marks to have licence to marry her, she being a widow. He was governor of Berwick upon Tweed and of Carlisle, and distinguished himself in the wars with Scotland. Shortly after his marriage with Margaret he sold, with her consent, their interest in the manors of Stanstead, Great Hoylands, and East Ham to Robert Burnel, Bishop of Bath and Wells.

Alice de Bolbec, the third daughter of Hugh and Margaret de Bolbec, was married to Walter, son of William de Huntercombe, a crusader with Prince Edward. He was summoned to parliament as a baron in 1295 and seems to have been the constant companion of King Edward in his Scottish wars. In 1298 he was governor of the castle of Edinburgh and died without issue in the year 1312. In the "post-mortem inquisition respecting Walter de Huntercombe and Alice his wife" a fourth part of the barony of Bolbec is recorded, but no mention is made of any property whatever in Essex, a circumstance which confirms the probability of MORANT's opinion, that Alice's share of the barony of Montfichet in that county was sold to Robert Burnel together with that of her sister Margaret.

Mathilda, the youngest of the daughters and heiresses of Hugh de Bolbec, was married to Hugh de la Val or de Laval, of whom little is known. She died in 1281, possessed of the manors of East and West Ham, which together with other portions of her inheritance passed on the death of her husband (in 1302) to her cousin and heir John de Lancaster.

Such were the marriages made by the four daughters and heiresses of Hugh de Bolbec and his wife Margaret de Montfichet, and it appears that of their descendants John de Lancaster alone retained any connexion with the ancient barony of their common ancestor Richard de Montfichet.

Before, however, leaving this branch of the family, we must not omit to mention a document, preserved in the unpublished "Close Rolls," which refers to the division of the third part of the knights' fees, held by Richard de Montfichet in capite, amongst these four granddaughters of his sister Margaret de Bolbec. The inconvenience resulting from such a sub-division, as is there displayed, must have been very great. The lord paramount had four capital tenants to look to for the same amount of service as had been previously rendered by one. To the under-tenant the inconvenience was greater still; he had, when holding of one superior, to pay his aid or his scutage to one seneschal, to render his suit and service at one court, and to perform his military service under one banner, but on the dismemberment of a barony he found three or four lords assigned to him. It is true that to each lord a smaller amount of service was due, but as a whole the burden must have been greatly magnified by this division of interest and fealty, indeed personal service to each lord became impossible. Equivalents and money payments necessarily resulted from such a state of things, and the old chivalric spirit of feudal allegiance gradually faded away, until nothing remained but antiquated forms, oppression, and inconvenience instead of life, energy, and perfect adaptation to the moral and physical condition of the society in which it existed.

Having thus traced the sub-division of the third part of the great possessions of Richard de Montfichet amongst the four daughters of his eldest sister Margaret or Margery de Bolbec, we now proceed to consider those portions which fell to the share of his other two sisters.

Aveline, second sister to Richard de Montfichet, was the wife of William de Fortibus, second Earl of Albemarle of that name, who was one of the twenty-five barons chosen to enforce the observance of Magna Charta. He afterwards espoused the cause of King John and of Henry III. and fought under the royal banner at Lincoln (1217), when his brother-in-law Richard de Montfichet was taken prisoner.

The Earl of Albemarle died at sea, in 1241, on his way to the Holy Land, and was succeeded in the earldom by his son William, who married Isabel, daughter of Baldwin de Rivers, Earl of Devon. They had three sons who all died in childhood, and one daughter, named after her grandmother Aveline.

William de Fortibus, third Earl of Albemarle, died at Amiens in 1259, leaving his only surviving daughter Aveline, aged about five years, sole heiress to the accumulated dignities and estates of both her parents. She became in her own right Countess of Albemarle and of Devon, Lady of Skipton in Yorkshire, sovereign of the Isle of Wight and possessor of the third part of the barony of Montfichet in Essex.

So great an heiress was thought a match for a king's son, and she was accordingly placed under the guardianship of Edward, the eldest son of King Henry III. In 1269, being then about sixteen years old, she was married in Westminster Abbey to Edmund, surnamed Crouchback, second son of King Henry III. "with great state and solempnitie, whereof the Kyng kept ther in the great Hall a great honourable feast the Sundaye following." On occasion of these splendid nuptials the king, queen, and most of the nobility of England were present. The following year her husband was signed with the cross and departed for the Holy Land. Aveline becoming of age sufficient to possess her lands, her husband Edmund doing his fealty had livery of them. "To these lands and castles however," DUGDALE says, "the King (Edward I.) had a mind and came to an agreement with her, in the fourth year of his reign, that she should by sufficient assurance pass them with a few exceptions unto him and his heirs, whilst he was to enfeoff her of other lands to the full extent and worth, and moreover to pay her 20,000 marks. But—he adds—it is reported, that the agreement was fraudulent, especially as to the Isle of Wight, that her mother, Isabel de Fortibus, always refused it, saying that she would not wrong her heirs so much as to pass that part of her ancient inheritance from them. And that thereupon the King set Sir — de Stratton, who had much interest and power with her, to work her to it, but when he saw that he could not prevail with her, he waited till her death, and then forged a grant thereof, and put her seal to it, of which he had the custody, and that by this means the right heirs were shamefully defrauded thereof."

Aveline was early attacked by disease and died at the age of twenty-two years at Stokewell, near London, in 1276, leaving no issue. She was buried in Westminster Abbey, where a magnificent monument was erected to her memory. The effigy, though now much mutilated, remains and is portrayed by STOTHARD in his "Monumental Effigies." The countenance is youthful and the figure

displays the costume of the day, the wimple worn round the throat, also the mantle and veil. Under the head are two cushions; the upper one embroidered with the arms of England, and a lion rampant in a field of gold, being the arms of Rivers, Earl of Devon,—the under cushion is figured with the arms of de Fortibus, Earl of Albemarle.

Of the personal history of the Lady Aveline nothing is known, yet through the dry hard facts, recorded of her in the driest of all books—"The Public Records"—a touching story is dimly shadowed forth. "Early an orphan; bereaved even in childhood of her brothers;

doubtless brought up in the train of her guardian, Prince Edward's Consort, Queen Eleanor of Castile; married in girlhood to his brother Edmund, who shortly after was separated from her on his distant voyage to the Holy Land. On coming of age to find her lands and castle and manor houses coveted by him, to whose hands they had so long been intrusted; the unwilling alienation of them; her illness and early death."

With the exception of the park at Langley and the manors of Langley and Wyrardesbury in Bucks, her third part of the barony of Montfichet appears to have reverted to the other coheirs. The next year after her death, King Edward I. bought the manors of Langley and Wyrardesbury, which belonged to Roger de Lancaster and Philippa, his wife, and Nicholas Corbet and Margery, his wife. LIPSCOMB, in his "History of Bucks," considers, that these manors were retained by the Crown in consequence of the minority of Ralph de Plaiz, who was cousin and heir to Aveline's share of the Montfichet estates. The Plaiz family, however, did not forego their claim; Sir John de Plaiz, who died in 1389, petitioned the Crown, as heir of Aveline, for the restoration of these manors, as did also Elizabeth, Countess of Oxford, as heir to Ralph de Plaiz, but both without avail.

Philippa de Montfichet, the third and youngest sister of Richard, was the wife of Hugh de Plaiz, who is said to have had three wives, of whom she was the second. With her a third part of the barony of Montfichet came into the family of de Plaiz, an ancient and noble race, seated in Norfolk, Suffolk and Sussex, immediately after the conquest. Their son Richard (I.) paid in 1269 his relief for the third part of the barony of Montfichet which, amongst other portions, included that part of the manor of Ham which has since been known as the manor of Plaiz and the village of Plaistow.

Richard was succeeded by Ralph, his son and heir, nine years old in 1275, on whose death his brother Richard (II.) became heir to the estate.

He again was succeeded by his son Giles who, being left a minor on the death of his father in 1287, was in ward of the Queen. In 1294 he was knighted and had summons to attend the king with divers other eminent persons, with his advice "touching the great affairs of the realm. Sir Giles de Plaiz died in the year 1303, possessed of nine or more manors, thirteen knights' fees, rents in East Ham from thirty tenements, woods in the parishes of East and West Ham, besides the advowson of seven churches and various other property.

His son Richard (III.) married Margaret, sister and heir of his cousin John de Lancaster, by which connexion the whole remnant of the barony of Montfichet centered in their descendants. At an inquisition of the united property of Richard and Margaret, made in the year 1327, nothing is recorded as at that time belonging to them in Ham, but £4 8s 10d rent in Stratford. The reader cannot fail to observe how large a portion of the barony of Montfichet was now absorbed by the Abbey of Stratford Langthorne. Margaret died before her husband, who went beyond sea and died in the year 1340, about thirty years old.

He was succeeded by his son, also named Richard (IV.) who was heir to John de Lancaster, of Stanstead Montfichet in Essex, and other places in that county. In 1353 he had licence from the King (Edward III.) as Sir Richard Plaiz, knight, to give to the Abbot and Convent of Stratford ten acres of wood, twelve acres of heath land, and £8 3s 4d rent with the appurtenances in West Ham, which he held of the king in capite. The same year it is stated in the "Inquisitiones ad quod damnum," that Sir Richard de Plaiz had given to the monks of the Abbey of St. Mary at Stratford all his rents and lands in East and West Ham, and West Ham Frith. He died beyond sea in 1359, leaving his son John his heir, then eighteen years old.

Under the designation of "Sir John de Plaiz, kinsman and sole heir of Richard de Montfichet," he obtained from the king a confirmation of the right of free warren in all his lands in Essex, Kent, and Bucks, and a market and fair in his manor of Acley or Oakley, in the county of Essex, which was at that time his residence. He there executed, in 1379, a deed which, extraordinary as it may appear to us, was perfectly consistent with the customs of that day. It is a deed completing the " sale " of his only daughter and heiress Margaret to Sir Robert Howard, as a wife for his son. As Sir John de Plaiz married her mother, Joan Stapleton, daughter of Sir Miles Stapleton of Ingham (Norfolk), in 1364, the bride cannot at that date have been

more than fourteen years old; it would be difficult to convey the real
meaning of this transaction by any other term than that of sale.

Sir John de Plaiz died in 1389 and was buried in the Priory
Church at Weeting. The great diminution in his property and estates
leads to the suggestion, that a large proportion had been settled upon
or given in "franc marriage" with his daughter Margaret. By his will,
dated 1385, he bequeathed many legacies to religious uses; amongst
others he left five marks to every house of Friars Mendicant in Norfolk,
Suffolk, Essex, and Cambridgeshire. To his wife he left all his utensils
and ornaments belonging to his house, not before bequeathed, with all
other goods in his various manors, also all his wardrobe and silver
vessels, and to his son-in-law, Sir John Howard, all his armour and
furniture of war. Joan, his wife, who died 1385, was buried in Ingham
Church, Norfolk, where a brass to her memory still exists.

The family of de Plaiz having thus become extinct in the male
line, their estates passed to Margaret, wife of Sir John Howard, in
whom now centered the whole of the estates of the families of
Montfichet and de Plaiz, with the exception of those portions which
had either been given to the Abbot and Convent of Stratford, or sold
to Robert Burnel, Bishop of Bath and Wells.

Sir John Howard and Margaret his wife are believed to have
resided in the castle at Weeting in Norfolk. WEEVER saw the effigy
of Sir John with the arms of the two families, in the south window of
the Church of Weeting, and has preserved in his "Funeral Monuments"
a picture of which the accompanying woodcut is a fac-simile.

John, the grandson of Sir John Howard and Margaret de Plaiz, died in 1410, leaving an only child Elizabeth, his heiress, who brought a very large fortune to her husband John de Vere, 12th Earl of Oxford. As she married without the King's licence, the Earl had to pay a fine of £2000 to the King.

With this marriage the history of the old barons of Montfichet and their descendants is brought to a close, their female representatives having been traced until they ceased to have any interest in the parishes of East and West Ham.

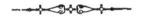

N

CHAPTER VII.

(CONTENTS).

HISTORY OF THE ABBEY OF STRATFORD LANGTHORNE, COMMONLY KNOWN AS WEST HAM ABBEY.

AMIDST the life and bustle of the numerous factories with their tall chimneys and steam engines, and the hasty traffic of the railroad, which we now find on the site of the ancient West Ham Abbey, it requires some effort of the imagination to realise the fact, that on this very spot once stood in tranquil solitude a Cistercian monastery and that, instead of the present busy population, hooded monks used to dwell in retirement amidst the cloisters, the gardens, and orchards which were enclosed within its walls and moats, passing their lives in the worship of God and in taking care of their own souls and making themselves fit for a better world than this, hereafter. They were men of another age, living in a different state of society, which they as faithfully represented in their day and generation, as we do that in which our existence has been placed.

Within the first hundred years after the conquest of this country by the Normans, a great number of abbeys and religious houses were founded by the Anglo-Norman kings and their barons, and also endowed by them with so prodigal a hand that, had not the legislature interfered, the whole landed property of the kingdom would have been in danger of falling into the hands of the monks. The Church of Rome inculcated the doctrine, that whatever was so given was consecrated to God and was good for the soul of the donor, who could also name for a participation in these benefits the deceased as well as the living members of his family, his king, and in short anyone he pleased. In their ignorance and superstition the men of that iron age were taught to believe, that a life of rapine and licentiousness could be atoned for by good works and almsdeeds, among which liberality to the church was esteemed one of the chief, and that by founding monasteries they could also purchase for themselves an interest in the good works of the monks, whose superior sanctity was supposed to leave an overplus for the benefit of their founders.

What those lives were of which they thus sought to expiate the guilt, some faint idea may be formed, when we reflect upon the forcible manner in which the Normans held possession of the soil. Armed in their strongholds they dwelt as conquerors amongst a hostile population, with whom they were perpetually in collision. The barons served even William the Conqueror and his sons with turbulent independence, which often assumed an attitude of defiance, and to the ordinary devastations of war, acts of the most flagrant individual injustice and cruelty were occasionally added throughout the whole length and breadth of the land.

From time to time an ascetic monk would go forth from a monastic order to establish one of still stricter rule. Such was the origin of the Cistercians who sprung from the order of St. Benedict in the year 1098, when Robert, the first Abbot of Molesme, with twenty-one zealous monks of the latter order, whose discipline they considered too lax, established themselves at Citeaux (Cistercium) in the duchy of Burgundy. Dedicating themselves to a contemplative life, their severe rule and assumption of superior sanctity brought them rapidly into notice. CARDINAL DE VITRY says: " They neither wore skins nor shirts, nor ate flesh except in sickness, and abstained from fish, eggs, milk, and cheese. They lay only on straw beds in their tunics and cowls, and rose at midnight singing praises to God till break of day; spent the day in labour, reading and prayer, and in all their exercises observed a strict and continual silence." It is computed, that within a hundred years of its foundation, this order embraced eighteen-hundred rich abbeys in different parts of Europe, of which St. Bernard, Abbot of Clairvaux, alone founded no less than one hundred and sixty. The Cistercian abbeys were all dedicated to the Virgin Mary and were generally built in solitary and uncultivated places, nor would the monks allow another monastery, even of the same order to be established near them.

The Cistercian monks were much devoted to agriculture and horticulture, which seem to have flourished under their care. Their selection of a site, although it might be solitary, was generally found in a fertile valley or well-watered plain; orchards and gardens abounded within the precincts of their abbeys, and it is very probable that some of the fruits, now known in this country were originally introduced by them.

The first house of Cistercians in England was established at Waverley, in Surrey, by William Giffard, Bishop of Winchester, in the year 1128. About six or seven years later William de Montfichet founded that of Stratford Langthorne or, as it is familiarly called, West Ham Abbey, by the advice of William Carbois, Archbishop of Canterbury, dedicating it to God and the blessed Virgin and endowing it with great munificence with a large portion of the vast barony, which he had inherited from his predecessor Robert Gernon.

Thither he brought monks from the Abbey of Savigny in Normandy, where the Abbot, Geoffrey by name, was of such high reputation for his wisdom and skill in the establishment of monasteries of his order, that he was consulted from all parts of Europe, and it is stated that nineteen Cistercian Houses were under his direction. He was attracted to Savigny by the sanctity of Vital, its first abbot and founder, who in the year 1105 commenced to build his abbey amidst the wild forests on the confines of Normandy and Brittany, at a place since called Savigny, and prescribed to his disciples the Cistercian rule with some additional peculiar statutes and ordinances of his own.

It is highly probable that Abbot Geoffrey, who governed Savigny as abbot from 1119 to 1139, was well known to William de Montfichet, being a man of noble family in Bayeux, and originally a monk of the Abbey of Cerisy in the immediate neighbourhood of the Castle of Montfichet. (*See page* 57).

Such was the parentage of the Abbey of Stratford Langthorne, placed amongst those, called "proprie filie" by the monks of Savigny, according to whose authority it was founded on the 10th of January, 1134.

The charter given on this occasion is a fair specimen of the documents originally used, but without date, as was commonly the case at that early period. It is printed in the " Monasticon " and is as follows:

Carta Willielmi de Montefichet facta monachis de Hamma de manerio de Hamma.

Willielmus de Montefichet omnibus praepositis et ministris' et hominibus suis, tam Francis quam Anglicis, salutem.

Notum sit omnibus quod ego Willielmus de Montefichet, gratia Dei praemonente, consilio Domini Willielmi Cantuar Archiepiscopi, et aliorum religiosorum virorum et consensu et voluntate uxoris meae Margaretae et concessu filiorum meorum, pro salute animae Regis Henrici, et meae, et uxoris meae M. et filiorum meorum et omnium antecessorum meorum, dedi in elemosinam ecclesiae Dei, et Sanctae Mariae, et omnium Sanctorum de Hamma, et abbati et monachis ibi Deo servientibus, totum dominium meum de Hamma, in terris, in culturis, in pratis, in mariscis, in aquis, et nominatim totam terram, quae fuit Ranulfi sacerdotis.

Et praeter pratum dominii mei XI acras quas excambiavi de Geraldo de Hamma pro XIIII acris terrae in marisco,

William de Montfichet to all his bailiffs, servants and vassals, whether French or English, greeting.

Be it known tc all, that I William de Montfichet forewarned by the Grace of God, by the advice of Lord William, Archbishop of Canterbury and other religious men, and with the consent and by the wish of Margaret my wife, and the consent of my sons, for the health of the soul of the King Henry, and mine, and my wife Margaret's, and my sons and all my ancestors, I have given in alms to the Church of God, and St. Mary, and all saints of Ham, and the abbot and monks there serving God, all my demesne of Ham, in land, in arable fields, in meadows, in marsh, in water, and especially all the land, which was Ranulph's the priest.

And besides the meadow in my demesne, the eleven acres, which I exchanged with Gerald de Ham for fourteen acres of land

et duo molendina juxta calceatam de Stratford, videlicet unum quod tenebat Aedwinus filius Algari, et aliud quod tenebat Ulwinus molendinarius, et boscum meum de Bocherst et decimam pasnagii mei de ....pastur.

Testibus :

Henrico episcopo Wintoniensi et Willielmo et Ricardo Archidiac. London, et Margareta uxore mea, et Ricardo de Poili et Johanne, ... et Mathis Gernun, et Willielmo filio Radulfi, et Willielmo de Montefichet nepote meo, Rogero Capellano etc.

in the marsh, and two mills near the Stratford causeway, namely one held by Edwin, son of Algar, and the other held by Ulwin the miller, and my wood of Bocherst and the tithe of my pannage at ....pasture.

Witnesses :

Henry, Bishop of Winchester and William and Richard, Archdeacons of London and Margaret my wife, and Richard de Poili and John, — and Mathew Gernon, and William son of Ralph, and William de Montfichet, my grandson, Roger the chaplain etc.

By a second charter William de Montfichet confirmed to the Abbot and Convent of Stratford the gifts of his feudal tenants, and at the same time exercised his power as superior lord by prohibiting any land, held of him, being given by them to any other monastery. This charter is preserved in WEEVER's " Funeral Monuments " who found it among the Cottonian M.S.S. It is not there now, and was probably burnt at the time of the fire in the cloisters at Westminster in 1731. WEEVER adds : " That the seale of this deed was in blouddy waxe " — but we are not informed what was the impress.

The confirmation of this charter by Henry II. was obtained by the monks of Stratford in the year 1182. Religious communities not being permitted by the ancient common law to hold land without the king's licence, all endowments and grants, made by private persons, required Royal confirmation. The following is a list of the benefactions enumerated in it :

Benefactions.

The place of the Abbot of Stratford in West Ham with the whole demesne of the said town.

Given by :

William de Montfichet.

Land in the same town.
Land.
Land, also church of Greeneforde.
Land in the City of London.
Grange of Ledehall and appurtenances.
Land at Thomely (Thomelea).
. Grange of Suineleia with all its appurtenances.
Land at Ginges Joyberd.
Manor of Cubige (Cowbridge).
Land at Takeley.
Land at Fuilmere (Fludmere) of the fee of Ralph Fitz-Urse.
Land at Wokendonne (Ockenden)
The Churches of Leyton and West Ham.

Luke, son of Martin de Hamme.
Walter de Baalun.
Sybille, wife of Norman.
Geoffrey de St. Elegio.
William, son of Eloy and Emma his wife.
Jordan and Ruald, his brother.
Monks of Abington.

Geoffrey de Revill (Peverel ?).
Mathew Germin.
William, son of Alice.
Richard de Montfichet.

William de Ane.
Gilbert de Montfichet.

There are also two charters granted by Richard Cœur de Lion, in the first of which he confirms to " God and the Church of the Blessed Virgin Mary of Stratford, and the brethren serving there ":

The Church of All Souls (Saints ?) in West Ham and the land in the same town, given by Gilbert de Montfichet.

The Church of St. Mary Magdalen of Burgstead and the estate there, being the gift of Geoffrey de Beauval.

Land at Billericay, given by the monks of Gant (Ghent).

A marsh at Hadleigh, given by Henry de Essex.

Land at Suthmerse or South Mersey, an island at the mouth of the rivers Colne and Blackwater, of the fee of Walter de Windsor.

Also the manor of Sudbury in West Ham, given by William Plantagenet, the king's uncle, and Alan de Falaise, his tenant.

To these benefactions were added on the part of the king himself the privilege of cutting wood and timber out of the forest of Essex, and liberty to take as much brushwood or thorns from Windsor Forest as was necessary for the use of their house; also immunity from molestation on the part of the foresters touching their Grange near the Frith (now known as Woodgrange and Ham Frith), and pasture in the heath land between the Frith and Walthamstow (now known as Wanstead Flats), for 800 sheep by the great hundred.

This was considered a great favour, sheep not being commonable animals in the royal forests, as their breath was supposed to taint the herbage for the deer.

The marsh in the parish of Hadleigh, which was given by Henry de Essex, was afterwards called Clerkenwick or Abbot's Marsh, and yielded in later years an annual income of £800. The family of Henry de Essex was of high distinction in this country before the Norman invasion, their barony comprising fifty lordships, of which Raleigh was the chief seat. Henry de Essex is chiefly known for the misfortune and disgrace which he incurred, when attending King Henry II. on an expedition against the Welsh in 1164. He was carrying the Royal Standard at the battle of Coleshull, in Wales, when he was suddenly seized with such a terrible panic that he threw it down and fled. This unworthy action much encouraged the Welsh, who supposed the king had fallen, and at the same time discouraged the English from the same cause, so that they turned and began to retreat, which ended in their being utterly routed. For this high misdemeanour he was charged with high treason by Robert de Montfort, an eminent nobleman, who vanquished him in trial by single combat at Reading. By the law he should have suffered death upon his defeat, but the king, exercising his clemency, spared his life and caused him instead to be shorn a monk in the adjacent abbey.

By a second charter King Richard I. gave to the monks of Stratford immunity from tolls and imposts at "Fairs and Markets," and it is worth noticing the fact that to both charters the following sentence was appended : " This was the tenour of our former charter under our former seal which, because it was sometime lost, and while we were captive in Germany, was constituted in another's authority, is changed, and of this renovation these are the witnesses etc."

" Dated from the Rock "les Andelys" in Normandy, in the tenth year of our reign."

Though but few words, they suggest scenes and events of such high importance and interest, that in a short digression from our immediate subject we may be permitted to glance at them, especially as there is little doubt that some of our Stratford monks were eye-witnesses of them. In the last year of his life, King Richard caused a new seal to be made, and directed that all the charters of his reign should be renewed and confirmed by the impression of his new seal, — a measure evidently the result of irregularities which had crept into the administration of public affairs during his absence. In consequence of this regulation the monks of Stratford, or their agents, followed the court into Normandy, where the lion-hearted king in the zenith of his fame and power was occupied in personally superintending the erection of a great fortress on the French frontier, known as the rock "les Andelys." This stupendous structure, whose ruins still embellish the banks of the Seine, was intended to check the incursions of the French King Philip II., surnamed the August, into Normandy. It was a masterpiece of the science of fortification, and stands first among the fortresses of the middle ages, crowning the summit of a perpendicular cliff, with vaults and foundations hewn out of the living rock. The impetuous monarch urged forward the work, notwithstanding papal interdicts, broken treaties, and forgotten oaths, until it was completed within one year of its commencement, and then in the pride of his heart he triumphantly exclaimed, as he saw it rising against the sky: "Qu'elle est belle, ma fille d'un an." (How pretty a child is mine, this child of but one year old.) In official writings both he and his brother John called it the "Rock les Andelys," but Richard is said always to have spoken of it as " Le Château Gaillard," his saucy Castle. Under this well known designation its ruins remain to this day, a monument of the military genius of Richard Cœur-de-Lion, of the imbecility of his brother John, and of the instability of all human greatness!

Scarcely six months after the monks of Stratford had seen the impression of King Richard's new seal affixed to their charter, he was dead, struck down by an arrow, as he was riding round the walls of Chalus to observe where the assault of the castle might be given with the fairest probability of success, and his sceptre, not his sword, had fallen into the feeble hands of his brother John. Only five years elapsed, when after a gallant struggle and lengthened defence the Château Gaillard succumbed to the victorious arms of the French King, followed by the loss of the whole of Normandy in one inglorious campaign. At the commencement of the siege King

o

John watched the proceedings from Ponte de l'Arche, a fortress on the Seine between Rouen and les Andelys, and it was there that on the 3rd of June 1203 the monks of Stratford obtained the royal permission to disafforest their wood of Bockurst (or Buckhurst) in Woodford and Chigwell.

The monks seem to have availed themselves of every occasion to obtain an augmentation of their wealth, or a new privilege, and

A Cistercian Monk.

to have been ever alive to the interests of their community, amidst the tumult of war as well as in the hour of peace. Indeed, the Cistercians were considered the most grasping and avaricious of all the monastic orders, and King Richard is reported to have said, that "he bestowed his daughter 'Avarice' to be married to the Cistercian Order." The brethren at West Ham formed no exception to this rule, for they never rested until they had obtained from the heirs of William de Montfichet the whole of the lordship of Ham, so far as it was in their power to bestow.

Having thus followed the thread of the great events enacted in Normandy, at which our Stratford monks were present, we must now return to their domestic interests at the abbey, amidst the marshes of the Lea. Early in the reign of King John, they obtained from John, son of Leonard de Venois (or de Venuz) the gift by charter of his land called Sudbirie in West Ham, paying an annual rent of £31 and 12 pence. This charter, though without date, was evidently executed at Ham, judging from the names of the witnesses, amongst whom were the chaplain and two clerks of Ham, — and was afterwards on the 24th December 1201 confirmed by King John at Argentan in Normandy, who reserved to himself the services due for that estate from the said John and his heirs. Payments, made by order of the Crown for this fee farm rent, frequently occur in the public records.

Up to this date we have no name of any Abbot of Stratford handed down to us, but afterwards they occasionally occur. The first abbot mentioned is

BENEDICT (1199).

We are told of him "that in 1199 he sold property in Hame to Joan, wife of Lucie, and others,"—and that in 1208 he bought property in Great Burstead of Beauvalle, a member of whose family, named Geoffrey, had already given to the monks the church of Burstead (or Burgstead).

By an entry in the "Close Rolls" it would appear that in 1214 the abbot was abroad, and sent John de Venuz to the king in England, who allowed him £10 for expences he had incurred.

The name of the abbot next mentioned is

RICHARD (1218).

It will be in the recollection of the reader that in the reign of King John, the rebellious barons called in the assistance of Lewis, son of the King of France. In order to satisfy his claims, the Regent Pembroke was obliged in the second year of the reign of King Henry III., son of King John, to borrow the sum of 6000 marks of the great nobility and heads of religious houses, among whom we find Richard, the Abbot of Stratford, who forwarded 100 marks as a loan.

In the following year the abbot was sent together with the abbot of Viterbe on an embassy to France, and they received 100 marks for their expences. In RYMER's "Foedera" we find a letter addressed by Randulph, the Pope's legate, to Hubert de Burgh, chief justiciary of England, dated from Bath, the 4th of January 1220, and enclosing a form of truce with the King of France. The letter is accompanied by a request that it may be forwarded without delay by the hand of some clergyman of discretion, and it is highly probable that Richard, the Abbot of Stratford, a discreet and able man, was the person selected to fulfil this mission, for on the 26th of this same January the Abbot of Stratford, with Philip de Albani and Allen Basset, had thirty marks allowed them for their expences going on the king's affairs into France.

In July of the next year (1221) the "Close Rolls" contain an entry of twenty marks allowed to the Abbot of Stratford for his expences going on an embassy into Germany, and being again sent on another embassy ten pounds was given to him and his companion Andrew de Cancello for their expences. Nor was the abbot the only member of the community at West Ham occupied in public affairs, for two months later brother Michael Besaunt, a monk of Stratford, receives two marks from the royal treasury for going on a commission for the king.

In 1222 Abbot Richard had a dispute with Maude, Prioress of Holywell, respecting the tithes of their property at Leyton in Essex. The advowson of the church of Leyton, the manor and an estate called "Carpetune" or "Leyton Carmidue," which formed part of the barony of Stanstead, belonged to the Abbey of Stratford by endowment of Gilbert de Montfichet, while the tithes of another portion of Leyton had been given to the nuns of Holywell by Gundrada de Valoines — hence the dispute. A translation of the charter, which settled this dispute as to the tithes of Leyton, is still preserved in the library of Trinity College, Dublin, and is as follows: "To all the children of our holie mother the Church this present writing. Seeing brother Richarde, Abbot of Stratford and Convent of the same place, and Maude, Prioresse of Holywell and Convent of the same place — sende greeting in our Lord. We will have it notified to all men, that a cause or matter being in variaunce betweene them upon tithe in the paroche of Leyton, it is agreed by the counseill of discrete men betweene us, that the ladie prioresse and nunne of Holywell shall receive and take all tithes, which they were wont to receive, except the tithes either of the demesne of Rockholde and of the demesne of Carmidue, which the lord abbot and Convente of Stratforde shall receive by reason of the right, that they have in the church of Leyton. And to the intent, that this composition may for ever persevere firme inviolable and immutable, to the present writing we have on either side sette our seales.

This was truly done in the yer of grace a thousand-two-hundred and XXII. at Easter."

This peaceable agreement with the nuns of Holywell affords another indication of the discretion of the Abbot Richard. The last occasion on which his name is mentioned is, that he bought property in Leyton of Thomas de Arderne, and land in Ginges of Richard de Ginges in the year 1233.

The next abbot mentioned is

HUGH (1237).

His name occurs in the alienation fines in connexion with various transfers of land in Leuiton, Ginges Mounteney, West Ham and Leyton; he also purchased the advowson of the church of St. Christopher at Willingale, and six years later, in 1243, of William Dun rents in East Ham and Barking, all which purchases formed a considerable addition to the estates of the abbey. During his time the prior of the abbey, Walter de London by name, was elected abbot of the Cistercian House of Crokesden or Croxden in Staffordshire, where he commenced his rule in the year 1242. In the annals of that place it is honourably recorded of him, "that the monks believed his accession to the abbey to have been a special blessing of God, that he wonderfully enlarged and greatly embellished their monastery, namely the gateway, the church, the chapter-house and refectory, the kitchen, parlour, infirmary and cloisters. The novice's house and other buildings were most skilfully erected in his time and various useful offices were most laudably prepared for his successors." This energetic lord abbot, Walter de London, died in the year 1268.

Everything recorded of the abbey of Stratford about this period conveys the idea of a flourishing and vigorous community. While Abbot Richard was honoured with duties of a diplomatic character, Abbot Hugh used every effort to increase its property by purchase.

The next record relating to the Abbey of Stratford is a charter of King Henry III. dated at Westminster the 24th of May 1253, permitting the monks to disafforest and make a park[1] of their wood at Leyton, called Carpetune, also granting a free warren[2] in all their demesne lands of West Hamme, Leyton, Chigwell, Woodford, Ginges Mounteney, Ginges Laundry, Ginges Joyberd, Ginges Radulphi, Dunton, East Horndon, Wand, Little Thurrock, Great and Little Burgstead, Caldwell, besides a weekly market aud annual fair at their manor of Great Burgstead.

The pleasures of the chase as well as a supply of game for the table were thus secured to the monks of Stratford, and fish they could obtain from their own waters, since they had a fishing-house and piscatories on the river Lea. It would appear as if the churchmen of that age had widely parted from the simplicity and self-denial of their ancient founders. An old writer says of them "Bacon, cheese, eggs, and even fish itself can no more please their nice palates; they only relish the flesh-pots of Egypt, pieces of boiled and roast pork, good fat veal, otters and hares, the best geese aud pullets, and in a word all sorts of flesh and fowl do now cover the tables of holy

---

[1] Parks were not then mere ornamental enclosures, but when established by royal authority the kings had legal and prescriptive rights over the game contained in them.

[2] Free warren is much the same right as that now coveted by sportsmen, namely to preserve from others and to destroy for themselves the beasts and fowls of warren, as rabbits, hares, roes, partridges, pheasants, rails, quails, woodcocks, mallards and herons.

monks. But what do I talk? These things are grown now too common, they are cloyed with them, they must have something more delicate, they would have got them kids, harts, boars and wild bears. One must for them beat the bushes with a great number of hunters and by the help of birds of prey must one chase the pheasants, and partridges and ring-doves, for fear the servants of God, who are good monks, should starve with hunger."

The sporting propensities of the mediaeval clergy are well known and, indeed, one of the earliest treatises on hunting, hawking, and fishing was written by Julia de Berners, Prioress of Sopewell, near St. Albans—"a gentlewoman endued with great gifts of body and mind." Another instance nearer home is found in the Abbess of Barking, who was permitted to keep dogs for hunting hares and foxes in the forest of Essex, and we may well suppose, that if such were the habits of ladies devoted to religious life, the men were not far behind them.

But, not only did the Abbey of Stratford continue to grow in wealth, it had also in the year 1267 the honour of becoming for a while the residence of King Henry III., and the scene of important historical transactions. This happened at the conclusion of the last war between the king and the barons, when the royal army lay encamped round London. After escaping by a postern from the Tower of London, Cardinal Ottoboni, the royal legate, joined the king at the abbey, and here for "streightnesse of lodging" the legate's horses and mules were stabled in the cloisters. Hither also resorted Prince Edward, the king's great and warlike son, and it became a common centre, where all the barons of the king's party as well as his foreign favourites and advisers used to assemble.

The long reign of Henry III. closed in the year 1272, and Edward I. commenced his glorious and vigorous career. At this period of our history the monastic orders had absorbed so large a portion of the landed property of the kingdom, as to become a serious national evil. Their estates rendered no due, or military service to the feudal lord; they paid neither contributions nor toll to the civil power, nor tithe to the parish priest. Exempt alike from civil, military, and ecclesiastical burdens they had fallen into a dead hand, "mortmain." But what was politically even worse still, the rents and revenues arising from church property, being chiefly under the control of foreigners, were too often carried beyond the sea to enrich some great mother church of the order in France or Italy, or to fill the coffers of the Roman Pontiff.

In the year 1237 three hundred Italians were sent by the Pope to be provided with benefices in England, and we are told that eight years later (1245) the church preferments possessed by Italians in this country amounted to sixty thousand marks per annum, a greater sum than the ordinary revenue of the crown. The following year the Pope demanded half the income of every non-resident, and one third of the income of every resident clergyman. It was calculated that the present of Sicily, offered to Prince Edward, was used as a pretext by the Pope to draw from this country a sum equal to twelve millions of our present money.

Such abuses as these could not pass unchecked, nor was it compatible with the prosperity of the kingdom to allow the land to fall into such hands. Accordingly the attention of the legislature was directed to the subject early in the reign of King Edward I. That monarch as wise in council as he was victorious in arms, "closed,' (to use the words of Sir William Blackstone) "the gulf in which all the landed property of the kingdom was in danger of being swallowed up, by his reiterated statutes of Mortmain.[1]" The first of these, in the seventh year of his reign, provided "that no person religious or otherwise should buy or sell any lands or tenements, or, under the colour of any gift or lease or any title whatever, receive the same or by any other craft shall appropriate lands in any wise to come into mortmain, on pain of forfeiture." It is a matter of curiosity, says the learned judge, "to observe the great address and subtle contrivances of the ecclesiastics in eluding from time to time the

---

[1] Mortmain; the term applies generally to alienations of lands or tenements to any corporation, ecclesiastical or temporal; but it is used especially with reference to "Religious Houses," whose enormous acquisitions of landed property and subtle evasions of the law gave rise to a series of restraining enactments, and were at length effectually met by the "Statute de religiosis" or as it is commonly called "of Mortmain," which forbade any further alienation of land to religious houses.

laws in being, and the zeal with which successive parliaments have pursued them through all their finesses, and how new remedies were still the parents of new evasions."

The various modes of evasion resorted to may be traced in the subsequent charters, given to the Abbey of Stratford Langthorne, and will repay the curious for a careful investigation.

In the Hundred Rolls of the third year of King Edward I. it is recorded that the jurors said, that the Abbot of Stratford held half a hide of land in Havering, and that he had there view of frank-pledge and claimed assize of bread and beer, but they knew not by what warrant. Also that the abbot possessed that estate (tenement) in West Ham called Sudbury or Sudbirie by gift of John de Venuz (Venois), and paid into the exchequer £31 and twelve pence, as the jurors believed, but they were ignorant whether he held it under a royal charter.

The next abbot whose name has been handed down to us is

ROBERT (1282).

He is first mentioned in the year 1282 in DEVON's Index to the "Alienation Fines." In 1294 he was summoned to attend a council of the clergy to be held before the king in person at Westminster, in consequence of the seizure of Gascony by the King of France. Heavy news must he have brought home that day to his monks from the council at Westminster, neither more nor less than that the royal treasury, impoverished by the wars, was to be replenished by one half of their revenue, whether spiritual or temporal. We can well imagine what anxious consultations must have been held in the Chapter House at West Ham, how to raise this money, and picture to ourselves the monks, speaking to one another in their cloister walks of the strange scene witnessed by their abbot at Westminster on this occasion, and of the personal audience to which the ecclesiastics were admitted by the king, whose frowns so overcame William de Montford, Dean of St. Paul's, pleading for a diminution of this heavy tax, that he sank down and died upon the spot; and how after this fatal accident the agitated churchmen returned to the Monk's Hall at Westminster Abbey, where their deliberations were interrupted by the intrusion of Sir John de Havering, governor of Guienne, who was

P

sent by the king, and with a fierce and menacing air addressed the assembly in this laconic speech : " Reverend Fathers, if any of you dare to contradict the king's demand in this business, let him stand forth into the midst of this assembly, that his person may be known and taken notice of as a breaker of the peace of the kingdom." To this speech no one had the courage to make any answer, for they knew that King Edward was not to be trifled with. He had already set bounds to the encroachments of the church by the Statute of Mortmain, and also resisted both the usurpations of the Church of Rome and the exactions of the Pope, being determined that the ecclesiastical estates should bear their share of the national burden.

It was between the year 1288 and 1290 that Pope Nicholas IV., on occasion of an expedition to the Holy Land, granted to King Edward I. the " tenthe " in England, towards defraying the expenses. A record of this has been preserved in the " Taxation of Pope Nicholas IV.," and from it we learn what the temporalities of the. abbey were at that date.

A.   Diocese of Rochester :

    In parochia de Leueseham (Lewisham) £7 11 8

B.   Diocese of London :

    Bona Abbatis de Stratford in Par. de St.
        Nicholas Cold Abbey 0 3 4
    In Parochia St. Petri in Temestrete (Thames
        Street), Summa 3s 11d, Decima 4¾d 0 0 7

C.   Archdeaconry of Essex :

      Deanery of Budstaple, Abbas and Stratforde...   4 15 0
    In Bournsted Magna (Great Burgstead)...   ...   33 9 10
    In Leyndon (Langdon) 0 15 0
    In Chaldwell 7 4 11½
    In Shenefend (Shenfield) 0 3 0
    In Felbinge or Febbing   :...   ...   .   6 0 6
    In Thurrock parva 12 19 0
      Deanery of Chafford :
    In Welde (South Weald) 3 10 8

      Deanery of Aurigre (Ongar) :
    In Chyggwelle (Chigwell) 12 17 2

Deanery of Berkynge (Barking) :

	£	s	d
In Berkynge	0	15	0
In Easthamme	2	13	8
In Westhamme	45	14	4
In Illesforde (Ilford)	11	12	1½
In Leyton	23	3	6½
In Wodeford (Buckhurst in Woodford)	1	0	0

Deanery of Chelmsford :

	£	s	d
In Botolph Ossury	8	11	0
In Gynge Mountneys	13	8	0

Deanery of Rochford :

	£	s	d
In Hadley (Hadleigh)	2	13	4

Diocese of Lincoln, Archdeaconry of Bucks, dues
from the Prior of St. Fritheswide :

	£	s	d
In Wychenden, Oxon	0	1	0

Diocese of Salisbury, Archdeaconry Berks :
Deanery of Reading in Wynkefelde

	£	s	d
Decima 3s 2½d	1	12	0

Total ... £200 14 8½

Unless their privileges as Cistercians exempted the monks of Stratford from some of these imposts, their coffers must have been nearly empty, before King Edward's tax of half their income was demanded.

In 1295, the year following the council of the clergy at Westminster afore mentioned, the abbot was again summoned to attend parliament, and likewise in the year 1307, when an Act of Parliament was enacted to restrain the great amount of contributions sent abroad by foreign superiors of the religious orders of the Praemonstratensians, the Clunatics and the Cistercians.

Another circumstance, relating to the monks at Stratford, is a royal letter or circular addressed to the abbot in common with the Archbishop of Canterbury, the bishops and thirty-eight other abbots, commanding them to perform solemn obsequies for the soul of

Edmund,[1] Duke of Lancaster, the king's brother, who died in 1296. They were to be performed "with great solemnity and devotion, commending his spirit to the Most High, chaunting of masses, and offering of devout prayers."

About the beginning of the fourteenth century, the old founders and patrons of the Abbey of Stratford Langthorne, bearing the name of Montfichet, were all gone, and their honours had devolved on their heir John de Lancaster, who, as has already been stated, was very liberal to the monks of Stratford, and gave them besides the advowson of the church of East Ham with lands adjoining (*see page* 81), also the reversion of the manor of East Ham, in conjunction with his wife Annora. Into possession of this manor the monks entered after the death of Annora, who survived her husband, but as they did so " without process of chancery or observing the proper legal forms," the manor was taken into the king's hands. This contempt or transgression was, however, afterwards forgiven, and on paying a fine of £20, the Abbot and Convent resumed the manor.

During the next few years nothing very remarkable appears to have occurred in connexion with the convent at West Ham, except that in 1315 the abbot received a summons to attend parliament, which was accompanied by the request that his monastery would lend fifty marks in aid of the war against the Scots. From the year 1295 to 1318 the abbot appears to have been summoned twelve times to attend parliament or convocations of the clergy, but finding that no similar summonses were issued after that date, we may suppose that Abbot Robert owed this distinction to some personal quality. The discontinuance may, however, have arisen from the policy pursued by King Edward, who reduced the number of abbots sitting

---

[1] Edmund Crouchback, Duke of Lancaster, was dispatched with a military force into Gascony, but his army being too inconsiderable to cope with that of the French, he was constrained to shut himself up in Bayonne where, suffering under mental vexation from his ill success, he sickened and died in 1296. A truce being concluded with France, his body was brought to England and buried in a sumptuous tomb in the Abbey Church at Westminster, near the spot where his first wife Aveline had been interred. (*See page* 85).

in parliament from sixty-four to twenty-four, and that of priors from thirty-six to only two.

Despite all enactments to the contrary, the monks contrived to add houses and land to their already large possessions, not always, however, without an official enquiry. A writ for this purpose was issued respecting their acquisition of one messuage and a hundred acres of land in East Ham from Thomas Pernested, besides several other writs of inquiry respecting land in Little Ilford and West Ham; also, whether it was prejudicial to the king's or any other interest, for Walter de Jernemuth to give to the Prior of Stratford land in West Ham, East Ham, and Burgstead, and to the abbot some manorial property in East Ham. An evasion of the Statute of Mortmain is also recorded, the King (Edward II.) granting letters patent, whereby Edmund Basset and Roger Samakyn, of Hatfield, were allowed to give to the Abbot and Convent of Stratford one messuage and 120 acres of land in Leyton, which were to be held by special licence. To this gift Edmund Basset afterwards added, in conjunction with Nicholas Cotes, one messuage and fifty acres in East Ham.

It was about this time that great disputes arose between the Abbot of Stratford, the Abbess of Barking, and the public, respecting the maintenance and repair of the two bridges at Bow and Stratford, and the causeway between them. The exact date is not known when the abbess transferred to the abbot the estate, settled by Queen Maude for this purpose, together with the duties attached to it. He had long coveted the mill, since so well-known as the "Abbey Mills," because it "lay near his house, and conveniently for the same," but the delegated responsibility respecting the bridges and causeway was neglected or evaded both by him and his successors. Complaint after complaint was made of the state of the bridges and the causeway, special enquiries and legal authorities seem to have been equally disregarded, until it became a question, whose duty it was to repair them. Such was the state of affairs, when in 1315 an enquiry or inquisition, as it was called, was instituted before the judges, who sat at Bow for that purpose. The jury there found the Abbess of Barking responsible, and the business was finally settled by a concord between the abbot and abbess, of which a full account has already been given in a previous chapter.

The same agreement under which afterwards the abbey landowners were liable as the successors of the abbot and monks of Stratford, both to maintain and to repair the bridges and the causeway between them, has been in force until recent years, but why the burden rested only on those holding abbey lands in the parish of West Ham, is not so clear.

What the position was of the abbots, as lay barons, is illustrated by the request, made in 1322 to the Abbot of Stratford, to raise as many men at arms and foot soldiers as he could, to march against the rebels and muster at Coventry on the first Sunday in Lent, on the occasion of the revolt of the English baronage against Edward II. and the two Despensers, which cost its leader, the unfortunate Earl of Lancaster, his life. When arrested at Boroughbridge, where his troops were dispersed, he was brought captive before Edward at Pontefract, and instantly ordered to death as a traitor. "Have mercy on me, King of Heaven," cried Lancaster, as mounted on a grey pony, without a bridle, he was hurried to execution, "for my earthly king has forsaken me." Cruel, unscrupulous, treacherous and selfish as Thomas of Lancaster is shown by every recorded act of his life to have been, yet there was something in so sudden and so great a fall, that cannot fail to touch men's hearts.

The next abbot mentioned is

WILLIAM (1330).

His name first occurs in the "Alienation Fines" in 1330. A few years later, in 1333, a subsidy was granted to Edward III. on occasion of the marriage of his sister Eleanor with the Earl of Gueldres, when one hundred and forty-one heads of religious houses, among whom was the Abbot of Stratford, endeavoured, but in vain, to excuse themselves from paying this tax.

It is at this period of our local history that we first obtain a glimpse of the structure of the abbey and its church. John de Bohun, Earl of Hereford and Essex, died in 1335 an invalid, at Kirby Thure, in Westmoreland, whence his body was brought for interment to the Abbey church at Stratford. His monument, if ever it existed, has totally disappeared with the Abbey church, nor do we know what the connexion was with the Abbey of Stratford Langthorne, that induced the interment of this great baron in its church.

There existed at that date, near the entrance gate of the monastery, a chapel belonging to the Abbot and Convent, where a daily mass was read for the souls of King Edward II., of William le Scroop, and Constantia, his wife, their son Geoffrey le Scroop, with Ivetta, his wife, and all faithful departed. To endow this mass Geoffrey le Scroop gave to the King (Edward III.), and the king granted to the abbot and convent two messuages, ten acres of land, seventy-two shillings and four-pence rent in Woolwich, also a certain rent of seven cocks, twenty-eight hens, and two-hundred and forty sheep, "to be held by the service of finding a monk or other fit person to celebrate a daily mass for the before-mentioned souls."

This giving to the Crown, and the Crown giving and confirming to the monks, was one of the methods by which the Statute of Mortmain was evaded. It occurs again in a second charter of the same king, dated four months later, in which it is rehearsed "that Simon Leythorne, vicar of West Ham, and John Duck, vicar of Great Burgstead, (both livings being in the gift of the abbot), had given to the king, and the king had given to the Abbot and Convent three messuages with four gardens, four shops, one dovecot, eighty-four acres of arable land, seven acres of meadow, twelve acres and a half of wood, and six shillings and sevenpence half-penny rent in Barking, in the hamlet of Great Ilford, and in the parish of Little Ilford, to be held by the service of finding a monk or other fit person to celebrate a daily mass for the souls of King Edward and of the members of the Scroop family, (already named), in the chapel near the gate of the monastery."

The vast stream of benefactions still kept flowing on, and during the whole reign of Edward III. the accumulation of land by the Abbot and Convent of Stratford remained unabated. In 1338 John Henry (Henny) and Rosa, his wife, bequeathed to the Abbot William sixty acres of land in Burgstead, and two years later Thomas de Harewolde, a citizen of London, granted to him, some land "in Woolwich, on the north part of the Thames, that formerly belonged to William de Rokyngham."

The next benefactor seems to have been John Charteney, who

gave to the Abbot and Convent a house with its appurtenances in St. Clement's Lane, in which William Peverel, a citizen of London, had an interest. This house was held of the king in capite, and of "free burgage,"[1] and was worth in all issues twelve marks by the year or £8. This house was afterwards known as the "Abbot's Inn,"—the word "Inn" being then applied to private town residences in the same way as the word "Hôtel" is now used in France. About two hundred years earlier than the date under consideration, FITZ-STEPHENS, in his account of London, mentions the custom of having town houses. He says: "Almost all the bishops, abbots, and great men of this kingdom are in a manner citizens and inhabitants of London, as having their respective and not inelegant habitations, to which they resort and where their disbursements are not sparing, whenever they are summoned from the country to attend councils or solemn meetings of the king or their metropolitan." If this description applied to the twelfth century when FITZ-STEPHENS wrote, it doubtless equally did so to the fourteenth.

In 1353 Sir Richard de Plaiz bestowed upon the monks all the property that he retained in East and West Ham, of the inheritance of the Montfichets, by a charter executed at West Ham. (*See page* 48).

In 1354 William de Dersham gave to the monks lands and rents in Ginges Mounteney and Hutton; and in 1374 Letters Patent were issued in favour of the Abbot of Stratford, by which William Langditch had permission to assign to the monks one messuage, two hundred and forty acres of land, fifteen acres of meadow, thirty-four acres of pasture and forty-four shillings and a half-penny rent in Burgstead, retaining for himself and Annor his wife the manor and its appurtenances. After the death of Annor, the monks intruded themselves into it without "the needful process in chancery," which contempt was, however, as in the case of the East Ham Manor, forgiven by the king on payment of £20. Nearly all the land in the parish of Burgstead now belonged to the Abbot of Stratford, having been given at different periods by different persons, many of whom

---

[1] Burgage tenure is an ancient tenure proper to boroughs, whereby the inhabitants by custom held their lands or tenements of the king or other person by a rent certain.

are not known.   Here also the abbot had a "grange,"[1] where he and the monks chiefly resided at this period, in consequence of a terrible calamity which had overtaken them in the destruction of their house.   It is alluded to by LELAND in his "Itinerary," who gives the following account: "This house first sett among the low marshes, was after with sore fludes defacy'd and remevid to a celle or graunge longynge to it, called Bergestede in Estsex, a mile or more from Billerica.   The monks remayned at Burgestede untyl entrete was made, that they might have some help otherwyse.   Then one of the Richards, King of England, toke the grounde and Abbaye of Stratford into his protection, and reedifienge it brought the foresayde monks agayne to Strateforde, where among the marshes they re-inhabytyd."

The impoverished circumstances of the abbey are more fully set forth in the following Letter Patent of King Richard II., whereby he took it under his own royal patronage.   This document records an astonishing proof of ignorance on the part of the monks, as well as of ingratitude towards their founder and his family, whose very existence is ignored, although it was through their bounty and successive gifts, that the Abbey of Stratford had been gradually enriched with nearly the whole of the two great parishes, which once formed the fee of Montfichet.   The document is as follows:—

LETTER PATENT OF KING RICHARD II.

24th May, 1397.

" Richard, by the Grace of God, King of England and France, and Lord of Ireland, &c., to all to whom these presents shall come, Greeting:

Know ye — that whereas a certain William de Montfichet, who began to found the Abbey of Stratford Langthorne, died

---

[1] The word "Grange" literally means a barn, but was applied also to the dwelling house and buildings constituting the farm establishment on conventual estates; such, no doubt, were the "Woodgrange" in the parish of West Ham, which has left its name to one of the existing manors, and also the "Abbey Farm" called "Ham Grange."   But when, as in this instance of Great Burgstead, it was attached to a considerable and distant estate, the abbotical "Grange" appears to have been equivalent to the manor house of the lay gentry, which it probably equalled in comfort and importance.

without heirs before that he was able to finish the said Abbey,
so that the Abbot and Convent aforesaid are become destitute
of a patron and guardian, who ought of right to help and
relieve, and defend them, whereby, as well as by the encroachments of the water and access of divers persons continually
resorting to their Mansion, as by divers other causes, they have
become liable to suits, heavy debts, wants and losses, and do
from day to day become more embarrassed, that it will in a
very short time behove them to repair · their Mansion, unless
they be by us graciously assisted ; We, at the supplication of
our well-beloved in Christ, the now Abbot and Convent of the
aforesaid place, and in consideration of the premises for the
avoiding of such like damages and dangers, of our Special Grace
have granted to the same Abbot and Convent, that we be from henceforth their Founder, and that the same Abbey as of our Foundation
and Patronage shall be held, reputed and deemed, and shall
have all the liberties and franchises which other Houses of our
Foundation of the Cistercian Order have in all things in virtue of
our Foundation and Patronage above-mentioned, so that the
said Abbot and Convent and their successors by the occasion
aforesaid of any —— pension or other burthens whatever, be
not by any means burthened. Nor in the time of the Vacation
of that Abbey by the death or deprivation or resignation of
the Abbot of the aforesaid place be holden, bound or compelled
to require the Royal Assent and licence or of our heirs, before
they proceed to the election of another Abbot. And that no
Escheator[1], Sheriff or other Minister of us or our heirs, may in
the time of such Vacation intermeddle with their temporalities or
other things belonging to their aforesaid house, otherwise than
before these times was accustomed to be done.

And as their liberties, ancient customs, and privileges do
require as to elections and other burthens, they may as freely

---

[1] Escheator — an officer who has to look after the escheats of the Crown —
escheats being land or tenements etc., falling to the Crown or the lord of the manor
as a forfeit, or on the death of a tenant having no heir.

exist as ever they were, and before this time ought to have been, for that the aforesaid house be of our Patronage and Foundation as is aforesaid, notwithstanding; And further of our more abundant Grace We have granted to the said Abbot, that he or his successors be not made or assigned collectors of tenths or other quotas or subsidies by the (aforesaid) Pope, or by the Clergy of our Realm of England, or by any other mode whatsoever granted or in future to be granted, against their will. In witness whereof We have caused this our letter to be made patent.

Witness ourself at Westminster the 24th day of May in the twentieth year of our reign (1397.)"

In the commencement of the reign of Henry IV. the monks of Stratford obtained "Letters Patent" to hold property in Aveley, Upminster, Chaldewell, East Tilbury and Little Thurrock, also a confirmation of their former charters. In the year 1446 "Letters Patent" were issued by King Henry VI., permitting Thomas Bernewell and William Hulyn, to grant to the Abbot and Convent and their successors for ever, a messuage and one hundred acres of arable, four acres of meadow, three roods of wood, and twenty-eight shillings and one penny of annual quit rents in West Ham. This West Ham estate was given in exchange for one in Havering, held of the king in capite by the annual service of two shillings or "one spur."

It was at this period, that the desolating wars of York and Lancaster commenced, and although their effects upon the Abbey of Stratford have not been recorded, there can be no doubt that they were the chief cause, that from this period the gifts to the Abbey became few and unimportant.

In 1467 King Edward IV. was at Stratford, and probably entertained at the abbey, for in the following year he made them by deed an annual gift of two casks of red wine (afterwards changed to an allowance in money) for the celebration of masses. This wine was to be received at the hand of the king's butler from the port of London, one cask at the feast of St. Martin and the other at Easter. The same monarch also confirmed to the abbey the grant, formerly made by Henry III., of two fairs and a market at Burgstead;

since these had been transferred to Billericay, a hamlet of that parish, it is possible that this circumstance rendered the confirmation desirable.

These appear to have been the last benefactions made to the monks of Stratford. Not only had the wars of York and Lancaster desolated and agitated the kingdom, but the influence of the early Reformers had also gradually weaned the national mind from dependence on the monastic orders. Consequently gifts to their houses ceased, not from their inability to receive, but rather from the disinclination to bestow on the part of the laymen.

As early as 1365, John Wyclif had commenced his open controversy with the clergy and mendicant friars, and in his divinity lectures at Oxford taught doctrines, which were entirely opposed to those of the Church of Rome. These reformed opinions spread so rapidly that shortly after his death, his followers, under the name of Lollards,[1] were computed at more than half the people of England, numbering among their ranks some of the most powerful nobles. In order to suppress their heresy, the "Statute of Heretics" was enacted. By the provisions of this infamous act, "bishops were not only permitted to arrest and imprison, so long as their heresy should last, all preachers of heresy, all schoolmasters infected with heretical teaching, all owners or writers of heretical books, but a refusal to abjure or a relapse after abjuration enabled them also to hand over the heretic to the civil officers, and by these — so ran the first legal enactment of religious bloodshed, which defiled our statute book — he was to be burnt on a high place before the people." The statute was hardly passed before William Sawtre, who had quitted the rectory of St. Margaret's, in the town of Lynn in Norfolk, to spread the new Lollardism, became its first victim and was committed to the flames in Smithfield, in the year 1401. While the Archbishops Arundel and Chichely, seconded by the Lancasterian kings, persecuted the Lollards to death, the people, sympathizing with

---

[1] Lollard — a word which probably means much the same as "idle babbler" was the nickname of scorn with which the orthodox churchmen chose to insult their assailants.

the Reformers, made their voice heard in an unmistakable manner through their representatives in parliament. One parliament refused to grant supplies, because their petition for the repeal of the recent statute "of burning heretics" was refused. Another parliament presented, upon the accession of Henry IV., a petition "that temporal lands, devoutly given but disorderately spent by spiritual persons, should be seized into the king's hand, stating at the same time, that these lands might suffice to maintain for the king's honour and defence of the realm, fifteen earls, one thousand five hundred knights, six thousand two hundred esquires, one hundred alms-houses for the poor and impotent, with a surplus of £20,000 for the king's coffers." The result of this movement was the suppression of one hundred and ten priories, whose revenues were given to the Crown.

In the following year, Henry Chichely, then Archbishop of Canterbury, averted a similar "thrust," by turning the attention of King Henry V. from the monastic orders, and inflaming his ambition with the glittering prospects of the crown of France. This prelate preferred to plunge two nations into all the horrors of a long and sanguinary war, rather than risk the quiet possession of monastic property in England, "so that," as FULLER quaintly observes, "putting the king upon the seeking of a new crown, kept the abbots' old mitres on their heads." Although the destruction of the abbeys, already tottering, was thus for a time averted, yet a severe blow had been struck at the root of monachism in England. The great principles of the Reformation were also secretly gaining a strong hold on men's minds, and the struggle was gradually commencing, which never really ceased, until the authority of the Church of Rome was finally overthrown in our land.

Since the time of the last-named abbot more than a hundred years elapse, before we meet with the name of another abbot, during the reign of Edward IV.

JOHN RIESIDE.

We are indebted for the preservation of his name to an ancient manuscript extant in Trinity College, Dublin, of which mention has already been made (*see page* 101), as containing a copy of the amicable agreement between Abbot Richard, and Maude, Prioress of

Holywell. It appears that, after the lapse of two centuries, the question of tithes was again agitated by their successors, John Rieside, Abbot of Stratford, and Jane Sevenoak, Prioress of Holywell, when the matter was arbitrated by William Wetynge and Robert Kereges. The instrument itself is without date, but on one of the leaves of the manuscript is this entry: "Tythes by the Abbot and Prioress in . . . . Edw: quart:" and one of the pages is headed "return of lands in Leyton, in the xxiii year of the reign of King Edward IV." whereby the date is fixed (1482.) The arbitrators decided, that the prioress was to receive the tithes of certain parcels of land, and of her demesne land in the Manor of Ruckholts,—and the abbot, those due from tenants and farmers of that manor, and all others in the parish of Leyton. Amongst the land entitled as the demesne of the prioress is " Halewell garden and acres, and Halywell-down, and Heswelldown, containing by estimation XXX acres." Holloway-down is probably a corruption of the ancient name here referred to, and both are clearly derived from their ancient possessors, the nuns of Holywell, near Shoreditch.

Rieside was succeeded by the abbot

HUGH (1483.)

His name is given in the list of abbots in the new edition of the Monasticon, quoting the Harleian M.S.S., where we find a warrant to aid and assist Hugh, Abbot of Stratford, and Robert, Abbot of Woburne, and the Abbot of Clyffe, " Reformatours and visitours of the order of Cisteaux." It was during his rule that King Henry VII., in 1487, granted to the abbey a charter of " Inspeximus and Confirmation," in which many of the more ancient charters, already quoted, are rehearsed; the same instrument was again inspected and confirmed in 1510, by a charter of King Henry VIII, which is preserved in the Public Record Office, and rehearses no less than thirteen charters or letters patent of former kings.

The abbot next mentioned is

WILLIAM (HICHMAN?) 1509.

This abbot granted in 1509, the first year of the reign of Henry VIII., to John Balle of London, haberdasher, and Anne his wife, and Margaret Mason, widow, a life lease of a house (tenement) and yard (curtilage), then called "Poor Firmary," also two gardens, one small and one large, called "The Poor Firmary Gardens," the whole situated within the precincts of the monastery, and abutting on the abbot's garden, on the court-yard of the monastery, on the church-yard of the Parochial Church of All Saints within the said monastery, on a mead called Tan House Mead, and on Garden Bradberry.

This lease as well as others of a subsequent date, afford a glimpse of the interior arrangements of the abbey, and show that there was a population, resident within the precincts, distinct from the monastery which was enclosed within, as the kernel in the shell of a nut, and overthrow the idea of extreme seclusion and exclusiveness of conventual life, or perhaps afford an example of the relaxation of discipline at this period, complained of in the monastic orders.

The Firmarie or Infirmarium in a monastery was a detached building, "wherein"—FULLER informs us—"persons down right sick, trouble to others, and troubled by others, had the benefit of attendance and physick privie to themselves," but the addition of the word "poor," and the fact that there were rents belonging to the "impotent poor of West Ham," mark this as a charity either fallen into disuse, or removed without the precincts of the abbey.

We have presumed that the family name of Abbot William was Hichman or Hycheman, because in the grant of abbey lands in East Ham, made to Richard Breame by King Henry VIII., a certain marsh is reserved which William Hichman or Hycheman, late (nuper) Abbot of Stratford, had recovered from the overflowing of the water. Since William Etherway was appointed abbot in 1516, and William Huddleston, the last abbot, granted leases from the year 1533 down to the dissolution of the monastery, it appears almost conclusive that William Hichman is the Abbot "William" alluded to in the above lease, dated 1509.

The next abbot is

WILLIAM ETHERWAY (1516.)

Of this abbot nothing is recorded beyond the fact that he was appointed in the year 1516.

He was succeeded by

ROBERT.

This abbot was present at the christening of Queen Elizabeth, on the 10th of September, 1533.

We have now arrived at the time when the Monastery was under the rule of the last abbot, whose name is

WILLIAM HUDDLESTON (1533.)

The earliest notice of him is contained in the abstract of the leases of abbey lands, rehearsed in the deed of gift by Henry VIII. to Sir Peter Meautas. The extremely low rents and the dates of these leases lead to the supposition that this abbot, foreseeing the probable fall of his house, secured the immediate advantage of large fines.

FULLER in his "Church History" informs us, that amongst other means, by which the monastic orders had acquired wealth, was the "renting and stocking of farms, keeping tan houses and brew houses in their own hands, for though the monks themselves were too fine-nosed to dabble in tan fats, yet they kept others, bred in that trade, to follow their work. These convents having bark of their own woods, hides of the cattle of their own breeding and killing, and which was the main, a large stock of money to buy at the best hand and to allow such chapmen, they sold to, a long day of payment, easily eat out those who were bred to that vocation. Whereupon in the twenty-first year of King Henry VIII. (1529) a statute was made, that no priest, either secular or regular, should on heavy penalties hereafter meddle with such mechanic employment."

This statute was complied with at Stratford, for Richard Parker, the tanner, ceased to carry on his vocation within the monastery, and settled in 1535 at Plaistow, whereupon the tan house, garden, orchard, and mead were let to Thomas Cole, of West Ham, and Anne, his wife. Richard Parker afterwards held, as tenant of the abbey, about twenty acres of land in different parts of the parish of West Ham, at a yearly rent of one hundred and six shillings and two pence, amongst which were four acres of land called " Bedfords," [1] and an acre and a half called " Hencotes Down."

Tanning was, however, not the only secular employment, carried on in the precincts of the abbey, for near the Abbey Mills was a kilnhouse, giving its name to a gate there, and it was probably in compliance with the statute already mentioned, that the kilnhouse was used as a barn in 1533, and let together with the mills to John Rowle, a carpenter.

At this date the mills were described as " those two mills situate and being under one roof within the precincts of the said monastery, together with all houses, chambers, etc., belonging to the said mills and bakehouse." These buildings with a garden, a small island to the north of the mills, called " Tonge Island," and some marsh land were let for the term of 40 years at an annual rent of £10, payable to the abbot, and of two shillings to the sexton of the monastery.

A slaughter-house, a grange or barn, a dove-house, a yard, stables, hay-barns, fish-ponds, gardens and orchards are also enumerated as being within the precincts of the abbey; the number of the latter, and the fact that the abbot had a private garden, are a proof of the horticultural tastes of the Cistercian monks.

In the leases granted by the Abbot Huddleston, there is also a mansion named, " late in the occupation of the Lady Margaret de Vere, widow," which stood within the precincts, nearly opposite to the present "Adam and Eve" public-house, while another mansion called " The Lodge" stood on the southern boundary of the precincts, surrounded by a moat, of which traces yet remain.

Respecting the monastery itself, little remains on record. The cloisters were used as stables for the horses and mules of the Pope's legate, Ottoboni, when the accommodation in the abbey was "too strait" for the whole court of King Henry III. The abbot had a private

---

[1] It is very probable that the cottage residence, so long known as " Bedfords" near Plaistow, and latterly as the " Willows," with the four acres of paddock attached to it, and its pond and ancient willows, for many years the residence of Captain Richard Pelly, R.N., is identical with the above. This estate is now being laid out for building purposes.

R

garden and in the monastery a library, in which LELAND informs us he found almost all the works of Stephen of Canterbury, the archbishop, who wrote commentaries on most of the books of Holy Scripture, and to whom the first division of the books of the Old and New Testament into chapters is ascribed.

The precincts of the monastery appear to have formed a parish, distinct from that of West Ham, and the "little church of St. Mary and All Saints within the precincts of the monastery" was considered the parish church, as distinct from West Ham parish church. This distinction between the two parishes is frequently specified in the leases granted by the last abbot, viz.:

In one instance—Peter Vanne's lease—"the little church, within the said monastery, called the Parish Church," is named. In another—Thomas Cole's lease—the abbot lets to Thomas Cole, of West Ham, and Ann, his wife, "a messuage, orchard and garden in the parish of All Saints, within the precincts of the said monastery," —also "a close of land in the said parish of West Ham, called Hobbley's close."

Again—the abbot lets to Robert Wright "land in the parish of West Ham," and to Richard Parker, and Agnes, his wife, "of the parish of All Saints within the precincts of the monastery, various parcels of land lying in the parish of West Ham."

Another lease—granted to John Balle, Ann, his wife, and Margaret Mason, widow—describes a house and garden within the abbey precincts, as abutting against the "Churchyard of the parochial church of All Saints within the said monastery."

Robert Snow, bailiff and collector of the rents of the abbey, at the period of the dissolution, enters as the first head in his accounts "the rents appertaining to the parish church of St. Mary and All Saints within the precincts of the monastery."

It is therefore very evident that the abbey precincts were regarded as a distinct parish, or, perhaps, "extra-parochial."

Of the abbey church itself little appears to be known. Whether the original Saxon, or early Norman building, which existed when William de Montfichet founded the abbey, remained till the period now under discussion, we have no means of ascertaining. We know that it was endowed with the tithe of the demesne by William de

Montfichet's chaplain, at the same time as the feudal baron himself endowed the monastery with his demesne, its mansion, and appurtenances for the residence of the monks.

About fifty years later (1184) we find that a parish church did exist at West Ham, which was given to the Abbot and Convent by Gilbert de Montfichet, and which from that time became a vicarage.

Besides the conventual church, there was within the precincts of the abbey, near the entrance gate, a chapel, dedicated to St. Richard,[1] which is mentioned in Henry VIII.'s grant of the Abbey site to Sir Peter Mewtas. This may have been the chapel, as described near the entrance gate of the Monastery, where daily masses were said for the Scroop family.

Of the various officers attached to the abbey there are but very few notices. The priors were not unfrequently promoted to abbots of other houses, as we have seen in the case of Walter de London, Prior of Stratford, who was promoted to the abbot's chair at Croxden (Crokesden).

The other officers were also great men in their day.

"Upon my faith thou art some officer,
Some worthy Sexton or some Cellarer,
No poor chorister, nor no novice,
But a governor both ware and wise"

says CHAUCER in his "Prologue to the Monk's Tale."

To the office of Sexton certain lands and rents were attached, twelve shillings annually from four acres of land, called "Bedfords," and two cottages or tenements situate in West Ham, also two shillings annually from the tenant of the Abbey Mills.

To the office of sub-cellarius rents accrued from eight different tenants, amounting to fifty-four shillings and four pence. The Cellarers, whose duties consisted in supplying all sorts of provisions and liquors consumed in the convent, were also often taken abroad by reason of

[1] St. Richard's Chapel. Morant supposes it was intended for a private altar or burying place, perhaps for Richard de Montfichet; it certainly cannot be from a dedication, there being no Saint of that name.

their office in connexion with the commissariat and other secular vocations. FULLER says of them "the Cellarers were brave blades, much affecting singular gallantry, for I find it complained of them that they used to swagger with swords by their sides like lay gentlemen."

There was also attached to the Monastery another functionary, the porter of the gate, an office of considerable trust, to know what guests and when, especially at the postern, were to be admitted thereunto. At the gatehouse leading to West Ham the "monk

Gateway of West Ham Abbey as it appeared in 1758.

porter, had a tenement, orchard, garden and yard, which in June 1535 were in farm to Robert Sknowe, porter there." But we hardly are prepared to find that, besides the monk porter, Robert Banks and Margaret, his wife, were lessees of a tenement and curtilage, "as well at as upon the great gate there," together with an adjacent orchard and garden, of which Agnes Hurst had been the previous tenant. That such an arrangement was liable to abuse, there can be little doubt, and the following injunction of the visitors, appointed to inspect the monasteries, under Cromwell in 1535, would probably apply among others also to the Abbey of Stratford—"that there be

no enteryng into the Monastery but one, and that by the Great
For-Gate of the same, which diligently shall be watched and kept
by some porter specially appoynted for that purpose, and shall be
shut and opened by the same bothe daye and nyght at convenient
and accustomed hours, which porter shall repell all manner of women
from entrance into the said Monastery."

Without the moated precincts, thirty acres of wood, called "the
Abbot's Grove," lay to the north of the abbey, and towards the east,
at about a quarter of a mile distant, lay the village of West Ham
clustered round the parish church.

*This sketch of West Ham Church was taken in 1832 from the site of the old "Lodge";
the water in the foreground is part of the original moat, which surrounded the Abbey.*

A road, called in ancient deeds "the Portway," led from the great
gate of the abbey to the village. It then passed along the churchyard to Upton Cross, until, winding on between fields and hedgerows,
it entered the parish of East Ham. Along the southern side

of the road the property of the abbey extended nearly, if not quite, to Upton Cross, and thence towards Plaistow, including "Bedfords," "Hencotes Down," and the "Lady Well Field," so called from a natural spring of very pure water, which until recently was still in existence, nearly opposite the present Plaistow Grove. Some picturesque superstitions were attached to this well, even in the memory of persons now living. Tradition says "that at midnight, or in the early mornings a lady was seen to float above the well, shrouded in a white mist, and that her voice might be heard singing in the air even in the day time." Having formed part of the possessions of the monks, it is probable that the name of the well was derived from the Virgin Mary, the lady of their adoration, and these romantic legends attached to it are probably founded on some miraculous qualities attributed to it by the monks. That the water of this old well was famous for the cure of sore eyes, we may accept as a fact, since frequent washing with clear, pure, and fresh spring water would unquestionably be beneficial to eyes, unaccustomed to its free use.

The demesne farm of the abbey, called Ham Grange, lay towards the south of the road leading from West Ham to Plaistow, amidst rich marshland pastures and not less productive arable land.

The western boundary of the estate was formed by the branch of the River Lea, known as the Channel-sea river, which was one of the artificial channels cut by King Alfred, and it is very probable that the ancient pollard willows, which stood on the borders of this stream, were planted by the monks. A winding road led—up to a recent date—from the old postern under the mills to the causeway, raised by Queen Maud, which it joined at a very short distance from Bow Bridge.

The view from this point of the abbey was uninterrupted; seated in the midst of green meadows and watered with abundant streams, it charmed the old topographers, who clearly did not participate in our modern fears of damp exhalations and malaria.

In addition to these demesnes, more immediately surrounding their house, the monks had a "fishing-house" and "all manner of piscatories" from the mouth of the river Lea to Bow Bridge.

We have seen that the abbot and monks, in process of time,

became lords of the Manors of West Ham,[1] Woodgrange, Sudbury, Plaiz, East West Ham and East Ham, that they were also patrons and rectors of the churches of East Ham, West Ham, and Leyton, that they possessed a park at Leyton, also woods stocked with game in Woodford and Chigwell, besides other valuable estates in different parts of the country. Their lands were let to tenants at the average rent of three shillings and four-pence, or four shillings an acre for pasture, and two shillings and eight-pence for arable land. Low as these rents appear to us, the annual income was estimated at £652 3s 1½d and amounted, one hundred and twenty years after the dissolution, to no less than £15,100 per annum.

The history of the Abbey of West Ham is now brought down to its close, the period having arrived, when these establishments were suppressed throughout the kingdom. In the twelfth, thirteenth, and fourteenth centuries, the monasteries were unquestionably lights compared to the atmosphere of darkness and superstition, by which they were surrounded; they were the centres of civilisation and refinement, from which radiated light and warmth and incalculable blessings far and wide; they were seats of literature and of religious retirement. Many valuable books and national records, as well as private evidences were preserved in their libraries—indeed they were the only places where they could have been safely lodged in those turbulent times. Nor were they useless in other respects, being the hospitals for the sick and poor, many of both being daily relieved by them; they also afforded lodging and entertainment to travellers, when there was no inn. But the monastic orders made no progress, and in the fifteenth and sixteenth centuries their relative position, as it concerned the world at large, was greatly changed; they had become dark spots in the fierce light of the dawning day that shone around, in short, they had outlived the work which they were created to perform. Whilst art and science, sound learning and experimental philosophy, commerce, industry, and maritime discovery were making constant progress among the lay

---

[1] Morant says that the demesnes of the Abbey in West Ham alone comprehended near 1500 acres.

population, and the doctrines and precepts of Holy Scripture became known and beloved by them, the monks still clung to their mediæval prejudices; their houses became the hiding places of indolence and superstition, and in many instances even of crime and imposture; false miracles disgraced their shrines, and idleness and vice their halls and cloisters.

The abbeys fell before the mandate of Henry VIII., but that mandate could hardly have been executed, had not public opinion—as we now call it—seconded the movement, and withdrawn the sympathies of the people from their inmates. That their fall had been foreseen by many members of their own church in England, we may conclude from the fact that Robert Whitgift, Abbot of Wellow in Lincolnshire, uncle of the Archbishop Whitgift, was wont to say "that they and their religion could not long continue, because he had read the whole scripture over and over, and could never find therein that their religion was founded of God." And for proof of his opinion, the abbot would allege that saying of our Saviour, "every planting, that my heavenly Father hath not planted, shall be rooted up."

The pious Bernard Gilpin, Rector of Houghton-le-Spring, who was contemporary with these transactions, writing to his nephew, Thomas Gelthorpe, lays stress on another point, saying "whereas ye are grieved at the fall of monasteries and abbeys, I am sorry you should be blinded in this case, for many of your own religion have confessed that they could not possibly subsist any longer, because the cry of them, like the cry of Sodom, was ascended into the ears of God, their crimes are so manifest, that they could no longer be concealed, the Lord would endure those wicked men no longer."

The first step taken towards this suppression was in 1535, when "Visitors" were sent into different counties, under the direction of Thomas Cromwell, to institute a searching enquiry into the condition of monastic houses, and to reform the abuses which should be found in them. The revelations resulting from this commission were such, that the entire suppression of the smaller houses followed within three years.

Stow informs us, that the visitors began by putting "forth all religious persons that would go, and all that were under the age of four-and-twenty years, and after "closed up" the remainder that would remain, so that they should not come out of their places, and took order, that no men should come to the houses of women, nor women to the houses of men, but only that they should hear service in their churches."

The remedy applied to an abuse is the surest proof of what the abuse was, and these regulations confirm the idea, that the residence of Lady Margaret de Vere and other women, however honourable, within the precincts of West Ham Abbey, arose from a relaxation of discipline.

DOCTOR LONDON gives a graphic picture of what he, as one of the visitors, saw of the weary lassitude that had crept over the monks, thus "closed up" within the precincts of their monasteries. "I perceive many monks and chanons, which be young, lusty men, always fat-fed, living in idleness and at rest, be sore perplexed that now, being priests, they may not return and marry. Most part of them be nothing learned, nor apt thereto and thereby in much worse case. I have given as well to some of them, as to their master such poor council as I might do, and have advised them that, where they be neither learned nor apt unto the same, to turn some of their sermons of idleness unto some bodily exercise, and not to sit all day lurking in the cloister idly." However, in common fairness and candour it must be admitted that, though there were scandalous brethren, the monks, as a class, were neither vicious nor profligate, neither drunken nor unchaste, and there was rarely, very rarely, a wicked abbot or prior.

It was not until the year 1538 that the Abbey of Stratford Langthorne was resigned into the hands of King Henry VIII. The deed of surrender, which is still extant in the "Public Record Office," was executed in the Chapter House of the Abbey, on the 18th day of March in the above-named year, in the presence of Richard Leyton, one of the clerks or masters in chancery, and was signed by William Huddleston, the Abbot, William Parsons, the Prior, John Meryst, the Chanter, John Ryddsdall, the Sacrist, and eleven monks, one of whom, named John Wyght, was so illiterate that he could not sign his name, but was obliged to make a cross, which is denoted as the mark "for John Wyght which cannot wrytte." A facsimile of the document is given on the next page.

S

per me William Abbate praedictum.

per me William Parsons Pryor.

per me Johannem Merystum cantorem.

per me Johannem Ryddsdall

Supp'orem et Sacristam.

per me Antonium Clercke Bacchalaureum.

per me Johannem Gybbs.

per me Christoferum Snow.

per me Wyllyam Danyells.

per me William Peyrson.

per me Thomas Solbey.

per me William Symonds.

per me Johannem Scott.

per me Richard Stanton.

per me Thomas Drake.

× for John Wyght which cannot wrytte.

The conventual seal—representing the Blessed Virgin Mary with the infant Jesus in her arms under a Gothic canopy—was appended.

Stratford Langthorne.

All that can be read of the legend is : " Sigill com — Stratforde."

In the Chapter House at West Ham Abbey on that day, many hearts must have been full of deep emotion. In the accompanying facsimile of the signatures the eye may detect this especially in that of William Huddleston, the abbot. It could not have been without feelings of pain and sorrow that each monk approached the table and signed away his old familiar home, and its to him sacred precincts, to the profanation of lay proprietors, its church, its cloisters, its chapter house to desecration, to give up his share in its quiet luxuries, its farm, its manors, the gardens he had tended, which, perhaps, he had himself planted, and instead of being a member of a wealthy community, whose sway was paramount around, he was to go forth a needy man into a world, from which he had been long estranged. However much we may concur in the judgement, as to the propriety of the suppression of the abbeys, it is impossible not to compassionate some of the individuals, old and infirm men, especially accustomed to the routine of conventual life, and unfitted from either habit or taste to battle with the stream of life. To such the change must have cost much effort. Nevertheless it should not be forgotten, that the abbey doors had been previously opened to all willing to go forth, that all under twenty-four years of age had been compelled to do so, and that those only remained who preferred their cloister life, and to whom a compulsory dismissal would necessarily be distasteful.

The monks of Stratford after their ejection from the Abbey are traditionally said to have been permitted to retire to a mansion —probably Hyde House—at Plaistow, part of their former possessions, and there to have resided in community. The house has disappeared, but part of the garden walls remain to the present day, and an ancient gateway, of a somewhat subsequent date, has only within the last thirty years been removed. Of this we shall have occasion to speak in a future chapter, relating to Plaistow.

CHAPTER VIII.

(CONTENTS).

TRADITIONS AND REMAINS OF THE ABBEY AND DISTRIBUTION OF THE ABBEY LANDS.

LTHOUGH but scanty fragments of the once important Abbey of Stratford Langthorne are to be seen at the present day, traces of its existence can yet be discovered, and there are still many old parishioners living who, besides other remains of the ancient monastery distinctly remember the old brick gateway, which formerly stood in the abbey road and formed the entrance to the conventual precincts. At different times objects of curiosity, articles of silver plate, and a large metal dish have also been found, which unfortunately have been dispersed, so that it is now quite impossible to obtain an accurate description of them. LYSON, who wrote about the end of the last century, observes in his Environs of London: "The foundations of the convent were dug up and removed by the present proprietor, Mr. Holbrook, in doing which no antiquities worthy of note were found, except a small onyx seal with the impression of a griffin, set in silver, and bearing

the following inscription: 'Nunc vobis gaudium et salutem,' perhaps the privy seal of one of the abbots."

MR. GALLOWAY, an old inhabitant of West Ham, gives in his manuscript an account of a " Chrystal relic," "found," he says " in the

ruins of the abbey and now in my possession; in it is a liquid, but confined, there being no place to put it in except the body of it; it is much broken top and bottom." This short notice is accompanied by a rough sketch, of which the above is a copy.

The same writer also mentions that he has in his possession "a silver ring, lacquered over with gold wash, that was found in 1791 among the ruins of the abbey, with the following letters

✳ GoD :Ebold: to : W̓CVC.

around it," which are difficult to decipher; also that, "as labourers were digging in a field near the 'Adam and Eve' public-house, two leaden coffins were found, both much decayed, from which he concluded that this field once was the burying place of the abbey."[1]

Several of the old arches and walls still existed about fifty years ago, but the numerous and extensive erections in connexion with Mr. Tucker's (afterwards James Kayess') factory, as well as the North Woolwich Railway, which was made (1845) through the abbey precincts from north to south, have almost entirely obliterated the many lingering proofs of antiquity, that might have served as way-marks to the curious archæologist.

Nearly the whole of the old site of the abbey, which comprised about sixteen acres, is now covered with ranges of factory buildings and yards, while the ancient "Mansion" and the "Gesten Hall" are completely razed to the ground. The mansion was at one time occupied by the Lady Margaret de Vere, and presumably also the residence of the unfortunate Countess of Salisbury,[2] a daughter of the Duke of Clarence, and a niece of Edward IV., whom the remorseless Henry VIII. caused to be beheaded in her old age, without the slightest evidence of criminality.

These large though much decayed mansions were still in existence about forty years ago; one of them was then occupied as a home for Lascars, who had been brought to London as sailors, and was afterwards by Captain Bronton, R.N., converted into a refuge for destitute boys.

---

[1] This opinion is borne out by the fact, that in May 1887, among the old foundation walls in the same field, several skulls were found.

[2] The aged countess was then 70 years of age, but behaved not the less with wonderful firmness. She was dragged to the scaffold, and one of the most frightful scenes in English history took place. When told by the executioner to lay her head on the block, she answered, "No, my head never committed treason; if you will have it, you must take it as you can." The executioners strove to detain her, but she ran swiftly round the scaffold, tossing her head from side to side, while the monsters struck at her with their axes, until at last, with her grey hair all dabbled in blood, she was held forcibly to the block, and an end put to her misery.

By reference to the accompanying map we are enabled to form some idea of the various groups of buildings and appurtenances

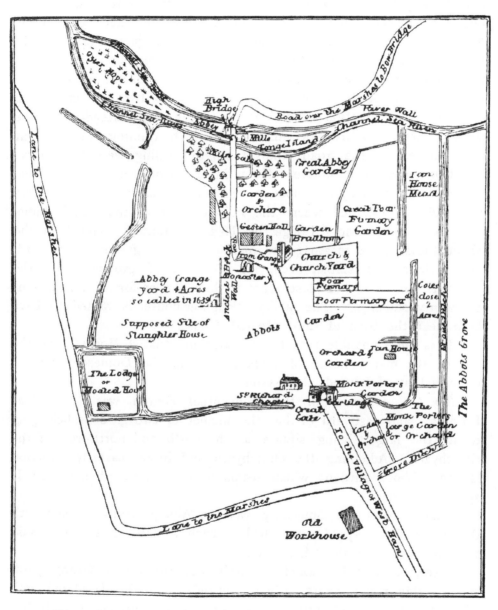

This plan has been designed from the old leases granted by the later abbots.

which once belonged to the monastery. Starting from West Ham, near the church, along the road called Abbey Road, we pass on our left hand the Leather Cloth Factory, the site of which was not many years ago occupied by the old parish workhouse. Some fifty yards beyond this building stood the great entrance gate of the monastery, a picture of which may be seen on page 124. It will be noticed that the road leads parallel to a ditch, which formed part of the moat that surrounded the precincts of the abbey. On the inner side of the moat or grove ditch were two gardens, which were in the occupation of the monk porter who attended to the gate. There was also an inner moat which, running southward at right angles to the road and at length turning westward, marks out four sides of a square. Here, in the south-east corner of the precincts, enclosed by the moat, portions of which could a few years ago still be discerned where the railroad crosses the Marsh Lane, was the site of the "Lodge or Moated House," defined in the abbot's lease as a messuage or mansion with a garden or orchard, and a barn and stable, occupying one acre of ground within the precincts, and let by the last abbot to John Hever for an annual rent of twenty shillings. The abbey slaughter-house is stated to have been near the barn of the "Moated House."

It is quite possible that the "Lodge or Moated House" was the site of the manor house of Robert Gernon, the Domesday tenant, or even that of Leured, the Saxon.

To the eastward of the conventual church was the "Poor Firmary," and eastward of that the smaller of two gardens belonging to it, the larger being situate at the north and north-west of the churchyard. Adjoining the churchyard and in an easterly direction lay the abbot's garden, which seems to have been of considerable size.

Southward of the monastery was the Abbey Grange, which with the Abbey Grange-yard—described as such as late as 1639—is said to have comprised about four acres.

Here, in a field, which formerly was the Abbey Grange-yard, stood within recent years, a very obtusely pointed, dilapidated arch of white stone, built into a wall of old red bricks, two inches thick, belonging to some modern farm buildings, and probably in

T

former ages forming the entrance from the court of the monastery to the grange or farm yard. The accompanying woodcut has been made from a sketch which was taken in the year 1854.

At right angles to this a red brick wall, ornamented with black bricks in the usual mode of Tudor building, ran westward for 170 feet, and then at right angles for about 70 feet, probably marking the line of way from the entrance gate of the grange to the little church of St. Mary. Some distance to the west, in the factory formerly belonging to James Kayess, may still be seen a piece of wall with two small two-light windows.

It is a well known fact that the churches of all Cistercian convents were built in the form of a cross, facing east and west, with central tower and three chapels attached to the east side of each of its transepts. Under the shelter of the nave and transept, usually on the south side of the church, was placed the cloister, the nave forming its north side, and the south transept part of its east side. The accompanying woodcut shows an ancient pointed

archway, with the remains of groining columns, which probably was one of the arches of the cloister. This archway was built up in the wall of the "Adam and Eve" Inn, but has some years since been removed.

In the kitchen of this Inn, which has always been considered to occupy the site of the old monastery, may still be seen a flag stone with brass studs, which seem to have affixed to it two figures beneath canopies, but the indent is almost obliterated. In the garden belonging to the "Adam and Eve" Inn was formerly a little grove of thickly planted yew trees, reputed to be of great antiquity; and it is stated in the "Ambulator" of 1806, that near there a stone coffin was found in the year 1770.

A curious discovery was made in the year 1845, while the workmen were excavating for the North Woolwich railway. Just where the line crosses the rise of the "Adam and Eve" garden, a subterranean passage was discovered, which communicated with the cellar of the Inn and extended eastward for some distance. This passage was again laid open at a distance of some hundred yards, whence it was supposed to have formed a subterraneous mode of escape to the inmates of the abbey. There has always been a tradition in the neighbourhood, that this passage extended from West Ham Abbey to that of Barking, and formed a way of secret communication, but the distance between the two places and the tidal channel of the river Roding render this most improbable. Moreover, some years ago the tenant of the adjoining land, which formerly was part of the abbey demesne, struck this passage again in a field, some distance from the precincts of the abbey, while ploughing deeply, and traced it to an outlet in a marsh ditch, which confirms the opinion that it had been an ancient sewer leading to the river.

During these excavations the workmen also lighted upon a reservoir, not more than two feet below the grassy surface; it was of an oblong shape, about twelve feet long, eight feet wide, and five feet in depth, and the sides were neatly lined with Dutch tiles, finely glazed and of a pure white. It was supposed to have been a lavatory; but it evidently formed no part of the old abbey, and was of much more recent date.

At the same time a leaden pipe was found and traced from a reservoir, near the pump in West Ham Lane, to the old workhouse, whence a wooden pipe conducted the water to the supposed sites of the tan-house and the "Poor Firmary," whilst the main pipe continued towards the "Adam and Eve" Inn.

The "Kiln House and Kiln Gate" were situate close to the Abbey Mills. These mills lay between the two branches of the Channelsea river, with Tonge island on the northern, and an ozier hope on the southern side of the river. The accompanying picture of the mills, as seen from the marshes, is an accurate representation of them as they were in the year 1830, surrounded by the ancient

willows, which grew amongst the ditches, and were believed to have been planted by the monks. Of these mills in their ancient condition, nothing now remains.

From the map it would appear as if a roadway passed through the precincts of the monastery in the time of the monks; there may have been a way leading from the gateway in the Abbey road past the mills to the marshes, but we cannot suppose the passage of a public roadway invading the privacy of the monks.

From the various leases which the abbot granted, it would appear that the precincts of the abbey were treated much in the same manner as we now treat a cathedral close. A population independent of the monks appears to have resided within its boundaries, carrying on various secular occupations. We find record of a slaughterhouse, a grange, a dove-house and yard, stables, hay-barns, a bakehouse near the mills, a tan-house, a farm garden and several orchards. While within the retirement of the cloister, fenced in with high walls, the monks were pursuing their daily avocations, and the real conventual life was going on, there was outside the cloister, though yet within the precincts, a vast hive of industry which it is difficult for us now to realise. Everything that was eaten, or drunk, or worn, almost everything that was made or used, seems to have been produced on the spot. The grain grew on their own land, the corn was ground in their own mill, they had their own sheep and their own dove-houses, they kept their own piscatories, they grew their own garden stuff and their own fruit, and they had their own tailors, shoemakers, and carpenters, almost within call.

The Abbot and Convent of Stratford Langthorne having surrendered their house (*see page* 129) with its estates and revenues to the king, they were, with the exception of some comparatively small reservations, gradually alienated by the Crown to various persons.

In the parishes of East and West Ham they were disposed of in the following manner:

1. THE MONASTERY.

The site of the same, the conventual church, belfry, churchyard, St. Richard's chapel, with all the other buildings and lands within the precincts, were granted by Henry VIII. to Peter Mewtas (Meautas, Meautis) and Johanna, his wife, for their true and faithful service, and to their heirs male, together with the demesne lands of the abbey, then worth a yearly rental of £35 7s 2d also the reversion of the messuages, lands, tenements, mills, meadow, pasture, etc., let by the last abbot, as well as the rents issuing from the abbot's leases, to be held by knight's service as the tenth part of a knight's fee, and £8 10s (£18 10s?) rent to the king and his successors.

Sir Peter Mewtas was of French extraction, being descended from an ancient Norman family, which took its name from the parish of Meautis—near Carenton in the duchy—which in ancient times was a considerable barony, whose lords were coeval with the conquest. Sir Peter was sent as ambassador to France by King Henry VIII. and also by Queen Elizabeth. Henry Mewtas, a descendant of Sir

Peter, in the year 1633, sold the site of the abbey with 240 acres of land, the abbey mills, etc., to Sir John Nulls, whose son in 1663 conveyed it to Thomas Meads and others, from whom it passed to Richard Knight. In his family it remained until the year 1786, when it was sold by Dudlas Knight to Mr. Thomas Holbrook, who left it to his nephew, Mr. Richardson. Afterwards it became divided, and was held by several proprietors. As the grant, made by King Henry VIII. to Sir Peter Mewtas and his wife, included the abbey house and demesne, it is probable that their successors were more especially considered to be the representatives of the Abbot of Stratford, and consequently charged with the repairs of the Bow and Channelsea bridges and the causeway.

2. THE MANOR OF WEST HAM.

This manor became vested in the Crown. In the year 1610 it was granted by King James I. to Henry, Prince of Wales, and after his death in 1616 assigned to trustees for his brother Charles I., then Prince of Wales and in his minority. Subsequently, in the year 1629, it became part of the jointure of Queen Henrietta Maria of France, Consort of Charles I., and then of Queen Catherine of Portugal, Consort of Charles II., hence called the "Queen's Manor." But before her decease, which took place in 1705, William III. had granted a ninety-nine years' lease of it to the Honourable George Booth, at a reserved rent. The lease having expired in 1804, the manor was, in the year 1805, purchased of the Crown in fee by Edward Humphreys and George Johnstone; afterwards, it descended to Thomas, nephew of Edward Humphreys, and on his death it devolved to his son Charles, who is the present Lord of the Manor.

3. THE MANOR OF EAST HAM.

This manor, with the tithes and a mansion, was granted by Henry VIII., in 1544, to Richard Bream, on payment of £385 15s 8d to the treasurer of the Court, for the augmentation of the revenues of the Crown. It continued in his family until the death of Giles Bream in 1621. Since then it was successively in the families of Allington, Draper, and Baker, until in 1766 it was bought by Sir John Henniker, in whose family it has remained until recent years, the present Lord Henniker having sold nearly the whole of the manor to Ynyr Burges, Esq., who now is the principal landowner in East Ham.

[The reader will remember, that two manors called East Ham and West Ham Burnels, were dismembered from the original manor, and came by purchase to Robert Burnel, Bishop of Bath and Wells. They were afterwards held successively by the Handlo, Lovel, Hungerford, Harvey, Mildmay, and other families, and were finally sold to the two branches of the Smyth family, of Upton, Sir Robert Smyth and Stephen Comyns. In 1810 they were purchased by Henry Hinde Pelly, Esq., and are now in the possession of his great-grandson, Sir Harold Pelly, Bart.]

There used to be a tradition current amongst the "homagers" of the different manors to the effect, that when a court was held for the manor of East Ham and some other adjoining manors in West Ham, the tenants of East Ham were obliged to treat those of West Ham, West Ham Burnels, and Plaiz, which is said to have originated from their predecessors in ancient times, having refused to contribute towards the ransom of their lord, when a prisoner.

4. THE MANORS OF EAST WEST HAM AND PLAIZ.

These two manors were in the year 1553 granted by Edward IV. to Sir Roger Cholmeley, whose co-heirs, Elizabeth wife of Christopher Kenne, and John Russell, enjoyed them after him. Having passed through several hands, they became together with the manor of East Ham and West Ham Burnels, vested in the Smyth family, who sold them in 1810 to Henry Hinde Pelly, Esq. They are now in the possession of Sir Harold Pelly, Bart., who is the present lord of the manors of East and West Ham Burnels, as well as of East West Ham and Plaiz.

5. THE MANOR OF WOODGRANGE.

This manor, with a portion of the tithes of West Ham, parcel of the possessions of the dissolved monastery, was leased, in 1535, to Morgan Philips, alias Wolfe, of London, goldsmith, for sixty years. Queen Elizabeth granted a reversionary lease to Robert, Earl of Leicester for seventy years. In 1649 it became the property of Thomas Campbell, whose son, Sir Henry Campbell, of Clay Hall, claimed the same right of common, and cutting wood in the forest as the Abbot and Convent had enjoyed. Dying without issue, the manor came by marriage to Thomas Price, whose son in 1738 sold it to John Pickering, merchant. It finally passed to John Pickering Peacock, and became afterwards divided, and was held in portions by several owners.

Some of the estates not situate in these parishes were disposed of as follows:

1. THE MANOR OF LEYTON.

This manor with the advowson of the church was granted by Henry VIII. to the Lord Chancellor, Thomas Lord Wriothesley, who sold it two days after to Sir Ralph Warren, then Lord Mayor of London, who died 1553.

2. THE ESTATE OF BURGSTEAD.

This estate together with the manors of Burgstead, Cowbridge, and others, was granted to Sir Richard Riche, whose descendants held it till 1660, when it was sold to Sir John Petre, an ancestor of Lord Petre, the present lord of the manor, who, being a Roman Catholic, is said to be permitted by Papal dispensation to hold these and other abbey lands.

3. THE MANOR OF BUMSTEAD IN AVELEY.

This manor was granted by Henry VIII., in 1540, to Edward North, Treasurer of the Court of Augmentation, afterwards Lord North. From him it passed to Lord Dacre.

4. BOCKURST, BUCKHURST, MONKEN HILL OR MONKET GROVE IN WOODFORD AND CHIGWELL.

These were granted by Edward VI., in 1547, to John Lyon and Alice his wife, to hold of the king as the fourth part of a knight's fee, together with the grove of the honour of Windsor.

5. THE ABBOT'S INN.

This house in St. Clement's Lane, London, was granted by Henry VIII., in 1543, to Sir Robert Southwell.

U

It has already been observed in a former chapter, that in the year 1628 a rate of £50 per annum was levied on all the lands formerly belonging to the abbey, for the purpose of maintaining and repairing the Bow and Channelsea Bridges and the Causeway between them. It appears, however, that all the outlying estates were exempt from this tax, and that the responsibility principally lay upon those lands which were situate in the parish of West Ham. As the Abbot, so also did his successors in vain endeavour to shift their responsibility of the repairs, until after various suits the matter was finally settled, by the abbey landowners of West Ham paying a fixed sum, which released them from all further responsibilities as regards the repairs of the bridges and the causeway. (*See page* 33.)

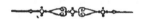

CHAPTER IX.

(Contents).

STRATFORD AND EVENTS.   THE HIGH ROAD AND TRAVELLERS.

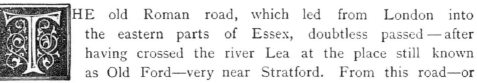

THE old Roman road, which led from London into the eastern parts of Essex, doubtless passed — after having crossed the river Lea at the place still known as Old Ford—very near Stratford. From this road—or in Saxon parlance Straet—by the ford, is derived the name of the present town of Stratford. Here it branched off, one way leading the traveller through the forest to the "Ford in the wood," where Woodford bridge is now, another tending more to the east, passing the river Roding by the "Il-ford."[1] The ancient legend connected with the removal of the body of St. Erkenwald from Barking to London (*see page* 5), in the year 685, is considered by some topographers as the earliest record in which this road is mentioned. The district through which it passed was called by the Saxons "Ham,"—meaning home or village—and included the whole of the present parishes of East and West Ham ; marsh, arable, and forest.

When Queen Maude erected Bow Bridge, and constructed the causeway, the road was with a considerable curve diverted to the southward, probably joining the ancient highway somewhere between

---

[1] Ilford, probably from the Saxon "eald, yld," meaning "old," and ford.

the fourth and fifth milestones. This new road having been established, two hamlets, both called Stratford, from the street by the ford, came into existence, namely, "Stratford atte Boghe" at the Middlesex end of the causeway, which originally belonged to Stepney, but is now a distinct parish called Bow,—and "Stratford Langthorne," on the Essex side, deriving its additional name of Langthorne, as MORANT supposes, either from some remarkable long thorn, or the length of thorns and underwood growing in this part of the forest. On the northern side of the road, which is intersected by several water-courses, three mills were situate, two of which— as has already been mentioned (*page* 33)—belonged to the London Bridge Estate, while the third was the property of the Hospital of St. Thomas of Acre.

With the increase of population, improvements quickly followed, and it is almost impossible to overrate the benefits which have accrued from this great public highway to both parishes of East and West Ham.

It is curious, and perhaps also instructive, to reflect upon the multitude and variety of travellers that passed along it, during the seven centuries which have elapsed since the time of Queen Maude. What hopes and fears, what joys and griefs must have agitated the generations of men by whose feet it has been trodden! An authentic anecdote occasionally affords us a glance at the varied scenes, but in general it is left to the imagination to draw the picture. The millers and the men, who lived near it, must have seen bands of warlike retainers following some mail-clad baron. The banners of the Bohuns, of the de Clares and the Fitzwalters, must have been well-known along the road; the Bigods too, no doubt, journeyed along it to their castles of Norwich and Bungay, as well as the Warrens to Castle Acre in Norfolk. These feudal times, however, passed away, and the descendants of the Conqueror's barons no longer dwelt in strong castles, grasping with an iron hand all within their power, but lived comparatively at peace in their spacious manor houses. These men rode slowly and deliberately by easy journeys to the magnificent court of the pomp-loving Tudors, attended by trains of liveried serving-men, with the waiting gentlewoman on a pillion behind "John of the Stable." They rested at the wayside inn, or perhaps turned aside to claim the hospitality of some neighbouring monastery, for we are told that the Abbot of Stratford often complained of being impoverished by the confluence of strangers at his house. Thus the Norfolk and Suffolk families, the Howards and the Boleyns, the Pastons and the Falstofs, the old knightly Lestrange, the great Lord Bacon, Keeper of the Seal, and his still more famous son, must have travelled along "our road;" but it is needless to dwell longer on what can only be a matter of supposition.

Though Stratford is only incidentally mentioned in records and chronicles, yet there are numerous notices of the place and events that occurred there, which sufficiently prove that it was much frequented and well known by name at an early period of our history. That it was a place of considerable importance, is proved by the fact of King Henry III. having, during his wars with the barons, taken up his temporary abode in the "Abbey of White Monks at Stratford." Thither came unto him the Pope's legate, Ottoboni, and was likewise lodged in the same abbey. The circumstance that, "for straitness of lodging, his horses and mules were set within the cloisters of the said abbey," would imply that the stable accommodation was at that time somewhat limited at Stratford.

This event took place in 1267, two years after the battle of Evesham, when a revolt broke out in London, which was one of the last acts of the struggle between the king and his people. To quell this dangerous insurrection, the king, accompanied by his warlike son, Prince Edward—afterwards King Edward I.—who had joined him with his army from the north, prepared to lay siege to London, and encamped at Stratford. The Pope's legate, Ottoboni, who had come for the express purpose of arranging terms of peace between the king and his rebellious barons, joined the king at West Ham Abbey, after having escaped from the Tower with considerable difficulty, by a postern on the side next the river, as is thus described by ROBERT OF GLOUCESTER in his "Rhyming Chronicle":

The King wende to Stratford to abide more migte,
And aboute London his pavilions pigte (pitched).
Bi a posterne the legate thoru quointise (cunning) and gile (guile)
Hii brogte to Stratford withoute London 2 mile.

Besides Prince Edward, the Counts of Boulogne and St. Paul with many others, were with the king at Stratford, while the siege lasted. The assertion of the Chronicler that King Henry III. was at Stratford, is confirmed by two deeds preserved in "RHYMER'S Foedera," which were witnessed by him there on the 28th of May, and the 16th of June, 1267. TYRREL, in his history of England, observes in alluding to this event, "that the king marched with his army to Stratford, a town within three miles of London and encamped there about two months, from the 24th of April to the 24th of June, 1267."

There is, however, mention made of Stratford even at an earlier date, when Henry III. levied an aid or tax on occasion of the marriage of his sister Isabella to Frederick II., Emperor of Germany, in the year 1235. We are told that Mauduit came to Stratford, and there on Thursday before the feast of St. Michael received various sums of money, which were due from the great feudatories in Essex, on this account. Robert Fitzwalter, lord of Dunmow, so distinguished in the previous reign as commander of the forces of the barons, sent by the hand of Sir William Fitz-Richard £17 6s 8d, for the twenty-six knights' fees he held in Essex, while his old confederate Richard de Montfichet paid by Michael Revel £16, for twenty-four knights' fees.

The Countess of Essex also sent by her bailiff £10 8s 8d, and by Ralph de Messingham £21 3s 4d on account of Pleshy. These payments were probably made on account of the Honour or Barony of which Pleshy Castle was the chief seat, and on account of the Earldom of Essex, as two distinct tenures. This lady, the daughter of Geoffery de Mandeville and heir to her brother William de Mandeville, the last Earl of Essex of that name, was at this time a widow, her husband Robert de Bohun, Earl of Hereford, having died in 1220. Another great heiress, who paid her "relief" at Stratford at the same time, was Margaret de Lucy, of the Honour of Ongar, the aged widow of Richard de Rivers. It would not interest the reader to prolong this list of names, which may be found in the record called "Testa de Nevill."

A further notice of Stratford occurs in the reign of Edward III. which furnishes proof that the king did not consider sanitary regulations beneath his notice, inasmuch as it was then thought "neither wholesome, nor consistent with the dignity of the city, that cattle should be driven into London or slaughtered within its walls." By an ordinance of the thirty-first year of his reign (1357), made with the consent of parliament, then sitting, the Mayor and Sheriffs of London were commanded, to make a public proclamation in the city and suburbs, strictly prohibiting "under pain of a year's imprisonment, that any ox, sheep, or pig should be driven nearer to London than Stratford on the one, or Knightsbridge on the other side of London." There they were to be slaughtered and after the intestines had been cleansed, these together with the flesh were permitted to be taken into the city for sale. Any butcher who dared to transgress this law was "to be whipped in the market place." The reason assigned for these regulations is, that the effluvia from the blood in the streets and from the offal thrown into the Thames, rendered the atmosphere unhealthy and engendered disease. Perhaps it is not hazarding an unreasonable conjecture, that "Butcher Row" Whitechapel, just outside Aldgate, may have originated in a meat market, supplied from the abatoires (shambles) at Stratford, or that, prohibited from approaching the city by its eastern or western avenues, the droves of cattle were gradually intruded nearer to its gates on the northern side, until "Smith's Field," near Newgate, became a cattle market.

Nor was meat the only article of provisions that the citizens of London received from Stratford, for it seems, that their bread was extensively made at Stratford, and that the trade was principally carried on by women. In January 1310, the following bakeresses of Stratford, viz: Sarah Foting, Christina Terrence, Godigeon Foting, Matilda de Bolington, Isabella Pouveste, Christina Prichet, Isabella Spirling, Alice Pegges, and Joanna de Cantebrigge were all found to be defaulters, having given short weight of bread in the half-penny loaf, four ounces and three-quarters in the loaf.

In the following year, William de Croton, of the county of Suffolk, was put in the pillory for pretending to be a sergeant of the Sheriff of London, and exacting a fine from Richolda and Mabel, of Stratford, bakeresses, whom he met with their carts bringing bread into the city for sale. He arrested the carts until they had paid him a fine, "he taking 10 pence from the said Mabel as such fine, to the great loss of the bakeresses, and the manifest scandal of the sheriff and their sergeants. Being accused of the matters aforesaid, William could not gainsay the same, and it was awarded that he should have the punishment of the pillory, and proclaim the cause why such judgment was given against him."

In the "Liber Albus" of the City of London, compiled by John Carpenter, the Town Clerk, in the mayoralty of the famous Whittington, may be found numerous regulations on this subject. Among the customs payable on victuals, are those that pertain unto the small trades in the market of London, as poultry, cheese, bread, etc;—" every basket of bread shall pay one half-penny per day—every cart of Bremble (Bromley) or of Stevenhethe (Stepney) that comes into the city with bread shall pay one half-penny—a cart that brings bread from another town shall pay each day one half-penny on a loaf, of whatever franchise the owner may be." From the same authority we learn, that a yearly assay of bread was made in London by the custom of the city, and that the regulations respecting bread and bakers were extremely strict. They seemed to have been infringed by the bakers of Stratford in the year 1419, for the following entry occurs in the regulations respecting bakers and their servants "Punishment of the hurdle[1] inflicted on the foreign bakers of Stratforde."

It has been supposed, and not without reason, that this trade of bread at Stratford and Bow was induced by the facility of procuring faggots for their ovens from the adjacent forest, as well as by the supply of flour from the Abbey Mills, and presumably also by the proximity of the London market.

The bakers of Stratford are also mentioned by HOLINSHED in his Chronicles. It appears "that in 1414, a certain Richard Hun, a merchant tailor of London, being accused of heresy, had been confined and murdered in the Lollard's Tower, by one Charles Joseph, the summoner, and John Spalding, alias Belringer, by

---

[1] The punishment of the hurdle consisted in being drawn on a hurdle through the principal streets of the city.

command, it not in the actual presence of Doctor Richard Horsley, chancellor of the Bishop of London. Rumours were afloat and the perpetrators became alarmed. Charles came home late at night and brought with him three bakers and a smith of Stratforde, and the same night they carried out of his house all his goods by the field side to the 'Bell at Shoreditch,' and conveyed them early next morning with carts to Stratforde."

We must now return to an earlier date in our history, when amongst our lanes, near the high road between Stratford and Ilford, a foul deed of treachery was perpetrated by Richard II., on his uncle Thomas, the good Duke of Gloucester, on a summer's night in the year 1397. The story may be read in the pages of FROISSART and other chroniclers. Thomas Woodstock, sixth son of King Edward III., afterwards Duke of Gloucester, was residing with his wife and children at the castle of Pleshy, near Chelmsford, of which he had become possessed in 1372, in right of his wife Eleanor, one of the heiresses of Humphrey de Bohun. Trained amongst the warriors of his father's court and camp, he had little sympathy with his royal nephew's weaker qualities; he saw with contempt his effeminate and luxurious habits, and his foreign predilections, which resulted in his marriage with Isabella, the daughter of Charles V., of France. Himself rough and blunt in manners, bold in speech and temperate in habit, the duke became the leader of the war party, and was especially beloved by the citizens of London, who flocked to Pleshy to consult him about their grievances. The jealousy of the king being excited, he resolved to remove his uncle from his path, and taking into his counsel his uncle Thomas de Mowbray, Duke of Norfolk, an unscrupulous and cruel man, Richard gave him most minute directions how to proceed. Mowbray is said to have kept the secret even from those who were employed in the execution of the orders he had received.

Leaving the queen at Eltham, the king, under the pretence of stag-hunting, went to Havering-atte-Bower, whence one fine hot summer afternoon he rode with few attendants to Pleshy, a distance of about twenty miles. His arrival was so sudden that no one knew of it, until the porter at the gate cried out, "Here is the king." The duke and the duchess with their children went out

x

with great respect to meet him in the court of the castle. It being five o'clock, the duke had already supped. The king entered the hall, and then an apartment where the table was relaid for him, and said to the duke: "Good uncle, order five or six of your horses to be saddled; you must go with me to London, for to-morrow I am to meet the Londoners, and we shall find there my uncles of York and Lancaster without fail, and I mean to take your opinion on a petition they are to present to me." The duke, suspecting no harm, obeyed forthwith. They rode hard, for the king was in haste to get to London, and all the way conversed with the duke. They avoided Brentwood and the other towns, and arrived between ten and eleven o'clock at night at a lane near Stratford, where Mowbray, the earl marshal, lay in ambush with a troop of men and horses, and sprang upon the duke, saying: "I arrest you by the king's orders." The king pressed on at full speed, deaf to the cries of Gloucester who, panic-struck, and aware of the extremity of his danger, called on him aloud for help and deliverance. Nor did Richard slacken his speed until he arrived at the Tower of London, where he passed the night. Meanwhile Mowbray hurried the duke "down the lane, that led from the road to the Thames," where he was forced into a boat which lay there at anchor for his reception, and conveyed to Calais. Here, after a few days' imprisonment, he was smothered by ruffians, engaged for the purpose, in September 1397.[1]

---

[1] The Parliamentary Records (Plac. Parl. vol. III. p. 452) contain the confession of John Halle, who was hanged for this murder. He was a valet of the Duke of Norfolk, and among other particulars stated: "That the duke and John Colfox, a squire of the duke, came to him at Calais and called him out of his bed, telling him, that the king and the duke of Aumerle had sent their valets, Serle and Franceys, for the purpose of murdering Gloucester, and that he must be present in the name of his master." Halle prayed that he might be suffered to go away, though with the loss of all his property; but the duke told him he must be present or forfeit his life, and therewith struck him on the head. The confederate valets first went to church and were sworn to secrecy; they then repaired to Gloucester's lodging at his inn, who, seeing Serle, asked him how his master was, saying: "Now, I know, I shall do well;" but Serle, taking Franceys with him, called Gloucester into another chamber, and they there told him, it was the king's will, that he should die. Gloucester answered that:

It is of course impossible to identify the lane, down which the unfortunate duke was hurried to the river. If we may hazard a conjecture, it would be in favour of the green lane, which divides the two parishes of East and West Ham, formerly known as Green Street and latterly called Gipsy Lane. This is the nearest lane to Stratford, that goes direct from the high road to the marshes of the Thames by a straight course, without passing through either village or hamlet. Its antiquity is marked by the ancient and, until recent years, still solitary Tudor Mansion, called Green Street House (locally known as Anne Boleyn's Castle) which abuts on it. Mowbray's ambush would be laid in a lonely place, or dark covert, not in the village of Stratford. Avoiding West Ham and all hamlets, where the cries of the prisoner might be heard, he would surely select a solitary and direct way to the river, like the old green lane.

It was in the year 1467 that Stratford Langthorne was honoured with the Royal presence of King Edward IV. as is related in the annals of WILLIAM DE WORCESTER. "Parliament was dissolved the third day of Penticost, and in the same week one Cornelius, a shoemaker, and servant of Whytingham, who was with Queen Margaret, was taken at Quenbourghe, bearing secretly letters from her into England. Upon him was found one, directed to Thomas Danvers, from the aforesaid Thomas Whytingham, whereupon the said Thomas Danvers about the middle of the night on the vigil of the Holy Trinity, being induced to leave the hospital of the Templars in London by stratagem on the part of Richard Widevile, a soldier, was arrested, and on the third day after taken before the king at Stratford Langthorne and forthwith committed to the tower to his great grief and alarm."

"If it was the king's will, it must be so." They asked him to have a chaplain, to which he agreed, and confessed; whereupon they compelled him to lie down on a bed. The two valets threw a feather-bed over him, three other persons held down its sides, whilst Serle and Franceys pressed on the mouth of the duke until he expired. There were three other persons in the chamber on their knees, weeping and praying for his soul, whilst Halle kept guard at the door. Then the Duke of Norfolk came to them and saw the body of murdered Gloucester.

Although Stratford is not mentioned by name in the following extract from Stow's Annals, yet there can be no doubt, that the magnificent company, so well described by the old historian, passed through Stratford, along Queen Maude's causeway, and defiled over her two ancient stone bridges. It requires therefore no apology to introduce the story in this place:

"Mary, the eldest daughter of King Henry VIII., began her raigne the sixth of July in the year 1553, when she dissolved her camp at Framlingham, which was to the number of 13,000 men. On the 30th of July the Lady Elizabeth, sister to the queen, rode from her place at Strande, where she had lien the night before, through the Cittie of London, out at Aldgate toward the queene, accompanied with a thousand horse of knights, ladies, gentlemenne and their servants. Queen Mary came from Wanstead, in Essex, to London on the third of August, being brought in with her nobles very honourably and strongly. The number of velvet coates, that did ride before her, as well strangers as others, were seven hundred and forty, and the number of ladies and gentlewomen that followed, was one hundred and eighty. The Earle of Arundell, riding next before her, bare a sword in his hand, and Sir Authony Browne did bear up her traine. The Lady Elizabeth, her sister, followed her next, and after her the Lord Marquesse of Excester's wife. The guard followed the ladies, and after them the Northamptonshire and Oxfordshire men, and then Buckinghamshire men, and after them the Lorde's servants; the whole nnmber of horsemen were esteemed to be about a thousand."

This must have been a magnificent sight for the inhabitants of Stratford. With pomp and royal splendour, and amid popular acclammation, Queen Mary passed along—at the same time carrying in her heart the seeds of that morose bigotry which has caused her name to be handed down to posterity with detestation. How many hearths were made desolate during her short reign! Into how many families were carried dismay and heartrending affliction to satisfy the jealousy with which she and her priestly advisers regarded the spread of the gospel truth! It is affecting to think of the mournful travellers that passed along the Stratford road, and of the tragic scenes enacted there, in consequence of her fierce persecution.

There can be no doubt that under the spirit-stirring ministry of Thomas Rose—one of the early reformers, who since the year 1551 had been Vicar of West Ham—the minds of his parishioners had been prepared to behold those scenes of cruelty, not only with deep emotion and sympathy for the persecuted victims, but also with detestation of the persecutors. Sad and mournful must have been to them the spectacle when, in 1552, Rowland Taylor, Vicar of Hadleigh, in Suffolk, passed through Stratford on his way to Oldham Common, near his own parish, where he was to be burnt at the stake.

The narrative of his sufferings is one of the most affecting and interesting stories connected with the history of the British reformation. Having been condemned to suffer death, Dr. Taylor was led by the sheriff and his officers to the Woolpack, an Inn without Aldgate, where the Sheriff of Essex was to take him in charge. His wife "suspecting that her husband would that night be carried away," went with one of her daughters and an orphan girl, and watched all night in the porch of St. Botolph's Church, beside Aldgate, by which she knew he must pass. " The sheriff and his company went without lights, but when they approached the church, the orphan heard them coming, and cried, saying 'O my dear father! Mother, mother, here is my father led away!' Then cried his wife, 'Rowland, Rowland, where art thou ?'—for it was so dark that they could not see one another. He answered her 'I am here, dear wife,' and stayed. The sheriff's men would have hurried on, but the sheriff desired them to let him stay awhile and speak to his wife. Taylor then took his daughter in his arms, and kneeling in the porch with his wife and the orphan girl, said the Lord's prayer. At which sight the sheriff wept apace and so did divers others of the company. After they had prayed he rose up, and kissed his wife, and shaking her by the hand, said ' Farewell, my dear wife, be of good comfort, for I am quiet in my conscience.' Then said his wife, 'God be with thee, dear Rowland; I will, with God's grace, meet thee at Hadleigh.' A little before noon the Sheriff of Essex arrived, Taylor was then placed on horseback and brought out of the Inn. And so they rode forth, the Sheriff of Essex with four yeomen of the guard and the sheriffs men leading him."

Passing along the high road, the people seem to have revolted at the cruelties practised upon the aged vicar, whose reverend and ancient face with its long white beard moved all beholders, notwith-standing the indignity, which Bishop Bonner—a monster of cruelty—put upon him, when he "disgraced him and notted his head evil favourably and clipped it much like as a man would clip a fool's head." When the Sheriff of Essex had brought him as far as Brentwood, he found it "expedient to conceal his prisoner's face by means of a close hood with two holes for his eyes and a slit for his mouth to breathe. This they did that no man should know him or he speak to any man; which practice they used also with others, their own consciences telling them, that they led innocent lambs to the slaughter. They halted for the night at Chelmsford, where the Sheriff of Suffolk met them. When they entered Suffolk a number of the gentry, who had been appointed to aid the sheriff, met them. At last they reached Hadleigh; the streets were lined with people, who with weeping eyes and lamentable voices cried out 'There goeth our good shepherd from us.' The journey was at last over. 'What place is this,' he asked, 'and what meaneth it, that so much people are gathered together?' It was answered 'it is Oldham Common, the place where you must suffer, and the people are come to look upon you.' Then said he 'Thanked be God, I am even at home.' But the people burst out crying 'God save thee, good Dr. Taylor, God strengthen thee and help thee.' When he had prayed, he went to the stake and kissed it, and set himself into a pitch-barrel, in which he was to stand, and stood upright, his hands folded and his eyes raised toward heaven in prayer, and so let himself be burned. So stood he still without either crying or moving, with his hands folded together, till Soyce, with a halberd, struck him on the head, that the brains fell out and the dead corpse fell down into the fire." [1]

The mode of discovering the poor protestants seems to have been by orders sent to the justices to look narrowly to the preachers of heresy, and to have secret spies in every parish. They were then

---

[1] At Oldham Common a stone yet marks the place where the martyr suffered; on it is rudely engraved "1555 Dr. Taylor in defending that was good, at this plas left his blude." A more finished monument was erected there in 1818.

sent up to Bishop Bonner, handed over to the civil power for the execution of the ecclesiastical sentence. Extraordinary as it may appear to us in the present day, the noblemen and gentry of the county lent themselves as instruments in these tyrannical proceedings, and even countenanced the burnings by their presence.

Sad and affecting as the spectacle of Dr. Rowland Taylor's procession, along our high road through Stratford, must have been to the beholder, still more distressing and revolting was the scene, when in June 1556 eleven men and two women were burnt at one fire at Stratford. Their names were: Henry Adlington, Lawrence Parnam, Henry Wye, William Hallywell, Thomas Bowyer, George Searles, Edmund Hurst, Lyon Cawch, Ralph Jackson, John Derifall, John Routh, Elizabeth Pepper, and Agnes George.

Early on the morning of the 27th of June (1556), being the day appointed for their execution, they were conducted from Newgate to Stratford. Delivered at Aldgate by the Sheriffs of London to the Sheriff of Essex, as in the case of Dr. Taylor, they were placed in three carts and pinioned, and thus commenced their last journey.

The cavalcade under guard moved through Whitechapel along the Mile End Road to Stratford, where they were to suffer death. By this time, no less than twenty-thousand persons had assembled to see, "how God's people could still endure the fiery furnace." The eleven men were tied to three stakes, the two women loose in the midst, without any stake, and so they were all burned in one fire "with much love to one another, that it made all the lookers-on marvel." William Harris of Cricksea, who was that year Sheriff of Essex, must have had a most unenviable office to discharge, when, alarmed by the signs of sympathy on the part of the people at the sight of the sufferers, he ordered the fire to be applied to the rushes, uttering the words: "God knoweth best when his corn is ripe." In a few minutes all was over, save the effect of this awful scene.

In the few years of Queen Mary's reign, three hundred victims had perished at the stake. The people sickened at the work of death, open sympathy began to be shown to the sufferers for conscience' sake, and it was the death of Queen Mary alone, which averted a general revolt. She left none to lament her, and there was not even the semblance of sorrow for her loss.

There has been much controversy on the question of locality, whether the martyrdom took place at Stratford-le-Bow, or Stratford in Essex. Fox in his "Martyrology" uses the two names interchangeably, but if we take into consideration, that twenty-thousand persons attended the great burning of the thirteen martyrs, we must look for a place capable of holding such a number. At that time and even within the memory of men, there was an open space, where now St. John's Church stands. Doubtless this open space was a portion of "Stratford Green," the memory of which is still preserved in the grass field surrounded by gentlemens' houses and gardens on the Romford road, known as "Stratford Green," whose ancient name was "Gallows Green."

The reader will remember, that in 1275 Richard de Montfichet, or his father, when Sheriff of Essex, had licence to "erect there a gallows in his lordship of Hamme." This green or common appears to have been a place of public execution, while the place near Stratford Church, at the junction of the two turnpike roads, was unquestionably the place of burning. The Rev. Bolton, Vicar of

St. John's in 1879, tells us in his story of the "Stratford Martyrs," that an aged parishioner accompanied him to St. John's churchyard, and there showed him the spot, which her grandfather had pointed out to her, when a girl, as the site of the ancient martyrdoms. She also affirmed, that one of her direct ancestors had been a friend of the martyrs. Moreover a picture, which may be found in an old folio edition of FOXE's "Book of Martyrs," represents the scene, as taking place at Stratford in an open space with only a few houses around, so that we may reasonably conclude, that the present memorial, erected in St. John's churchyard, stands near the spot, where these thirteen martyrs suffered their martyrdom in 1556.

Far different from the sad scenes we have just related was the spectacle, which a noisy and mirthful crowd went out to see on the first Monday in Lent, in the year 1599. Assembled by the wayside at Stratford, the eager crowd anxiously waited for the arrival of William Kemp, the distinguished comedian and buffoon, who had undertaken, "being merrily dispos'd in a Morrice," to dance the whole

way from London to Norwich. Will Kemp was a comedian in the same company with Shakespeare, in whose plays, when they were originally brought upon the stage, he performed such parts as Peter, Dogberry, Launce, Touchstone, the Grave-Digger, Justice Shallow, and Launcelot; he was also much admired in the performance of

Y

"jigs," a kind of ludicrous metrical composition either spoken or sung by the clown, and occasionally accompanied by dancing and playing on the pipe and tabour. He tells us himself, that he had spent his life in mad "Jigges and merry Jestes." That he was a practised dancer, is proved by the feat, of which he published an account in a tract, called "Kemp's nine daies wonder, performed in a daunce from London to Norwich."

The legs of "Morrice dancers" were garnished with bells to the number of twenty or even forty on each leg; the handkerchiefs or napkins were held in the hands or fastened on the shoulders, as is shown in the picture.

Kemp passed through Mile End and Stratford to Romford on his first day's journey—but his own account will be more acceptable, than any other form of narration.

"The first mundaye in Lent, the close morning promising a cleere day [attended on by Thomas Slye my Taberer, William Bee my servant, and George Sprat, appointed for my overseer, that I should take no other ease by my prescribed order] my selfe, thats I, otherwise called Cavaliero Kemp, head master of 'Morrice dances' etc. etc., began frolickly to foote it from the Right Honorable the Lord Mayor's of London towards the right worshipfull (and truely bountifull) Master Mayor's of Norwich.

My setting forward was somewhat before seaven in the morning; my Taberer stroke up merrily; and as fast as kinde peoples thronging together would give mee leave, thorow London I leapt. By the way many good olde people and divers others of yonger yeers, of meere kindness gave me bowd sixepences and grotes, blessing me with their hearty prayers and God-speedes.

Being past White-Chappell and having left faire London with all that north-east suburb before named, multitudes of Londoners left not me; but eyther to keepe a custome which many holde, that Mile-end is no walke without a recreation at Stratford Bow with Creame and Cakes, or else for love they beare toward me, or perhappes to make themselves merry, if I should chance (as many thought) to give over my Morrice within a mile of Mile-end; how ever, many a thousand brought me to Bow; where I rested a while from dancing, but had small rests with those, that would have urg'd me to drinking. But,

I warrant you, Will Kemp was wise enough: to their full cups, kinde thanks was my returne, with gentlemanlike protestations, as 'truly, sir, I dare not—it stands not with the congruitie of my health.' Congruitie said I? How came that strange language in my mouth? I thinke scarcely that it is any christian worde, an yet it may be a good worde for ought I knowe, though I never made it, nor doe verye well understand it; yet I am sure I have bought it at the word-mongers, at as deare a rate as I could have had a whole 100 of Bavines (small faggots) at the wood-mongers. Farewell, Congruitie, for I meane now to be more concise and stand upon eevener bases; but I must neither stand nor sit, the Tab'rer strikes alarum. Tickel it, good Tom, Ile follow thee. Farewell, Bowe; have over the bridge, where I heard say honest conscience was once drown'd; its pittye if it were so; but thats no matter belonging to our Morrice, lets now along to Stratford Langton.

Many good fellows being there met and knowing, how well I loved the sporte, had prepared a Beare-bayting; but so unreasonably were the multitudes of people, that I could only heare the beare roare and the dogges howle; therefore forward I went with my hey-de-gaies (a kind of rural dance) to Ilford where I again rested and was by the people of the towne and countreye there-about very wel welcomed, being offered carowses in the great spoon (a great spoone in Ilford, holding above a quart), one whole draught being able at that time to have drawne my little wit drye; but being afrayde of the old Proverbe (He had need of a long spoone that eates with the devill) I soberly gave my boone companyons the slip.

From Ilford, by moon-shine, I set forward, dauncing within a quarter of a myle of Romford. There being the end of my first dayes Morrice, a kinde gentleman of London lighting from his horse, would have no nay but I should leap into his saddle. To be plain with ye I was not proud, but kinldy tooke his kindlyer offer, chiefly thereto urged by my wearines, so I rid to my Inne at Romford. In that towne to give rest to my well-laboured limbs I continued two dayes being much beholding to the townsmen for their love, but more to the Londoners, that came hourly thither in great numbers to visite me, offring much more kindness, than I was willing to accept."

At Chelmsford an adventurous maid, not passing fourteen years of age, would dance a morrice with him in a "great large room;" she, fitted with bells, and "besides she would have the old fashion with napking on her arms," and to their jumps they fell. In this instance the object of ambition was the same as that of the

"Dancing pair, who simply sought renown
By holding out to tire each other down."

The woodcut (*see page* 161) shows the appearance of Kemp as he went along with bells on his legs, the whole figure full of movement. Tom Sly is evidently walking fast to keep up with his master, whose "pace in dancing was not ordinary." Indeed if the Tabourer travelled on foot, his performance can have been little less remarkable than that of Kemp himself, who records, that from Hingham to Barford Bridge, near Norwich, he was accompanied by five young men "running all the way with me, for otherwise my pace was not for footmen."

The whole narrative is full of amusing incidents. Ever attended by a group of spectators, often by large crowds, he danced along, through miry country ways, the water and mud over his ankles; he "had the heaviest way, that ever mad morrice-dauncer trod." At another time over a heath, "where" he says "I far'd like one that had escaped the stockes, and tride the use of his legs to out-run the constable; so light was my heeles, that I counted the ten miles no better, than a leap." These ten miles between Bury and Thetford he accomplished in three hours. At Bury he was detained some days by the great snow that fell.

In Suffolk a "lusty country lasse borrowed a leash of his belles, with which she garnished her thicke short legs, tucked up her russet petticoate, shooke her fat sides and footed it merrily to Melfoord, being a long myle." At Thetford the noble gentleman Sir Edwin Rich gave him a bountiful entertainment. His adventures with mine host at Rockland in Norfolk, "who was a very boone companion," are celebrated in rhymes, that have been attributed to Shakespeare. The journey was concluded on the evening of the ninth day by leaping over the wall of St. John's Church-yard in Norwich, and getting into the "Mayor's gates a neerer way." The measure of this leap was to be seen in the Guildhall at Norwich, where also the buskins, in which he had danced the whole way, were nailed to the wall; both have, however, long since disappeared.

After this long digression we must return to subjects more immediately connected with the history of our two parishes of East and West Ham. It was in 1588, that the nation was roused to arms by the fear of a Spanish invasion. Philip, King of Spain, the husband of Mary, late Queen of England, formed a design to invade this kingdom. Offended at the assistance, which Queen Elizabeth had offered to his oppressed protestant subjects in the Low Conntries, anxious to re-establish the ascendancy of popery in England, and to extend his already vast dominions, Philip fitted out his famous expedition for the invasion of England, upon a most formidable scale. He had spent three years in preparing his fleet "the Invincible Armada," as it was called, with incredible expence; it consisted of 130 ships in all, manned by troops, sailors and galley-slaves, to the amount of nearly 30,000 men, together with 2,000 Spanish nobles and their retainers. The plan was for the Armada, which was anchored off Calais, to sail up the Thames and land the whole Spanish army upon its banks.

The danger was imminent and the circumstances of Queen Elizabeth were at that time very critical; however, she found "effective resources in her own indomitable courage, the wisdom of her ministers, and the skill and valour of her distinguished officers." The English army, raised for the defence of the realm, was disposed in three divisions, one of which, consisting of 22,000 foot and 2,000 horse under the Earl of Leicester, was encamped at Tilbury to cover the capital. Both the excitement and traffic along the road and through Stratford must have been very great at that time. It was suggested by Leicester, in a letter to the Queen, that the army should be encamped in the parishes of East and West Ham. From this letter the following is an abstract:

"MY MOST DERE AND GRACIOUS LADY:

And this far yf ẏt please you, you may doe, to draw yourself to your howse at Havering and your army being about London, as Stratford, East Ham, Hackney, and the vyllages there abowt shal be alway not only a defence but a reddy suplye to these countreys, Essex and Kent, yf nede be, and in the meane tyme your Majesty to comforte this army and people of both these countreys may yf yt please you spend two or three (days) to se both the Camp and the Fortes, hit ys not abowt 14 myle at most from Havering and a very convenyent place for your Majesty to lye in by the way, and so rest you at the Camp. I trust you wyl be pleasyd with your pore Lyvetenants cabyn and within a myle ther ys a gentleman's house,[1] where your Majesty may also lye, you shall comfort not only these thousands, but many more, that shall hear of yt. And this farr but no furder can I consent to adventure your person, and by the Grace of God there can be no danger in this, though the enemye shuld pass by your flete, but your Majesty may without dishonour return to yonr owne forces being but at hand, and you may have 2000 horss well to be loged at Romford and other vyllages nere Havering and you fotemen to be loged nerer London."

Dated from Gravesend on the 27th July, 1588.

The plan proposed by Leicester was, however, not executed; no other camp was formed, but that at Tilbury Fort, where the queen arrived by water, in her barge, on the 8th of August. The dispersion and destruction of the Armada by the storm and the deadly English fire, which followed soon after, rendered any further arrangements needless.

When Philip received the news of the disaster, so contrary to his expectation, he thanked God "it was no greater." England was filled with universal joy, and Queen Elizabeth ordered a public thanksgiving for this deliverance to be made in all the churches of the kingdom, and went herself to St. Paul's in great solemnity, to perform the same duty.

That Stratford had already become a place of considerable importance during the reign of Edward II., may be gathered from the fact, that Aylmer de Valence, Earl of Pembroke, held there the

---

[1] Belhus, near Avely, a stately mansion, built in the time of Henry VIII., now the seat of Sir Thomas Barrett Lennard.

Court of Pleas for the forest, in the year 1324. Three centuries later, in the reign of King Charles I., who attempted to enlarge the forest, and to extort exorbitant fines from those, who held land within the enlarged boundaries, with a view to raising money independent of parliament, the Forest Court was again summoned to sit at Stratford, on the 8th of April 1636. The Earl of Holland, Chief Justiciary of the forest, assisted by four judges, presided at the Court of Justice Seat, which the chamberlains of the Court of Exchequer were commanded to attend, with all such "writeinge and recorde" as were in their charge. Robert Rich, Earl of Warwick, a distinguished leader of the popular party and the country in general, employed serjeants-at-law for counsel to defend their cause, anxious to prove the old forest bounds according to the perambulations made in the time of King Edward I. But the manuscript, which they offered to support their claim, was not admitted by the Court, who denied it to be of the age of Edward I., and by the handwriting affirmed it to be about the time of Elizabeth. Heath, the Attorney-General, on the other hand attempted to prove from divers records, that many places, which the serjeants of the county maintained to be out of the forest, were actually in it, and produced mulcts and punishments upon whole parishes and particular persons, inflicted in different ages, which showed them to have been constantly under forest laws. At length the Earl of Holland and the judges hastely broke up the Court, pronouncing, that the demands of the county were ill founded and should not be complied with.

Such was the clamour and discontent upon this occasion, that the king appointed a second Justice Seat the year after, to be held at Stratford, before the Lord Chief Justice in Eyre and the same four judges, who by command, in order to satisfy the people, gave separately their decision, as at the former Court, and added the grounds and reasons of their sentence. Then the Earl of Holland confirmed and approved it without relaxation or abatement, and before the Court rose, the Solicitor-General in form demanded, "that the fences should be kept down to such a height, that a doe with her fawn could readily jump them." Such a regulation, enforced from Bow Bridge to Colchester, would naturally have destroyed the agriculture of half the county.

The old forest laws were very stringent and oppressive to those who lived within their jurisdiction; enormous fines were often imposed by King Charles I. and his advisers upon the neighbouring landowners for their encroachments on Crown lands. To insist on disputed enlargements, to restore obsolete boundaries, and to strain the dormant powers of the prerogative of the Crown to their utmost was, however, highly unpopular, caused great annoyance and discontent, and provoked most determined opposition.

Thus was enacted at Stratford one of those fatal mistakes of the reign of Charles I., which brought about the civil war, and ultimately led to his own death and the fall of his dynasty.

The following extract from RUSHWORTH's Collections more fully shows the contemporary feeling:

"We did forget to mention (1639) in order of time some proceedings concerning the forests in England, especially in the County of Essex, before the Chief Justice in Eyre (circuit), and those joined in commission with him, against whose proceedings the country made grievous complaints, that the Meets, Meers, Limits and Bounds of forests were adjudged by them to extend further, than they were taken to be in the 20th year of King James (1622) and contrary to those bounds, by which the county had enjoyed them, near the space of three hundred years and also complained that the said Court, to effect their designs, did unlawfully procure undue returns to be made by jurors, in joining with them other persons, who were not sworn, the Court also using threatening speeches to make them give a verdict for the king. And when the country, who found themselves hardly dealt withal, did desire to traverse the proceedings against them, having just cause to except against the evidence, yet the Court denied the same, except what they should verbally speak.

Whereupon the counsel for the county told the Justice Seat, that their proceedings were contrary to law and to the charter of the liberties of the forests, and other charters, and divers acts of parliament. Nevertheless the Court obtained a verdict for the king; at which time the Justice Seat was called by adjournment to sit, and continued sitting, to maintain and confirm the verdict given against the country.

It so happened, that when the Court was to declare their final

decree and sentence against the people inhabiting in the forests
in Essex, sitting at Stratford Langton near Bow, about three miles
distant from London, that there came a drove of calves passing
through the town towards London. And when they were at the
open place in that town, over against the Justice Seat, they suddenly
made a stand and a great bleating, with such a united and
unmeasurable noise, as the Court could not hear themselves to declare
what was intended in giving judgement; so that after they had
forbore speaking till the noise was over, and the calves with much
difficulty removed towards London, then the Court proceeded to
give their final sentence, as to the forests in Essex against the
County, by which many inhabitants were fined great sums of money
or forthwith depart from their houses and estates, and retire out
of the forests, for that they were found by verdict, given against
them, to have encroached upon the forests."

There is one incident connected with these proceedings, which
it may not be improper here to insert, namely, that a knight of the
county of Suffolk, having lands within the forest, upon this occasion
told a knight of the county of Essex, that the "Essex calves did
make that bleating, as if the dumb creatures did understand that
sentence was to be pronounced against the inhabitants in the forest,
in whose grounds they fed." But the Essex knight took exception
to the words "Essex calves," and told the other knight, they were
"Suffolk calves, driven through Essex; therefore" said the Essex
knight, "let not calves hereafter be cast upon Essex alone, but let
Suffolk bear a share."

No account of our high road would be complete without mention
of the highwaymen, with whom it was infested during the last
century. One of these, called Henry Cook, was the son of respectable
parents in Houndsditch, who having given him a decent education,
apprenticed him to a leather cutter; when out of his time, his father
took a shop of a shoemaker in Stratford, in which he placed his son.
Having some knowledge of the shoemaking business, he was soon
well established, and married a young woman at Stratford, by whom
he had three children. It was not long after his marriage, before his
association with bad company and neglect of business involved him so far
in debt, that he was obliged to quit his house in apprehension of bailiffs.

z

Among the idle acquaintances, that Cook had made at Stratford, was an apothecary named Young, with whom he robbed gardens, fishponds, and poultry yards. A warrant having been granted against him, Cook left the neighbourhood and concealed himself for two months at the house of a relative at Grays. After that he commenced the life of a highwayman, and chiefly frequented the northern roads about Enfield, Barnet, and Tottenham, generally taking both the horse and money from the victims. On the adjustment of his affairs, Cook returned to Stratford and resided there with his wife, ostensibly carrying on his trade of shoemaker, but in reality stopping and robbing coaches, on the borders of Epping Forest, wherein he was assisted by his journeyman, named Taylor. They acted with such extreme caution, that for a long time they were entirely unsuspected. The neighbourhood was terified by repeated outrages, until Captain Mawley took a place in the "basket of the Colchester coach, to make discoveries." When Cook and Taylor came up to demand the money of the passengers, Taylor was shot through the head, whereupon Cook ran to the Captain and robbed him of his money, on threat of instant death. The carriage driving on, Cook began to search his deceased companion for his money, but some neighbours coming up, he retired behind a hedge to listen, and finding that they knew the deceased and intimated he had been accompanied by Cook, he became alarmed and crossed the fields towards London.

Having spent three days in riot and dissipation, and being informed that several warrants were issued against him, he bought a horse and rode to Brentwood, where he heard little conversation but of Cook, the famous highwayman of Stratford. On the next day he followed a coach from the Inn, where he had put up, and took about £30 from the passengers. He now connected himself with a gang of desperate highwaymen in London, in conjunction with whom he stopped a coach at Bow, in which were some young gentlemen from a boarding school. A gentleman, riding up at the instant, was killed. After this, Cook abandoned the neighbourhood, and was at length apprehended and hanged at Tyburn in 1741.

A still more notorious highwayman was also resident in these parishes, and although his exploits are not particularly connected with our high road, this seems the most suitable place to mention the connexion of Dick Turpin with East and West Ham. He was the son of John Turpin, a farmer at Hempstead, near Saffron Walden in Essex, and having received a common school education, he was apprenticed to a butcher at Whitechapel. His early youth was distinguished by the impropriety of his conduct and the brutality of his manners. At the expiration of his apprenticeship he lived for some time with Mr. Giles, a butcher at Plaistow, and afterwards married a young woman, named Palmer, of East Ham, where he appears to have resided. He had not long been married, before he took to the practice of stealing his neighbour's cattle, and cutting them up for sale. Having stolen two oxen, belonging to his old master, Mr. Giles at Plaistow, he drove them to his own house at East Ham. Two of Mr. Giles' servants, suspecting the robber, went to Turpin's, where they found two beasts agreeing in size with those that had been lost, but could not identify them, as the hides had been stripped off. Understanding that Turpin was accustomed to dispose of his booty at Waltham market, they went thither and saw the hides of the stolen cattle. A warrant was accordingly procured for his apprehension, but he made his escape from a back window, at the very moment the officers were entering the door. He then connected himself with a gang of smugglers, but thrown out of this kind of business, he joined a gang of deer-stealers, whose depredations were principally committed on Epping Forest and the parks in its neighbourhood; this not succeeding to the expectations of the robbers, they determined, as a more profitable pursuit, to commence housebreaking. Their exploits were generally performed towards nightfall, whilst the inhabitants were still up, and the houses were entered by stratagem. While one of them knocked at the door, the others would rush in and seize whatever they might deem worthy of their notice. It is probable that the walled enclosures, high iron gates, and other defences of that period rendered a forcible entrance more difficult than it is now. Their plan was to fix on houses which they presumed to contain valuable property, and having become aware that there was an old woman at Loughton, who was in possession of £700 or £800, they agreed to rob her. On coming to the door one of them knocked, and the rest, forcing their way into the house, tied handkerchiefs over the eyes of the old woman and her maid. Turpin then demanded what there was in the house, and the owner hesitating to tell him, he threatened to set her on the fire if she did not make an immediate disclosure. Still, however, she declined to give the desired information, when the villains actually placed her on the fire, where she sat till the tormenting pain compelled her to disclose her hidden treasure, and they, taking possession of above £400, made their escape.

Some little time after they agreed to rob the house of a farmer near Barking, and knocking at the door, the people declined to open it, on which they broke it open, and having bound the farmer, his wife, his son-in-law, and the servant maid, they robbed the house of £700. Turpin was so delighted that he exclaimed: "Aye, this will do, if it would always be so." On the dispersion of this gang, Turpin became a highwayman, attacking travellers chiefly in Epping Forest. He is said to have resided with his companion King in a cave, whence, through the thicket that enclosed it, they could see the passengers on the road. An excavation near Loughton, towards High Beach, is still pointed out to the curious traveller or the loitering pic-nic party as "Turpin's Cave." Various adventures are related of Turpin, connected with Epping Forest and its vicinity, until he was searched for with bloodhounds by the huntsmen of a neighbouring gentleman. Ultimately he retreated into Lincolnshire and Yorkshire, and ended his guilty career at York, where he was hanged for horsestealing in 1739.

For a long period after this, the roads still continued to be unsafe, foot-pads and highwaymen infesting most parts of the county.

After this long digression we must return to the hamlet of Stratford Langthorne, or Langton, as it is sometimes called. From the fact that the Forest Courts were occasionally held there, and from the noble assembly that used to meet there on those occasions we may conclude that there was at that time a Court House or Hall of some pretension. There cannot, however, have been many buildings, since from "the Green" could be seen a mansion, called "Woodgrange," which NORDEN, who lived in the reign of King James I. mentions amongst his list of "Houses, having special names in Essex." It is possible that there were also a few habitations at

Forest Gate, but with the exception of two wayside Inns, the road seems to have led from Stratford to Ilford without passing scarcely any buildings, and to have formed the southern boundary of the Forest, as it had been in the time of Edward I.

Mention is also made of an ancient mansion, called "Rokeby House," standing by the road side, and being in former years the residence of the Rokeby family, after the sequestration of their old property. The house has been new fronted, but the garden side still shows marks of antiquity; one of the rooms bears evident signs of the times of James I., and over the mantlepiece are carved in wood the arms of (probably) some branch of the Rokeby family, representing a chevron between three unicorns' heads three crescents. The pleasure grounds at the rear of the house extended nearly as far as West Ham Church, and there can be no doubt, that the present Rokeby Estate once formed part of the property belonging to the Rokeby family.

About the end of last century this house was in the possession of two maiden ladies, named Hills, who are said to have had a very old coachman, very old horses, and above all a very old coach, which was esteemed a great curiosity in those days, being painted, gilt, and carved like the Lord Mayor's coach, but never used.

In later years the house was used as a school, and is now in the occupation of the family of the late Mr. Robt. Anderson.

Another old mansion, called "Stratford House" situate in the grove, was the residence of Sir John Henniker, who served the office of High Sheriff for this county in 1758. In 1765 King George III. granted him the dignity of a baronet, and raised him subsequently (in 1800) to the peerage. On his death, Stratford House became the property and occasional residence of his son, Lord Henniker, who disposed of it. The appearance of the House which is still in existence, is much altered, in consequence of some additional erections in front, now used as shops.

In the "British Traveller" of 1771, the hamlet of Stratford is described, as formerly a small village, but now greatly increased by a vast number of buildings. Since then, however, great changes have taken place, many important improvements have been made, and the "small village" has become, not only one of the most populous suburbs of London, but also a hive of producing industry. Numerous flour mills and manufacturing establishments, chemical works and other factories, have sprung up in its immediate vicinity. A large market for vegetables,

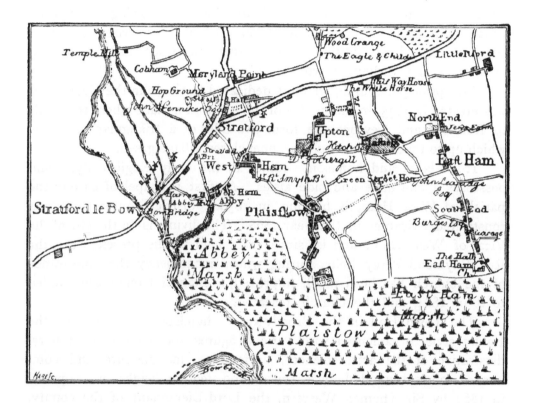

fruit, roots and straw, has also within recent years been constructed, close to the Stratford Bridge Station, for the development of the trade in vegetables from the Eastern Counties.

Here also is the Central Railway Station, where the two main branches of the Great Eastern Railway diverge, leading respectively to Cambridge and Colchester; there are also branches to North Woolwich, Woodford and Loughton, and to Barking on the Tilbury and Southend line. Adjacent to the station, the Company has established its chief factory for making carriages, engines and rolling stock, which with its various yards covers a large extent of ground, and gives employment to upwards of 3000 hands.

Tramways have also been laid down from the Broadway to Aldgate, Leytonstone, Forest Gate and Manor Park, to facilitate the increasing traffic. Numerous cottages and private residences have been erected on all sides to meet the demand of the ever-growing population, which from about 3,500 inhabitants in 1800 has now risen to about 50,000, — forming additional proof that Stratford has become a prosperous and thriving town.

The principal church, which is dedicated to St. John the Evangelist, was erected in 1835, in the centre of the town, at a place where the roads to Romford and Leytonstone form two sides of a triangular enclosure, which up to that time had been an unenclosed village green.

It is a large and handsome edifice in the early English style, and possesses a fine nave and side aisles. At first a chapel of ease to the parish of West Ham, it became in 1859 a district church, and was constituted a vicarage in the year 1868. The living is in the gift of the Vicar of West Ham, and is, since 1881, held by the present vicar, the Rev. Raymond Percy Pelly, during whose incumbency the appearance of the church has been much improved, a chancel having been added to it in 1884, and the church reseated.

The Town Hall in the Broadway, a handsome structure in the Italian style, ornamented with various figures and groups of statuary, illustrative of the arts, sciences, agriculture, manufacture and commerce, and surmounted by a tower, 100 feet in height, was opened in 1869 by Sir Thomas Western, the Lord-Lieutenant of the county, having been erected by the late Board of Health from the designs of Messrs. Lewis Angell and John Giles as joint architects. The lower part of the building consists of a large vestibule and commodious public offices, and has also a large room for the Town Council; on the first floor there is a spacious hall for public meetings, richly and artistically ornamented, which is acknowledged to be one of the finest halls in the vicinity of the metropolis. Extensive additions have recently been made to the building, and the public hall has also been enlarged, so as to accommodate 1000 persons.

Before concluding the chapter on Stratford, it is perhaps worthy of record, that there was in former years a tradition that, at the time of the great plague in London, the contagion did not cross Bow Bridge, or penetrate the fumes arising from the lime-kilns there. However, the following extracts from the parish register of West Ham completely refute this tradition, and give ample proof, that many deaths from plague occurred there.

On the 18th of July, 1665, the year of the plague in London, is the following entry:

A child was burried at West Ham, who died of plague.

On the 24th of July two other cases occurred.

On the 27th July a nurse child from Nan Smith's of Stratford was burried. Plague.

After this nameless nursling only one other instance is recorded in July, but in August sixteen persons were buried at West Ham, who died of plague, four of them in one day.

On August 28th a maide from Charlesbridge probably the (present Harrowbridge), at the glasse sellers was burried. Plague.

In September the mortality was fearful in some houses, the number being thirty, six of whom were buried on the 12th, and eight on the 29th September.

September 1st. Mr. Massinger from G^cilles house burried. Plague.

September 2nd. Ann Wall from G^cilles house. Plague.

September 5th. Ffuller's boye from Stratford. Plague.

September 8th. Ffuller's childe at "the Rents." Plague.

The family of the glass-maker and seller by Charlesbridge seems to have suffered severely from that dreadful disease. Besides the cases above mentioned are the following entries:

September 12th. A childe from the glassman's at Charlesbridge. Plague.

September 14th. The glassmaker's wife was burried. Plague.

Many names of persons are recorded in the parish register, as dying of plague, without their places of abode being mentioned, and other interments without mentioning names, a sufficient proof of the great consternation which must have prevailed during that time.

October 3rd. A blackman from Bedwell's house. Plague.

October 4th. Two children from Mrs. Middleton's house. Plague.

October 5th. A 'souldyer' from the 'Blew Anker' at Stratford. Plague.

October 7th. Goodman Dog's child. Plague.

Goodman Cross' child, same day. Plague.

A man from the Abbey mills, same day. Plague.

October 10th. Goodman Dog's wife. Plague.

October 11th. John, son of John Taylor. Plague.

October 20th. John Taylor from Bow Bridge. Plague.

October 27th. Rebecca, daughter of Randolph Hews. Plague.

October 28th. Ann, daughter of Randolph Hews. Plague.

Although mitigated, the plague seems to have lingered in the parish until May 1666, when it entirely ceased. Among the last victims were:

April 7th, 1666. A nurse child from the house of John Hills, of Stratford. Plague.

April 9th. Another nurse child from John Hill's house in Stratford. Plague.

April 11th. John, the son of John Hills, of Stratford. Plague.

April 24th. A nurse child from Hills, of Stratford. Plague.

With these entries we close our account of Stratford, and leaving its plague-stricken nurslings sleeping in West Ham churchyard, we will endeavour to give in the next chapter some account of the parish church of West Ham and the village around it.

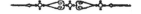

CHAPTER X.

(CONTENTS).

WEST HAM CHURCH. VICARS. PARISH REGISTER, ETC.

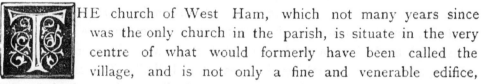HE church of West Ham, which not many years since was the only church in the parish, is situate in the very centre of what would formerly have been called the village, and is not only a fine and venerable edifice, but also from its antiquity, or the associations connected with it, an object of great curiosity and interest. When first a church stood upon the site it now occupies, it is impossible to say, but that there was a church before the year 1181, is proved by the fact that it was given to the Abbot and Convent of Stratford Langthorne by Gilbert, son of William de Montfichet, during the reign of Henry II., who by his charter, dated from Winchester, 1181, confirmed the gift.

This church, however, which is dedicated to " All Saints " must not be confounded with the " little church within the precincts of the monastery," which may have been a separate church, but more probably was part of the conventual church, and undoubtedly was (as we have seen from the various leases granted by the Abbots) the parish church of that district, though quite distinct from the West Ham parish church, of which we are now treating. The conventual church was dedicated to " St. Mary "—as all Cistercian monasteries were—and " All Saints," part of this conventual church, either an aisle, a transept, or the nave, with an entrance separate from that of the monks and with probably distinct services. This idea of the Abbey precincts forming a distinct parish of its own, is certainly curious, but may perhaps be accounted for by the supposition that, while the conventual church was for the use of the monks only, the "little church" was intended for the lay inhabitants of the abbey precincts.

The present parish church, which is essentially English in its plan and arrangements, and of grand almost cathedral-like proportions, consist of a nave and aisles, divided by circular columns, which support somewhat acute pointed arches. The south aisle is modern and incongruous and of white brick, while the north aisle is of flint, with stone dressings and bold buttresses in the "Perpendicular" style. The chancel, which is of later date, has a north and south chapel, and was divided from the church by a screen, which was taken down in the beginning of the last century.

At the western end is a fine square embattled tower of stone, 74 feet high, and containing a peal of ten excellent bells. From an old manuscript volume[1] we learn, that originally "there were only six bells, but by order of the vestry they were, in the year 1736, recast and made into a peal of eight bells; two bells were added by subscription in 1752, making the peal ten bells." The same author also informs us, that "in 1710 a new gallery was erected at the west end, commencing at the steeple, and in this gallery an organ was put up by subscription, in 1731, at a cost of £240. Before this gallery was built, the pulpit was against the fourth pillar, but on its erection, it was removed to the sixth." The other two galleries on the north and south sides (the latter of which is still in existence) were built at a later date.

There is appended to this record an old ground plan of the church and the pews, each pew having written upon it the name of the person to whom it was then allotted. Some of the names will be recognised in families yet residing in the neighbourhood; descendants of the Kilners, Frys, Reeves, Colliers, Newmans, and others are still to be found living among us.

One or two other curious notes from this volume are worth quoting, viz: "In the north-west corner was the old christening pew,

---

[1] The author of this MS. is Mr. John James, who was appointed bailiff of the manor of West Ham in 1753, by Francis Smart, Esq., then lord thereof.

and the north side was appropriated to 'servants and others of small note.' In 1738 the Rev Mr. Finch, lecturer of West Ham, brought into the vestry three large silver dishes, said to be the gift of a person unknown—but he adds in an appended note that the giver was Mr. Edward Flower of Maryland Point—and by order of the vestry two old dishes were 'molted down' and a new dish made exactly like the three given."

Another not uninteresting portion of the record is, that Nicholas Reader was appointed parish clerk in 1656, with the consent of the vestry, but that Jno. Warner, Vicar, appointed John Barber, in 1773, without the consent of the parish, — that the salary of the clerk was £40 per annum, — and that the 'Cookes' held the office of Sexton, which was worth £50 per annum, from time immemorial. A list of the burial fees is also given, from which we gather, that the fees varied according to the bells; 6th bell for instance, was 6s 8d, 5th bell 5s and so on.

The interior of the church has undergone many changes, restorations and renovations, more than are recorded or ever will be ascertained. During the restoration of 1848, when the hugh pews and other obstructions were swept away, and the church was reseated, a large mural painting was disclosed on the wall of the clerestory at the eastern end of the north aisle, which had been previously discovered during some cleaning in 1844. It excited at the time a great deal of interest, but was after a brief exposure again white-washed over with the rest of the walls.

In 1865, the interior underwent another vigorous restoration; the west gallery was taken down and the organ removed to its present position in the north chapel. The REV. R. H. CLUTTERBUCK, then curate of St. Mary's Church, Plaistow, has given, in the Transactions of the Essex Archaeological Society (vol. iv., p. 45) the following description of this restoration:

"The chief improvements, that are now being carried out, are the opening out of the great tower arch by the demolition of the huge west gallery, and the removal of the paint and whitewash from the stone work, as well as of the plaster from the clerestory walls. This last operation has brought to light a most curious and interesting fact, namely, the existence of a series of 'Norman or Transition' clerestory windows over the 'Decorated' arches 'of the nave.

Before the commencement of these works, it appeared as though the whole of the nave was of one date, and though the caps of the columns of the north and south arcades were known to be modern shams of plaster, and the bases had been so 'made good' with the same material, that the original outline was entirely altered, and, therefore, mouldings were no indication of the style or date—yet it seemed probable, as subsequent discoveries have confirmed, that this part of the church could not have been built long after the year 1300.

When the plastering was removed, it was seen from the masonry, that the two easternmost bays were of later date than the other four, the wall over these last being of that small rubble work with tile and clunch, which one would expect to find in Norman buildings. Above them is now seen a series of roundheaded windows, not ranging in any way with the arches below, and blocked with material precisely similar to the wall around them, and not extending into the more recent work of the two eastern bays. The sills of these windows had been removed, and in some cases the crown of the nave arch goes right through where the sill would have been, while in others the crown of the roundheaded windows has been destroyed. These two circumstances show, that they could not have been built at the same time as the great arches, and it is evident that they are of considerably earlier date than the arches below them.

The only solution of this extraordinary fact is the probability that at the time, when it was desirable to enlarge the arches of the original church, the roof and the clerestory walls were too good to be destroyed, and were, therefore, shored up, while the Norman arches were one by one cut away, and 'decorated ones' built up, the clerestory windows being blocked, for the sake of uniformity, with the old material, of which there would be of course abundance at hand.

The character of the masonry over the last two bays, one whole and one three-quarter arch, showed a somewhat later date; it appears also, that the columns of the arches are of different stone from the others; the bases also show later mouldings. The western columns were all built of white free stone with very hard grey stone capitals, resembling Kentish rag, while the later ones are of the hard stone throughout.

On pulling down the western gallery, part of two of the original caps were found remaining, and it was observed that the fictitious ones had been placed about four inches lower down than the original.

It may, perhaps, be well to mention, that a third alteration of the church apparently took place in pure 'Perpendicular' times, when the tower and side aisles were built on the foundation upon which they at present stand. The chancel with its aisles was subsequent some years. And then the north aisle of the chancel was re-built in that beautifully wrought brickwork of which there are so many fine specimens in this neighbourhood. Abutting on the wall of this chapel is a turret, which formerly gave admission to the rood loft, but this, at the time of the re-building of the chapel walls, was not pulled down, but encased in brick, and carried up some feet higher, the stone newel being continued in wood for the purpose of access to the roof.

The process of removing the plaster showed, that the whole building had been freely polychromed, but no patterns of any of the diaper could be secured, except in one place, and that on the wall of the latest portion, which had been covered with a very coarse and vulgar fret pattern, painted in distemper in two shades of red.

On the removal of the whitewash, it was found, that the painting which was first discovered in 1844, was too much dilapidated to be copied; it remained only on the eastern part of the south clerestory over the three-quarter arch, and as far as the second roof pendant, measuring eight feet in width by five in height. It does not appear, that more than this was visible, when previously exposed; but from some heads, found on the south side of the chancel arch, it seems clear, that this is only one wing of the subject, which probably extended over the east wall of the nave, and to an equal distance on the north and south sides. The picture appeared to be the work of the latter part of the 15th century, and was generally of inferior though somewhat elaborate execution. It was painted in oil colours on exceedingly rough plastering, and covered also part of the stones of the arch; in one place, where a beam of the aisle roof comes through the wall, it was continued upon the surface afforded by its section.

The whole subject undoubtedly represented the 'Final Doom of Mankind.' Upon the east wall was depicted our Lord as judge. The right wing, which remained, represented the 'Reward of the Righteous,' aud the left the 'Condemnation of the Wicked,' but not a trace of the latter could be discovered. The picture on the north wall represented the 'Resurrection of the Just.'

The upper part of the painting, extending as high as the wall plate and forming a background to the whole, was richly grouped, though rudely executed, 'tabernacle work,' chiefly white, shaded with grey, the windows aud crockets strongly outlined in black; some of the windows were coloured red. In the niches were several celestials, each wearing a circlet with a small cross over the forehead, and among them two of the heavenly choir playing upon gitterns.

At the lower part of the painting, below the basement of the canopy, were two angels raising the righteous by the hand; they seem to have issued through the portcullised gates behind them. There are two of these gates at the lower part of the picture, besides that in the upper part of the canopy, into which one of the redeemed is entering. From one of them, the angels, who are assisting the risen, seem themselves to have issued, and to be leading the righteous into the other.

The risen saints were grouped all along the line of the arch in that crowded manner, usual with mediaeval limners. They are singularly irregular in size, the largest being placed just over the crown of the arch, and diminishing as they approached the cap of the column. All were nude, with their hands either joined in prayer or extended as if in admiration. Among the group were two ecclesiastics with red mitres and a cardinal with a red hat.

The two angels, above mentioned as raising the righteous, were larger than the other figures and in tolerable preservation; they were vested in long white albs without cincture or apparels, and their faces painted with care and not without dignity.

Close to the angle of the wall three demons were visible, painted greyish blue, but the figures generally as void of expression as most paintings of this date."

As the whole painting was very imperfect and of an inferior order and moreover in that state, in which it was found, of no practical value, Mr. Clutterbuck, under whose careful superintendence this interesting example of mural decoration was developed, was of opinion, that there was not sufficient reason for its preservation, all the rest of the plastering having, moreover, to be removed, for the purpose of pointing the inner masonry.

Soon after the parish church of West Ham, dedicated to All Saints, had been appropriated to the Abbey of Stratford Langthorne by Gilbert de Montfichet, a perpetual vicarage was ordained by Gilbert Foliot, Bishop of London, between the years 1163 and 1187, "with the consent of the said Gilbert de Montfichet, the feudal lord of Hamme," which bishop endowed it as follows:

Vicarius quicunque fuerit, percipiet omnes oblationes et obventiones ad praefatam ecclesiam pertinentes, praeter decimationes bladi et liguminum, quas praedicti monachi percipient, totam etiam terram ad ecclesiam praefatam pertinentem cum hominibus et redditibus sibi excolendam habebit vicarius praeter Curiam ubi horrea sita sunt, et duos campos parvos hinc inde ipsi Curiae adjacentes, scilicet Asfeld et Estfeld, solvendo annuatim pro ipsis monachis canonicis Sanctae Trinitatis London: quatuor marcas argenti. Ipse quoque Vicarius omnes consuetudines debitas Episcopis London: et officialibus suis reddet et omnia onera episcopalia sustinebit.

The vicar shall enjoy all oblations and revenues which pertain to the aforesaid church, with the exception of the tithes of corn and pulse, which the aforesaid monks shall enjoy; the vicar shall also have all the arable land belonging to the aforesaid church with the men and revenues, except the court-yard where the barns are situate, and two small fields adjoining thereto, called Asfeld and Estfeld, by paying annually to the monks of Holy Trinity, London, four marks of silver. The vicar shall also render the accustomed dues to the Bishops of London and his officials, and bear all episcopal burdens.

This settlement was confirmed by Bishop Richard Fitz-Neal, the successor of Foliot, and the Abbot and Convent continued proprietaries of the rectory and patrons of the vicarage till their suppression. But in after times, in the years 1514, 1515 and 1516, a tedious suit arose, first in the Archbishop's Court, and then in the Court of Rome, between William Shragger, then vicar, and the said Abbot and Convent, which was finally settled by way of composition, on the 17th February 1516, and confirmed by Leo X. in 1519. By this agreement the Abbot aud Convent were allowed to set aside the endowment of the vicarage, and in lieu of it settled upon the vicar and his successors an annual pension of £39 13s 8d, together with the vicarage, dove-house and appurtenances, reserving to themselves all the tithes and profits. This pension which did not increase in value as the tithes did, was paid in four equal parts, at the feasts of Easter, Nativity of St. John the Baptist, St. Michael, and the birth of our Lord.

Although this stipend seems to us miserably small, it must not be forgotten, that in the time in which it was assigned to the vicar, circumstances were very different from what they now are;— that the priests were all single men and that to many of them, who had been brought up in the rigorous discipline of a convent, such a stipend would provide even many luxuries. Moreover, as late as 1414, seven marks[1] a year was considered a sufficient salary for a priest or clerk.

After the dissolution of the Abbey, in 1538, all the tithes came to the Crown, and were leased out from time to time, the vicar being allowed the £39 13s 8d, which formed nearly the whole income of the vicarage, till the 11th of January, 1638, when King Charles I. granted the small tithes, glebe land, and surplice fees to Peter Blower, and thenceforth the stipend of £39 13s 8d, paid by the Crown, ceased. In OGBORNE's "History of Essex," however, it is stated, and perhaps correctly, that William Blower purchased the existing lease of the vicarial tithes, and that his son and successor procured from the Crown a renewal of the old endowment, which was to consist of all the tithes, except corn and pulse, and that he

---

[1] A mark was equal to thirteen shillings and four pence of our money.

BB

resigned for himself and his successors for ever the pension of £39 13s 8d, paid out of the exchequer.

The family of Blower seems to have been long settled in West Ham, for we are told, that Peter Blower, of West Ham, gentleman, by deed dated July 26th 1616, gave to the poor one acre of land in Brady Mead, New Marsh, formerly the property of Richard Fox, and it is very probable, that this Peter Blower was the father of the above-named William, and grandfather of the second Peter.

The following list of the Vicars of West Ham, which is taken from NEWCOURT's "Repertorium" and commences with the year 1334, is probably correct and has therefore been here inserted :

LIST OF VICARS OF WEST HAM.	PATRONS.
William de Billingston, pr. 13 Kal. Nov. 1334.	The Abbot and Convent.
Joh. Farmer, was Vicar in 1338; he had license to exchange this for the church of Milstred, in the diocese of Cant., with	,,
Joh. Foucher.	,,
Joh. de Fakenham.	,,
William Salman, 17 Kal. Oct. 1365, per resig. Fakenham.	,,
Joh. Ward.	,,
Joh. Stondon, 20 April 1384, per resig. Ward. ...	,,
Ric. Clerke, cap. 16 Nov. 1384, per mort. Stondon.	,,
Will. Brede, pr. 20 April 1394, per mort. Clerke.	,,
Rad. Martell.	,,
Rob. Blakelowe, 24th Oct. 1438, per resig. Martell. ...	,,
Jac. Hamelyn, 30th March 1447, per resig. Blakelowe.	,,
Joh. White.	,,
Thomas Gore, pr. 2 Maii 1485, per resig. White. ...	,,
Will. Shragger, 8th Dec. 1499, per mort. Gore. ...	,,
Tho. Wodington, D.D., 1st July 1519, per mort. Shragger.	,,
Rob. Paynter, cap. 30th June 1522, per mort. Wodington.	,,
Ant. Barker, pr. 28 Sept. 1538, per mort. Paynter.	Henry VIII.

Thomas Rose, cl. 27 Jan. 1551, per mort. Barker.	Edward VI.
Joh. Peerse, pr. Jun. 1554, per priv. Rose. ...	Maria reg.
Thomas Rose, restitutus.	Elizabeth reg.
Will. King, cl. 8 March 1563, per resig. Rose. ...	„
Henry Stedd, cl. 12 Sept. 1590, per resig. King. ...	„
Robert Jenings, A.M., 12 July 1592.	„
Gabriel Weaver, A.M., 22 Oct. 1630, per mort. Jenings.	Carolus I. rex.
Will. Blower, A.M., 25 Maii 1635, per mort. Weaver.	„
Peter Blower, A.M., 20 April 1638, per mort. Wm. Blower.	„
Will. Marketman, cl. 22nd Sept. 1660.	Carolus II. rex.
Ric. Hollingworth, cl. 18th April 1672.	„
Josh. Stanley, A.M., 10th April 1682, per resig. Hollingworth.	„
Joh. Smith, A.M., 28th Aug. 1690, per resig. Stanley.	William rex. and Mary reg.
Charles Vernon, 13 Oct. 1708, per mort. Smith. ...	Ann reg.
Benjamin Carter, 1725, cessit Vernon.	George I. rex.
Hugo Wyat, 31st Jan. 1727, per mort. Carter. ...	„
James Trail, D.D., 9th July 1762, per mort. Wyat.	George III. rex.
John Warner, 30 Nov. 1765, per resig. Trail. ...	„
William Cropley, B.A. 23rd March 1775, per resig. Warner.	„
George Gregory, D.D., 2nd June 1804, per mort. Cropley.	„
Hon. Gerald Valerian Wellesley, M.A.. 16 June 1809, per mort. Gregory.	„
Hugh Chambres Jones, 22nd Nov. 1809, per resig. Wellesley.	„
Abel John Ram, M.A., 30 Oct. 1845, per resig. Jones.	Victoria reg.
Thomas Scott, M.A., 1868, per. resig. Ram.... ...	„

Of the early Vicars of West Ham, there is, as a general rule, but little information come down to us. Thomas Rose, who was instituted to the Vicarage in 1551, was amongst the first preachers of the reformed doctrines in this part of England. About the same time that Bilney and Latimer were moving at Cambridge, and preached against purgatory, praying to saints, and other doctrinal errors of the Church of Rome, Rose was pursuing the same course at Hadleigh, in Suffolk, which was one of the first towns in England that received the word of God and the true doctrine of the Gospel. He was an eloquent powerful preacher, and vehemently inveighed against the idolatrous worship of images. It happened that there was an idol, named "the Rood of Dovercourt," a full-sized figure of Christ, to which many people resorted, the monks giving it out, that it had miraculous powers, and that no man had power to shut the door which continually stood open both night and day. Several young men of Dedham, hearing Mr. Rose denounce this image, went one moonlight night over to Dovercourt (a distance of ten miles), took the idol from its shrine and burnt it in a field close by. In consequence of this desecration four persons were apprehended and condemned to be burnt. They were, however, offered their lives, if they would inform against Mr. Rose, who was suspected of being privy to the robbery, which on refusing to do, three were hung in chains, but the fourth escaped and fled. Thomas Rose was thereupon seized on suspicion and committed to prison, where he was placed with his body on the ground, and his feet in a pair of high stocks, until he was benumbed and nearly dead. Being released he was made one of Lord Cromwell's chaplains, but by the persecution of the Duke of Norfolk he was obliged to go abroad, when he was taken prisoner on his passage. After his liberation, he received from Edward VI. the Vicarage of West Ham, of which he was, however, deprived by Queen Mary, and again brought before the bishops. He then made his escape to the Continent, but returned upon the accession of Queen Elizabeth, and again took possession of the Vicarage of West Ham. He resigned it in 1563, when he was presented by the Crown with the living of Luton in Bedfordshire, which formed a quiet retreat for the persecuted preacher. Here he spent nearly 13 years, and died in the year 1576, at the age of 74.

Peter Blower, who was Vicar of West Ham at the commencement of the civil wars, seems during the Commonwealth to have either resigned, or to have been ejected, as were many others, if not all the parish clergy, and in some places the clerks also.

Dr. George Gregory, to whose memory a tablet is dedicated on the south wall of the chancel, was Vicar of West Ham from 1804 till his death 1808. He was the son of a clergyman in Ireland, and in his early years clerk to a merchant in Liverpool, but feeling a distaste for commercial pursuits he studied at the University of Edinburgh, and at length took orders in the Established Church. In 1782 he settled in London and became evening preacher at the Foundling Hospital, and afterwards Vicar of West Ham, for which preferment he was indebted to Mr. Addington, afterwards Lord Sidmouth, who employed him to defend his administration. He distinguished himself as an author, by several useful compilations and some original works. He published "Essays historical and moral," "the life of Chatterton," a "translation of Lowth's lectures on the sacred poetry of the Hebrews," "Church History," "the Economy of Nature," and "Sermons."

Although never Vicar of West Ham, the name of the unhappy Dr. William Dodd must not be omitted among the clergy of that place, where he was appointed lecturer in the year 1752. At that period he was already celebrated as a popular preacher, and writer of sermons and religious tracts. He was also zealous in promoting charitable institutions, especially the Magdalen Hospital. It is, however, to be feared, that these appearances of piety concealed a heart devoted to the world, for he is said to have been "vain and pompous." For a dishonourable attempt to obtain the chaplaincy of St. George's, Hanover Square, his name was struck off the list of chaplains. Upon this he went abroad, where his extravagance continued undiminished, until in 1777 he forged a bond for £4,200 from his former pupil, the Earl of Chesterfield, for which he was hanged at Tyburn. The house in which he resided at Plaistow is still in existence, and traditions respecting him and his pupil, the Hon. Philip Stanhope, afterwards Lord Chesterfield, are still retained there.

It may interest some of our readers to insert here a short biographical sketch of Dr. William Dodd. He was the eldest son of a clergyman, who held the Vicarage of Bourne, in Lincolnshire, and was born in 1729; handsome, genteel and elegant in his person, he was also a man of great talent. Having embraced the clerical profession, the first service, in which he was engaged, was to assist the Rev. Hugh Wyat, Vicar of West Ham, as his curate, and there he spent the happiest moments of his life, which he describes in the following lines :

"Dear were thy shades, O Ham, and dear the hours
In manly musings 'midst the forest passed,
And antique woods of sober solitude." — — And again :
"Expelled
From Ham's lost paradise and driv'n to seek
Another place of rest.—Yes, beauteous Fane !
To bright religion dedicate, thou well
My happy public labours canst attest ;
Unwearied and successful in the cause,
The glorious, honoured cause of Him, whose love
Bled for the human race ! Thou canst attest
The Sabbath days, delightful, when the throng
Crowded thy hallow'd walls with eager joy,
To hear Truth evangelical, the sound
Of gospel comfort, when attentive sate
Or at the holy altar humbly knelt
Persuasive, pleasing patterns, Athol's duke,
The polished Hervey, Kingston, the humane,
Aylesbury and Marchmont, Romney all rever'd ;
With numbers more, by splendid titles less
Than piety distinguish'd and pure zeal."

His abilities had at this time every opportunity of being shown to advantage, and his exertions were so properly directed, that he soon gained the respect of his parishioners, and on the death of their lecturer (1752) was chosen to succeed him. He soon became a popular preacher and was indefatigable in his vocation as minister.

From the time he entered the service of the church, he resided at Plaistow and made up the deficiences of his income by superintending the education of some young gentlemen, who were placed under his care. On leaving West Ham he launched out into scenes of expense, which his income was unequal to support.

In 1772 he obtained the Rectory of Hockliffe in Bedfordshire, the first cure of souls he ever had. In the following year, the Earl of Chesterfield died and was succeeded by his son the Hon. Philip Stanhope the former pupil of Dr. Dodd, who appointed his preceptor, his chaplain. At this period he seems to have been in the zenith of his popularity. Beloved and respected by all orders of people, he would have reached in all probability the situation, which was the object of his wishes, had he possessed patience to have waited for it, and prudence sufficient to keep himself out of difficulties. But the habits of dissipation and expense had acquired too much influence over him, so that he became involved in considerable debts. To extricate himself from them, he was tempted to an act, which entirely cut off every hope which he could entertain of rising in his profession, and totally ruined him in the opinion of the world.

On the translation of Bishop Moss (1774) to the see of Bath and Wells, the valuable Rectory of St. George, Hanover Square, fell to the disposal of the Crown by virtue of the king's prerogative. On this occasion he took a step, of all others, the most wild and extravagant, and least likely to be attended with success. He caused an anonymous letter to be sent to Lady Apsley, offering the sum of £3000, if, by her means, he could be presented to the living. The letter was immediately communicated to the chancellor, and after being traced to the sender, was laid before his majesty. The insult, offered to so high an officer by the proposal, was followed by instant punishment, and Dr. Dodd's name was ordered to be struck off the list of chaplains.

Stung with remorse and feelingly alive to the disgrace he had brought on himself, he hastily went abroad, and meeting his former pupil, then Lord Chesterfield, at Geneva, that nobleman presented him to the living of Winge, in Buckinghamshire. Though encumbered with debts, he might still have retrieved his circumstances, if not his character, had he attended to the lessons of prudence, but his extravagance continued undiminishingly and drove him to schemes, which overwhelmed him with additional infamy.

From this period, every step led to complete his ruin. In the summer of 1776 he went to France, and returning to England about the beginning of the winter, continued to exercise the duties of his function, particularly at the chapel of the Magdalen Hospital, where he still was heard with approbation, and where his last sermon was preached February 2nd 1777, two days before he signed that fatal instrument, which brought him to an ignominious death.

Pressed at length by creditors, whose importunity he was unable longer to soothe, he fell upon an expedient, from the consequences of which he could not escape. He forged a bond from his former pupil Lord Chesterfield for the sum of £4,200, in the hope of being able to meet it before it was due. Detection of the fraud almost immediately followed. At the sessions held at the Old Bailey, his trial commenced on February 24th 1777, and the commission of the offence being proved, he was pronounced guilty.

When brought to the bar to receive his sentence, and asked, what he had to allege, why it should not be pronounced upon him, he addressed the Court in an animated and pathetic speech, imploring the judge to recommend him to the clemency of his majesty.

Then he sank down, quite overwhelmed with agony, and after some little time the sentence of death was pronounced upon him.

The friends of Dr. Dodd were assiduously employed in endeavouring to save his life. Besides the petitions of many individuals, the members of the several charities, which had been benefited by him, joined in the application to the throne for mercy;—the City of London likewise, in its corporate capacity, solicited a remission of the punishment, in consideration of the advantages, which the public had derived from his various and laudable exertions, both as preacher and author. No less than 30,000 persons were supposed to have signed the petitions;—they were, however, of no avail. On the 15th of June, the Privy Council assembled, and after some deliberation the warrant was ordered to be made out for the execution of Dr. Dodd, and he was hanged at Tyburn on June 27th 1777.

Thus ended the life of a man, who had spent the greatest part of his life in doing good to his fellow creatures, but by one rash step was brought to this fatal exit.

Passing on to more recent days, we come to the name of a vicar, whose memory will always be regarded with feelings of respect and veneration—the Rev. Abel John Ram. At the time of his appointment in the year 1845, there were but three churches and five clergymen in the whole parish, to meet the spiritual wants of the population, then amounting to about 18,000 souls. During his incumbency of twenty-three years the population increased more than three-fold, not so much by any gradual increase, as by a vast flood of immigration, which the large public works in this locality caused to flow in. It became necessary to erect new churches and schools; untiring efforts were made, in which Mr. Ram took a prominent share, that the church extension might keep pace with the rapid growth of the population. Five churches were built and consecrated, and each with its appropriate group of schools. Besides the Pelly Memorial Schools for boys, a new school for Girls was erected, and the Boys' old school room converted into one for Infants. A vicarage house, the want of which had long been felt, was also purchased during his incumbency. Mr. Ram, who some years before had been appointed Honorary Canon of Rochester, resigned his office in the year 1868, and had a worthy successor in the present vicar, the Rev. Canon Thomas Scott.

Mr. Scott was appointed by the Crown, during the first Premiership of Lord Beaconsfield, then Mr. Disraeli, and has since 1870 also been Rural Dean of Barking. In 1881 he was appointed Hon. Canon of St. Albans, and has sat in the late and present Convocation of Canterbury as one of the two representatives of the clergy of the diocese. During his incumbency of nearly 20 years the parish of West Ham has increased more rapidly, than, perhaps, any other parish in the United Kingdom, numbering at the present time no less than 180,000 souls. With it have also increased the difficulties in satisfying the spiritual requirements of so large and extensive a district, chiefly inhabited by poor people. Great efforts have been made during his incumbency to provide churches or temporary iron places of worship in various parts of the parish. Several ecclesiastical districts have been formed, Mr. Scott taking a leading part in the formation of that of St. Gabriel, Canning Town, of which he was at first vicar. His zeal and activity are also manifested in such enterprises as the new Church Hall, in Meeson Road, which is the home of a number of agencies for the religious and social welfare of his parishioners. The foundation stone was laid by the Lord

Mayor of London, Sir R. N. Fowler, Bart., in 1884. The Hall, which can accommodate over 600, is used for Mission services, meetings of all kinds, concerts, etc., and on the ground floor are various commodious class rooms in connexion with the Working Lads' Institute, which was organized by the Rev. Edward Sant, senior curate of West Ham, and has under his able and careful superintendence proved a most successful and prosperous undertaking.

It has been already observed that during the turbulent times in the history of our church, at the commencement of the civil wars, many of the clergy were deprived of their livings; prosecutions and sequestrations were frequent, and there is no doubt, that to this circumstance may be attributed the loss of the early registers in so many parishes. Hence also arises the extreme difficulty, which genealogists so often find about that period, in connecting the links of more recent generations of a family with those of the same race, living before the civil wars.

To remedy this evil, an Act of the Parliament of the Commonwealth of England was passed in 1653, touching marriages, births and burials, by which it was provided "that a Registrar should be appointed and chosen in every parish of the Commonwealth, who was to be sworn to the faithful discharge of the duties intrusted to him."

The parishioners of West Ham record that in compliance with this act "they have at a meeting chosen Edward Lawford for the said office of a 'Register,' and recommend him unto Robert Smyth, Esq., one of the Justices of Peace for the county of Essex, to settle and establish him in the said office for the term of three years, according to the said Act of Parliament Sept. 11th, Anno Dom. 1653."

THE OATH WAS AS FOLLOWS:

"You shall swear in the presence of God, the searcher of all hearts, to be true, just, and faithful in your office of a 'Publique Register,' unto which you were chosen Sept. 11th Anno 1653, and shall neither ask, demand, nor require anie more for publications of marriages, births nor burialls, than what is allowed and appointed by the Act of Parliament of the Common Wealth in England, bearing date the 24th day of August an. 1653, observing and having things concerning your said office, according to the true meaning of the said statute. So helpe you God."

Edward Lawford, having taken the required oath before Alderman Robert Smyth, entered upon his office, registering births, deaths, and marriages with their previous publications of bans, with punctilious care. That he was a strict puritan is evident from his quaint habit of recording dates by their scripture names, in addition to those generally used, which he stigmatized as heathenish and common.

The Society of "Friends" maintained a somewhat similar custom to within recent years, which was evidently derived fron their puritan forerunners.

The following instances taken from different parts of the register will show the method, pursued by Edward Lawford in the registration. In the fly-leaf of the book is the following receipt for its purchase:

"Received Oct. the 16th, 1653, of Mr. George Bowerman for a Register Booke containing 100 leaves of parchment, being for the use of the parish of West Ham, the sume of one pound fifteen shillings (£1 15s) per me Thos. Euztre, statyoner at the Ship and Star over against the Exchange in Cornhill."

Having thus entered in due form the purchase of the Register book, Edward Lawford proceeded to fulfil the duties of the Parish Registrar.

The first entry in it is as follows:

BIRTHS.

Ethanim. Rebecca and Barbara Rossiter, twin daughters of Edward Rossiter and Marie his wife, was borne the seventeenth day of Sept. an. 1653, being Satterday.

Adar. John, the sonne of John and Margaret ffowler, was borne the tenth day day of ffebruary an. 1653, in Plaistow ward; the scripture moneth is called Adar.

Joseph, the sonne of Mr. George and Ann Bowerman of Stratford Langthorne ward, was borne on Satterday the eighteenth day of the month Abib or Nisan, called March, 1653.

The next entry is only twelve days later, but it must be borne in mind that these dates are according to the old style, when the year commenced in March.

1654.   Hanna, the daughter of Mr. Thomas and Judith Leddington, was borne at the Abbey in West Ham parish, the thirtieth day of the first month, called in scripture Abib or Nisan, vulgarlie March, in the year of our Lord God 1654.

Thomas, the sonne of John and — Monnam of Plaistowe ward, was borne the 21st day of August 1654, and baptized the 30th of August, called in scripture Elul.

Ethanim the 7th month.   Elizabeth, the daughter of Mr. Richard Nichols and Anne his wife, was borne the 5th day of Sept. and baptized the 6th day of the said moneth; Plaistowe 1654.

Adar.   Micah, the sonne of fferdinando and Anne Muxloc^d, was baptized on Thursday the sixth day of ffebruary, called in scripture Adar an. 1654. Upton warde nat. 4 die idem ffebr.

Ab. Hebr.   The 5th moneth is called Ab in scripture. Elizabeth, the daughter of Henrie and Abigail Hayfield, was borne on the Lord's day Jun 24th, and baptized the first day of Julie being Sabbath day 1655.

ffrances, the sonne of Mr. Henrie and Mrs. Dorothy ffauntkland of Stratford Langthorne, was borne the sixth day of Julie an. 1655. The month is called Ab by the Hebrew account.

Daniel, the sonne of Daniel and Elizabeth ffuller of Stratford Langthorne warde, was borne the 18th day of the (5th) month, called Ab in Hebr. vulgar acct: Julie 1655.

Thomas, the sonne of William and Marie Wight of Plaistowe warde, was borne the 25th day of the fifth month, called in scripture Ab, which signifieth (father), vulgar account Julie anno 1655.

Elul the 6th month.   Sarah, the daughter of John and Margaret Emmet, at Mr. John ffoote his Oyle Mill in Stratford warde, was baptized the 19th day of (6th) month called Elul, or Julie vulgarlie, anno 1655.

Thomasine, the daughter of Thomas Sheppard deceased and Marie his wife, was borne and baptized the 22nd day of Ethanim (September) 1655, two days after her father's buriall.

Among later dates we find the followiug entries:

Richard Jebb,[1] son of Samuel Jebb M.D. and Jane his wife, Oct. 30th 1729.

John, Henry and Sarah, sons and daughters of John and Esther flowerday — three children at a birth — baptized December 16th 1789.

MARRIAGES.

We find it recorded in the Parish Register that marriages were published in "West Ham Meeting Place," otherwise called "the Church," and took place before a Justice of the Peace. One of them is thus recorded:

Scrip.
Kissen.
Richard Smith, of Anne's Blackfriars parish, and Mrs. Kathtrine Walsingham, of this parish, after three several publications on the Lord's Dayes in the close of the morning exercises, as appeareth on the left hand page at letter (b), certificate being made thereof, were married in the parish by the Worsh^p. Alderman Robert Smyth, Esq.

Script.
Shebar.
and Justice of the Peace, ibid., on ffryday the sixth day of Januario, anno 1653, in the presence of us:

Vallentine Hutton.   The mark of
Thomas Baker.   E. O. Elizabeth Ourton.

Witness, William Plaile.
Meign, Edward Lawford.

---

[1] It appears by this entry that Dr. Samuel Jebb resided at Stratford and not at Stratford Bow, as stated in "Anecdotes of Bowyer" and that his son Richard, the celebrated physician, was born there. Dr. Samuel Jebb, was born at Nottingham, in 1690, and settled as physician at Stratford, where he resided till a short time before his death in 1772. His son Richard was, in 1780, appointed one of the physicians in ordinary to George III., who conferred upon him a baronetcy. But this office he did not enjoy long, for being in attendance upon two of the princesses, who were affected with the measles, he was suddenly attacked with a fever in their appartments at Windsor, and fell a victim to the disease after a few days' illness, on the 4th of July, 1787, in the 58th year of his age and was buried in the cloisters of Westminster Abbey.

Another marriage is thus recorded in the following year:

Parish reg. sub anno 1654. The publications of the marriage solemnized between William Wight, the sonne of Thomas Wight, of this parish, and Maria Pratt, the daughter of Mrs. Susanna Pratt, of ffinchley, in the county of Middlesex, wid., were made in a publique meeting place or church, 3 several sabbath daies at the close of the morning "exercises" viz. the 8th day, the 15th day and the 22nd day of the eighth month, called October an. 1654, married in the county of Middlesex, Nov. the second 1654.

The first entry of a marriage by a minister occurs the same year (1654), and is as follows:

Philipp Hall de Bromley, Com. Midd., and Susan Ward, of Plaistow, were married in our parish church, the 25th day of Oct., by Mr. Ley Kett, minister.

Coram: Thos. Ward. Hn. Reader.
Ed. Langford et aliis.

On the same day, however, a couple were married before the "Worshipful Mr. Robert Smyth, Justice of the Peace;" nor does another marriage by a minister occur for two years, when it is recorded, that:

A.D. 1656. Peter Drogus and Hester Toolye (french) both parties of West Ham parish, were married the 29th of September, called Michaelmas day, the publications were made in London (ut annt.), married by Mr. Kett in Ecclesia, married by justice Cooper at Bowe.

Mr. Kett married another couple in 1657, and Mr. Thomas Walton, minister, performed the same office in the same year.

In 1658, a marriage was solemnized by Benjamin Peiorke, minister; his name and that of Walton occur till the 5th of May, 1660, when Robert Spooner and Mary Walton were married by Mr. Marketman, minister, who henceforth continued to officiate. In August he is styled vicar, and from that date no more marriages before a justice are recorded.

The morning "exercises" mentioned were lectures or sermons, delivered by different ministers, and ceased with the Restoration.

Before leaving the subject of West Ham Church registers, we must revert to the subject of the plague, which evidently fell heavily on several families. It broke out in West Ham during the time that the Rev. William Marketman was vicar (1660—1672). In August 1665, it had spread to Plaistow, and carried off four members of the family of Chamberlain. In October the total number of deaths recorded in the parish of West Ham was sixty-four, fifty-three of which were of plague; the other cases were undefined, perhaps from the dread of the terror-stricken families to admit the fact.

In November the interment of Nicholas Reader, the parish clerk, is recorded, as well as that of William Bird, churchwarden, of Stratford, both of plague. The mortality, however, had then greatly lessened, the number in that month being fourteen, in December ten, in January sixteen; but the pestilence still raged fiercely in certain families, as we see from the following entries in the parish register.

BURYALS.

John, the sonne of John ffootes the younger, 11th December. Plague.

John ffootes of Plaistow, January 11th. Plague.

ffrances, the daughter of ffrancis Too, 20th December. Plague.
ffrances Too, the daughter of ffrancis Too, January 13th. Plague.
ffrancis Too of Plaistow, January 14th. Plague.
Susan, daughter of Edward Pilkinton, the 3rd day of January. Plague.

Margaret, daughter of Edward Pilkinton, 4th of January. Plague.
Widdow Pilkinton, 11th January. Plague.
—, daughter of Edward Pilkinton, January 14th. Plague.

Although mitigated, the plague continued to linger in the parish until May 1666, when it entirely ceased. One hundred and fifty-eight victims to this terrible scourge are recorded in the West Ham registers during the ten months that it infected the neighbourhood. As the mortality, from other causes, was during that period considerably above the average, we may conclude that it generally was an unhealthy season.

There is a tone of great simplicity in the registration of the deaths at this period, which implies that the population was small and primitive. Thus :

Richard Tanner, that was drowned in a pond at Playstowe, was burried January 9th, 1660.

A poor childe, named John, burried from Stratford, November 10th, 1662.

Joane Clarke, of the Dog's hed in the pott, was burried March 12th, 1663.

A man that was killed and throwne into a pond at Gallow's Green, was burried the 12th day of May, 1664.

Richard, a stranger from Goodwife Wetherall's at the Abbey, was burried the 4th day of December, 1666.

Henry Archer, a poor boy, was burried the 15th day of December, 1666.

The register also records a name so singular, that, did not recurrence of the same name exclude the possibility of error, it would be taken for a mark rather than a surname. During the time of the plague we find the following entry :

Mary, the daughter of was burried the 10th of November, 1665.

And later on :

David, son of was burried 16th of January, 1669.

Whether it was plague or some other awful contagion is not said, but in 1682 a Mr. Millington with Joan his wife, Henry his son, and Susan his daughter, all died in one day the 20th of August and are burried in the north aisle of the church.

If the dates, attached to the vicars in the list afore-mentioned, be correct, the following entry in the parish register must relate to the time that the Rev. John Stanley was vicar :

April 16th, 1689, Peter Paine and his wife and his son Peter and his daughter An, and the parson and his made was blowne up all in one day.

Two instances of longevity are also recorded in the parish register: ·

George Westwood, aged 102, burried April 19th, 1696. and

Arthur Bradshaw, aged about 100, burried September 5th, 1703.

—◇━◇◇◇━—

We now give a list of the monuments and inscriptions, commencing with those inside the church.

MONUMENTS AND INSCRIPTIONS.

There are several monuments of eminent persons, some of which have, in consequence of the renovations and restorations, that have from time to time been made, been removed from their original positions, while the effect of others is almost destroyed by a number of additional seats for the accommodation of an increasing congregation. The inscriptions also on some of the slabs on the floor are more or less obliterated, and others are covered by the pews.

In the Chancel.

On the wall to the right of the altar are two tablets, one in memory of John, eldest son of Robert Faldo, Esq., who died 1613, ten years old. Puer pius, generosus et eruditus.

The other is in memory of Francis, fifth son of Robert Faldo, who died 1632, and of John Fawcitt, gentleman, married to Jane, second sister of the said Francis, who died 1625, and of William Fawcitt, the only son of John, and Ann his eldest daughter, who rest hereunder interred in the dormitory of the Saints and assured hope of the common salvation, 1636. Nondum manifestum quid erimus.

Above these tablets is a monument in memory of the most affectionate husband, the kindest father, and the warmest friend, the Rev. George Gregory, D.D., vicar of this parish, who died May 12th, 1808, aged 53.

His varied learning and distinguished abilities were devoted to the benefit of mankind, excelling in the duties of his sacred profession, religious without bigotry, and pious without ostentation, he enforced by example the precepts he inculcated, by his knowledge, benevolence, and candour, promoting private happiness and public good.

DD

Also a tablet to the memory of Elizabeth Gregory, relict of the Rev. George Gregory, on which is inscribed by her children: In obedience to her wishes they erect no other than this simple memorial of her virtues and their affection.

In the North Aisle of the Chancel.

There is a curious altar tomb,[1] with Gothic ornaments, of considerable antiquity, to which no name has as yet been assigned with any degree of certainty. On the side exposed to view are angels bearing coats of arms, but so choked with repeated coats of whitewash as well as worn by age, that it is difficult, if not impossible to decipher their bearings. The Goldsmiths' arms are easily distinguishable, and in another escutcheon are three coats, one of which resembles that of the see of Canterbury.

In removing this tomb from its former position, between the two pillars on the north side of the altar, to the place it now occupies at the west end of the aisle, a signet ring was found, now in the possession of Mr. Jeremiah Self—of which the accompanying woodcut is a facsimile.

Against the east wall is a handsome monument to the memory of Sir Thomas Foot, late Alderman, and Lord Mayor of London in the year 1650, who departed this life the 12th of October, 1688, in the 96th year of his age, and of dame Elizabeth, his wife, who departed this life 1667. The effigies of the deceased and his lady are life sized, and in an erect position, Sir Thomas dressed in robes, and his lady in an elegant dress, ornamented with lace. The inscription records, that they had four daughters, of whom

The first was married to Sir John Cutler, of London, Knt. and Bart.

---

[1] There is a tradition that this was the tomb of the last abbot Wm. Huddleston.

The second to Sir Arthur Onslow, of Clandon in Surrey, Bart.

The third to Sir John Lewis, of Ledstone in Yorkshire, Knt. and Bart.

The fourth to Sir Francis Rolle, of Tuderley, Hants. Knt.

Adjoining it is a monument to the memory of Mr. James Cooper, with the effigies of the deceased in white marble, as large as life, with a book open in his hand, and of his lady standing by him. Sir James died aged 80, in 1743, and desired that under his effigie, after his name and age, to be written this (or to this purpose):

I believed
In one God, Father, Son and Holy Ghost
Also the Resurrection
And whilst I liv'd I firmly put my trust
In His divine protection.
But now interred I'm covered o'er with dust,
Reader prepare for thereunto you must.

Cooper was a good christian and sincere friend and liberal benefactor to the poor of the parish; besides his other extensive charities, too large to be here inserted. This truth was added by his friends and executors.

These two monuments of Foot and Cooper originally stood in the arches of the north side of the chancel, but were afterwards removed to the place they now occupy.

On the north wall is a monument in memory of Thomas Curtis, of Salway House, Stratford, who died 1862, aged 67, and of Mary, wife of the above, who died 1884, in the 73rd year of her age.

Another monument, partly hidden by the organ, is to the memory of Robert Rookes, Captain of the trained band of this Hundred, descended of the ancient family of Rookes of this parish who hath given a yearly contribution of five pounds to this parish for ever. He had two wives and seven children, and dyed October 5th, 1630. Above the inscription are the effigies of the deceased and his two wives, as well as of his three sons and four daughters in posture of devotion.

Also a monument in memory of Joseph Cleypole of this parish, who died 1826, aged 68, and of Sarah his wife, who died 1837, and of their children.

In the same aisle is a large altar tomb of unusual size to the memory of Sir Philip Hall, Knt., who departed this life 1745, aged 68, of dame Sarah his wife, who died, aged 46, in 1742, of Henry Hall citizen and merchant of London, and Stephen Hall, M.D. son of Henry Hall.

In the South Aisle of the Chancel.

There is a handsome marble monument to Sir James Smyth, Knt.,[1] sometime Lord Mayor of London (1684) who was the second son of Sir Robert Smyth, of Upton, Knt. and Bart., (who also lyes interred near this place) and of Elizabeth, wife of the said Sir James Smyth, who was the eldest daughter and one of the coheirs of Arthur Shurley, Esq., of an ancient family at Isfield in Sussex, and departed this life 1689 in the 29th year of her age, and of Elizabeth and Shurley, their two daughters, who dyed in their minority, and of Sir James, their son, who was created a baronet of Great Brittain, the 2nd day of December in the first year of King George, and dyed 1716, in the 32nd year of his age, and of Mirabella his wife, who was one of the daughters of Sir Robert Legard, Knt., and died in the 30th year of her age.

On the wall is a tablet to the memory of Sir Hervey Smyth, Bart., who died 1811, aged 77, an accomplished scholar, reared in the Court of George II. and trained to the military profession under Prince Ferdinand, a man of honour and enterprise; he was selected by General Wolfe as one of his companions in arms; at the battle of Quebec he recieved a wound, which impaired his health and abridged his usefulness; the latter part of his life was spent in continual suffering.

This tribute of respect is placed near his remains by his affectionate sister Anne Mirabella Henrietta Brand.

Another monument, of alabaster with columns of black marble, is to the memory of William Fawcitt, gentleman, of Upton. He endowed with an honest salary a chapel of Haughton Gil and built

---

[1] The family of Smyth resided at Upton, in the mansion afterwards known as Ham House, the residence of Samuel Gurney, Esq.

there a free school and gave 20s for a yearly sermon on the 5th of November. He died 1631, aged 60. Over the tablet are the effigies of the deceased in a recumbent position, leaning on a skull with a book in his hand, and above him, kneeling at a desk, of his widow, and her second husband William Toppesfield, a Justice of Peace, at whose expense the monument was erected in the year 1636.

Also a monument in brass to the memory of Thomas Staples, of West Ham, deceased 1592, hath given XXs. a yeare for ever yearly to be distributed to the poore of the saide parishe. The tablet contains the effigies of the deceased and his four wives, Anne, Margary, Denise and Alice.

Above it is a tablet to the memory of John Carstairs, F.R.S., merchant of London, of Stratford Green in this parish and of Warboys and Woodthurst in Hunts, who died 1837, aged 80 years, and of Cecil his wife, who died 1834, aged 76, and of Margaret their second daughter, wife of Henry Cheape, Esq., of Rossie Co. of Fife, N.B., who died without issue aged 35 years.

Also a tablet to the memory of Sarah Maria Jones, second daughter of John Chambres Jones of Brynsteddford, in Denbighshire, by Sarah, his second wife. She died of consumption, 1835.

On the south wall of the same aisle is a marble tablet to the memory of Sir John Henry Pelly, Bart., F.R.S., late of Upton in this parish, born 1777, died 1852. He was for 18 years Deputy Master of the Corporation of Trinity House, for 30 years Governor of the Hudson Bay Company, also Governor of the Bank of England, all of which most responsible and important offices he filled with the most uncompromising principle, undeviating integrity, and remarkable industry and ability, added to which he always took an active part in parochial matters and exercised a most beneficent influence on all local interests. He died universally honoured and beloved, and his loss will be long severely felt and regretted. For salvation he looked to Jesus the author and finisher of our faith. His remains are interred in the family vault at Plaistow.

Another tablet is to the memory of Samuel Jones Vachell, Esq., who died 1831. He was for 31 years a resident of this parish, to which he was upon his death a considerable benefactor.

Also Mary Ann Jenyns—only surviving child of Samuel John

Vachell and Sarah his wife — wife of Charles Jenyns, Esq. She died without issue 1837.

Also a monument in memory of Lieut. Col. Scott of the third regiment of Foot Guards, only son of Hugh Scott of Galashiels in the Shire of Tiviot Dale, North Britain. He married Elizabeth, daughter of Robert Harward, Esq., Captain in the Royal Navy. By her he had three children, namely, John and Sarah, who lie here interred, and Elizabeth still surviving. He was a person deservedly esteemed as having to his merits in the military capacity happily added the truly valuable character of the gentleman and the christian. Born 1685, died 1737.

On the opposite side of the chancel is a large monument erected by the Rev. Nicholas Buckeridge, A.M., to the memory of all his children deceased, with the figures of a son in a gown, and his daughter, both kneeling, and of another daughter on the top of the monument also kneeling, besides the heads in marble of four more children dying young—bearing the following inscription:

Near this place lie interred the bodies of Amhurst, eldest son of Nicholas and Eleonore Buckeridge, A.M., and fellow of St. John's College, Oxon., who died 1709, in the 29th year of his age, and of Elizabeth, their eldest daughter, who died 1698, in the 16th year of her age, and of Eleonore their second daughter, who died 1710, and of Arabella, their third daughter, who died about 11 months old. Of these, Amhurst and Eleonore lived to be remarkable for their great dutifulness to their parents, for their most affectionate kindness to and fondness for one another, and for their being inoffensive and obliging to everybody. These both died of small-pox in 13 days' time, one after the other. and whether the grief of Eleonore for her brother's death or the small-pox contributed most to her death, is uncertain. They were indeed lovely and pleasant in their lives, and but a very little divided in their deaths. And to their dear memory is this monument erected.

Below is the following inscription :

To the memory of the Rev. Nicholas Buckeridge, A.M., sometime Fellow of the St. John Baptist College in Oxford, and Rector of Bradwell juxta mare in this county, who departed this life 1727 in the 79th year of his age. And is gone to receive the reward of a long life, well spent in the constant exercise of all christian and social virtues.

Go reader and do thou likewise.

At the foot of the monument is a slab in memory of Eleonore, wife of Nicholas Buckeridge. She died 1724, 68 years old.

On the floor in the Chancel.

Mrs. Jane Pyot, wife of John Pyot, daughter of Sir Robert Smyth, died 1684, aged 28.

The Right Honourable Louisa Carolina Isabella Hervey, daughter of John, Earl of Bristol, and wife of Sir Robert Smyth of Isfield in Sussex. As a matron equal to all stations, worthy of the highest, content with the humblest, in beauty an ornament even to her race, in economy an example to her sex, in benevolence an honour to her species.

James Wittewrongle, the son of James Wittewrongle, a Fleming, a singular friend to the ministers of the city, a Maecenas of studious youth, a favourer of piety and learning. Died the 5th of June, 1622. aged 64.

Mrs. Mary Batailhey, alias Shirley, 1702. Resurgam.

Sarah Grimstead, wife of Valentine Grimstead, many years inhabitant of this parish, died 1804, aged 70. She was the fourth daughter of the late James Hatch, Esq.

William Tuder, citizen and merchant tailor, 1653, and Elizabeth his wife, 1654.

Walter Cope, 1767, and Elizabeth his wife, 1771.

Zachariah Taylor of Stratford Langthorne, mariner, who died 1710, in the 77th year of his age, his daughter Priscilla, who died 1690, and Mrs. Elizabeth Taylor.

Rachel Burford. She was the daughter of the late Roger Burrow, Esq., of the city of Exeter, and wife of the Rev. James Burford, A.M., curate and lecturer of the parish.

In suavity of temper, accomplishment of mind, and the truly christian virtues of simplicity and love she never was surpassed. She died 1814, leaving her children too young to appreciate the irreparable loss of a most exemplary and affectionate mother in her 31st year.

Samuel James Vachell, 1831.

Daniel Prat, citizen of London, 1666. Jane, his widow, 1709, aged 92. John Prat, gentleman, son of Daniel Prat, 1699.

Hic jacet Edwardus Salwey, obiit xxii July, Anno Dom. MDCCXXXI, aet. LXXIX. Vir bonus.

Elizabeth Tollet,[1] daughter of George Tollet, Esq., Commissioner of the navy in the reign of Queen Anne, died 1754, aged 60. Religion, justice and benevolence appeared in all her actions, and her poems in various languages are adorned with extensive learning applied to the best purposes.

Edward Towne, Esq., a gentleman esteemed for his great probity, candour, and generosity. He died 1744, aged 38 years. Also Sarah his wife, daughter of Benjamin Milner, 1730, and Lydia his second wife, 1750.

Also a slab in memory of John Shadwell of Plaistow, who died 1798, 77 years old, and of Mrs. Ann Shadwell, wife of John, who died 1807, aged 87.

In the South Aisle of the Church.

On the south wall are several tablets:

In memory of David Morgan, son of John and Sophia Morgan, born 1778, died 1857, also of Maria his wife, daughter of Robert Morris, Esq., of Barnwood, Co. of Gloucester, born 1785, died 1857, for nearly 40 years respected inhabitants of this parish.

---

[1] Elizabeth Tollet, who in early life was honoured by the friendship of Sir Isaac Newton and whose nephew George Tollet is well known for his valuable notes on Shakespeare, was born in 1694. Her father observing her extraordinary genius gave her so excellent an education, that besides great skill in music and drawing, she spoke fluently and correctly the Latin, Italian and French languages, and well understood history, poetry and the mathematics. These qualifications were dignified by an unfeigned piety and the moral virtues, which she possessed and practised in an eminent degree. The former part of her life was spent in the Tower of London, where her father had a house—the latter at Stratford and West Ham. She would not suffer her works to appear until she herself was beyond the reach of envy and applause. Her Latin poems are written in a truly classical taste. (Nichol's Coll. of Literary Notes.)

Sacred to the memory of Judith Smith, born 1754, at the Grove, Stratford, in this parish; where she passed a long and useful life, died 1832, aged 77. Universally esteemed and regretted.

To Samuel Billingay, Esq., and Ann Billingay, of Plaistow in Essex, 1823 and 1837, aged 70 and 74.

To Carolus Spearman, died 19 years old, 1725.

On the floor in the same aisle are the following slabs:

Robert Wright, and Mrs. Katherine Dennis, daughter of the above.

Thomas Shirley, who died 1793, in the 86th year of his age.

Mary Anne, wife of Rear Admiral John Gascoigne, 1748.

Her truly righteous spirit was recalled to heaven 1748, in the 46th year of her age, where only her inestimable goodness whilst on earth can be exceeded. It was accompanied by that of their tenth child, preceded by those of their two first-born sons, Nicholas and James, and one daughter Anne, who all died infants, and followed by the fourth son John, 1749, in the 13th year of his age.

Also the above named Rear Admiral John Gascoigne, who died 1753, aged 61. Likewise William Gascoigne, who died 1793, and James who died 1793, aged 83 years

John Dallaway, Surgeon of Stratford.

Mrs. Jane Lodge, daughter of John Lodge, late of London, Hamborough merchant, 1752.

Susannah Newell, wife of Richard Keys, Esq., 1787.

Roach, daughter of Thomas Roach and Katherine his wife, 1728.

Jeremiah Dummer, of New England, distinguished by his excellent learning, probity and humanity, who died 1739, aged 58.

In the North Aisle of the Church.

There are on the wall several hatchments, besides a monument in memory of Catherine, eldest daughter of George and Mary Dick of Bombay, who died 1791, on her voyage from England to India.

Also of Ann, the second daughter of the said George and Mary.

Also of William and James.

EE

On the floor in the North Aisle are the following slabs:

Edmund Montague, sometime the Deputy Governor of Fort St. David's in the East Indies, who departed this life 1730. Aged 78.

William Millington, who with Joan his wife, Henry his son, and Susan his daughter, all died on the 20th of August, 1683.

> Stay, courteous reader, spend a teare
> Upon the dust that slumbers here,
> And whilst thou read'st the state of me
> Think on the glass that runs for thee.

Also Catherine his daughter, wife of Daniel Ingole, 1689. Daniel Ingole, citizen and pewterer of London, who died 1691, aged 53.

In memory of James Allen Furnass, 1793.

Thomas Hewlett, 1775.

Thomas Haynes, of the parish of St. Botolph, citizen, armourer, and brazier of London, who died 1713, aged 62.

> Here lies the best of men
> Whose life is at an end,
> The best of husbands
> And the truest friend;
> Who feels I hope, as I do hope to be
> Happy with him to all eternity.

Phillip Dermitte, late of this parish, 1752.

William Vooght, 1819, and Mrs. Catherine Vooght, wife of the above.

Mary Tilson, wife of Walter Tilson, 1665.

In the Nave.

On the north wall is a tablet to the memory of William Ravenscroft, citizen and mercer of London, who died 1718, aged 84 years, also of Margaret his wife, who died 1741, aged 95 years.

> She did good and not evil
> All the days of her life,
> She opened her mouth with wisdom
> And on her tongue was the law of kindness.

Here also lie the bodies of two children of M. Frances Ball, daughter of William and Mary Ravenscroft, who in her dutiful regard to the memory of the best of parents has caused this monument to be erected.

On the same wall is a tablet to the memory of Honor, wife of John Pickering Peacock, of Whalebone House, in the parish of Dagenham, in this county, who died 1831, aged 45. Also of the above named John Pickering Peacock, who died 1845, aged 75.

On the south wall is a tablet to the memory of Baynbridge Buckeridge, 1732.

Another to the memory of William Ravenscroft, merchant, 1718.

His widow Margaret died 1741, aged 95. Also two children of Mrs. Frances Ball, daughter of the above.

On the walls of the chancel arch are two monuments, one to the memory of the Venerable Hugh Chambres Jones, M.A., Archdeacon of Essex, and Treasurer of the Cathedral of St. Paul in London, Vicar of West Ham from 1809 to 1845. During his incumbency, marked throughout by sound judgment, sagacity and uniform kindness of heart, two district churches were built in this parish. He died at Brynsteddford, near Conway, in 1869, 87 years old.

Also in memory of Ellen his wife, eldest daughter of John Carstairs, Esq., of Stratford Green, Essex, and Warboys, Hunts. She died at Brynsteddford 1861, in the 69th year of her age.

This monument is erected by M. G. Jones, the only surviving sister of her beloved brother.

The other monument is erected in affectionate remembrance of the Rev. Abel John Ram, M.A., of Clonatin, County of Wexford, born 1804, died 1883. Honorary Canon of Rochester, Rural Dean of Barking, and Vicar of this parish A.D. 1845 to 1868.

Holding forth the word of life.—Phil. 2. 16.

A workman that needeth not to be ashamed.—2 Tim. 2. 15.

On the floor are the following monuments, now covered by pews:

William Wight of this parish, who departed this life 1683, aged 51. Also Mary his wife, 1688, aged 51. Also John Wight, son of William and Mary Wight, died 1704, aged 45. Also Richard Wight who died 1713, aged 53, and Martha his wife, who died 1726, aged 58.

Major John Wicks, who died 1728, aged 80, and Mary his wife, aged 75.

John Pickering Peacock, merchant tailor, who died 1755, aged 73. Also John Peacock, who died 1801, aged 61 years, and Mary Peacock, wife of the above, who died 1805, aged 61. Also Mrs. Honor Peacock, wife of John Pickering Peacock. Also a son of John and Mary Peacock, who died 1831, aged 45. Also John Pickering Peacock, who died 1845, aged 75.

John Gray, who died 1826, aged 36.

Peter Hartopp, who died 1713, aged 61 years, and M. Hartopp, who died, 1712.

Susan Peck, of this parish, who died . . . . aged 22 years.

Jonathan Winthorp, also his eldest daughter, and Elizabeth, wife of Jonathan Winthorp, 1738.

In the Gallery of the south aisle are the following monuments:

Anne, relict of the Hon. James Mighells, sometime Vice Admiral of the Blue and afterwards Comptroller of the Royal Navy (who was buried at Lowestoft, the place of his birth 1733). In gratitude to the memory of so excellent a mother, who in every other character of life was also truely deserving, the three surviving daughters have caused this monument to be erected. She died 1741.

Henry Colchester and Penelope his wife who lived together in the greatest union and friendship. As they conducted themselves by the strictest rules of virtue and religion, so they passed through the duties of husband and wife, father and mother, master and mistress with the greatest satisfaction and pleasure to themselves, their children, and servants. The many charitable and good offices they did, while living, make their memory valuable to all that knew them and their deaths much lamented.

Four children and two grandchildren are also here interred. He died 1700. She survived him 19 years, during which time she continued a widow, and dedicated her time to the service and the good of her posterity. She died 1719.

The Rev. Jonathan Reeves, late lecturer of this parish during the space of 17 years, died 1787, aged 68, leaving a widow and eight children; likewise Mrs. Elizabeth Reeves and their children, 1790.

In the west end of the church under the belfry is a monumental pillar in memory of the Rev. John Finch, LL.B., who officiated in this church, and was lecturer of St. Peter's the Poor, in Broad Street. He left this vale of sorrow the 6th day of May, 1748, in the 50th year of his age. He was a divine, truly pious, affable, humane, sincere and excellent preacher. Benevolent to all, charitable, a most kind master, esteemed and loved by everybody, especially his most intimate friends, who lament the loss of so worthy a man.

On the floor are the following monuments:

Thomas Bland, of Maryland Point, died 1738.
Captain William Hill, died 1703.
Thomas Selby, of Mitcham, 1745.
John Hiett, 1719.
John Draigall, 1771.
Mark Macarthy, merchant, 1738.

In the Vestry is a mural tablet which has the following inscription:

Here lieth Nicolas Avenant, once merchant tailor of London, who gave five pounds and four shillings a year for ever to be distributed in breade upon every Sunday after morning prayer two shillings amongst four-and-twenty of the poorest dwellers in the parishe, by the discretion of the churchwardens for the time being, for ever and for performance hereof he gave six acres and a rood of land in Wytteringes Meade in this parishe and died the first day of July, Anno Dom. 1599.

WEEVER, in his "Funeral Monuments," records several tombs and inscriptions, of which, however, now no traces can be discovered; some of them rather confirm the tradition of King Henry VIII's. occasional residence at Green Street House, an ancient mansion on the confines of the two parishes.

Hîc jacet Henricus Kettleby quondam serviens illustrissimi Principis Henrici filii metuendissimi Regis Henrici septimi, qui obiit 8 die Augusti 1508.

Hîc sub pede jacet Margarete quondam uxor John Kettleby de com. Wigorn: armig. quae obiit 10 m. Januarii.

Here lieth John Hamerton, Esquyr, Sergeant at arms to Kinge

Henry the eyght, and Edith his wife, and Richard Hamerton his brother, of the parishe of Fedston in the countye of Yorke, which both fell sicke in an houre, and died both in one houre, An. Dom. 1512, on whose sowles Jesus have mercy. Amen.

Of your charite pray for the sowles of Jos. Eglesfield, who died the 13th Aug. 1504, and for the sowle of Edith his wyfe, who died 22nd June, 1533.

Of your charite pray for the sowles of Walter Froste, of West Ham, Esquyr, and Sewar to King Henry the eight, and of Anne his wyff, daughter of . . . . and widow of Richard Caly, merchant of the Staple of Calais, which Anne died the 23rd Oct. 1527.

——◦>•⊂══>•◦<◦——

In the Churchyard.

There are the following monuments:

William Pragell, 1579.　　John Pragell, Sen., 1590..
Richard Pragell, 1618.

Urselina, wife of Captain John Pragell, Governor of Berwick and Chief General under Queen Elizabeth for the North 1616. Clement Pragell, who was born in this parish. He left for ever 5 pounds a year to the poor of the same and twenty shillings a year for ever for the keeping this and the next tomb in repair. He died 1680, aged 37 years.

> Richard Gregory, gentleman, 1658.
> Nathaniel Wickham, M.D., 1727.
> Mr. Robert Watts, 1730.
> John Tennant, merchant, 1737.
> John Henniker, merchant, 1749. Dame Anne, wife of Sir
> 　　John Henniker, Bart. (buried in Rochester Cathedral),
> 　　1792.
> Henry Turner, Esq., (married 50 odd years).
> Middleton Howard, gentleman, 1759.
> Joseph Ball, barrister at law, 1760.
> Mrs. Sarah Jennings, 1773, aged 95.
> John Oxenford, Esq., 1780.
> Edward Waldo, Esq., 1783.
> William Palmer, Esq., 1786.

The Rev. Charles Cropley, M.A., Fellow of King's College,
  Cambridge, 1794.

Mrs. Thomasine Gouge, widow, 1755.

John Newe, Esq., 1763, aged 85, and Mrs. Elizabeth
  Newe, 1743.

Elizabeth wife of William Vere, Esq., 1759.

Theodore Hodshon, Sen., Esq., 1768.

John Davy, Esq., 1769.

Mrs Jane Holbrook, late wife of Thomas Holbrook, Esq., of
this parish, who died 1806, in the 89th year of her age, and of
Thomas Holbrook, many years an inhabitant of this parish, who
died 1811, aged 72. Also Thomas Willis, who died 1809 aged 58,
and three of his children,—and Mrs. Sarah Willis, who died 1833,
aged 66.

Robert Hill, late of the Minories in the parish of St. Botolph,
Aldgate, (1791), also Mr. James Hill, brother of the above, (1805),
likewise Mrs. Rose Hill, mother of the above Robert and James
Hill, (1805), also Mr. Robert Hill, father of the above Robert and
James, who died 1806, in the 80th year of his age.

Thomas Cooper, blacksmith and farrier of Stratford, who died
1768, aged 53.

His tombstone bears the following quaint inscription:

> "My sledge and hammer hath declin'd,
> My bellows too have lost their wind,
> My fire's extinct, my forge decay'd
> And in the dust my vice is laid.
> My coal is spent, my iron's gone
> My last nail's driven, my work is done."

John Atkins,[1] died 1757, aged 73.

---

[1] John Atkins was a surgeon in the navy and resided during the latter part of
his life at Plaistow, where he died. He has published a book called "The Navy
Surgeon" (1732), and "A Voyage to Guinea, Brazil, and the West Indies" (1735).

James Anderson,[1] LL.D., died 1808 aged 69.

George Edwards,[2] F.R.S., died 1773, aged 81 years, formerly Librarian to the Royal College of Physicians, in which capacity as well as in private life he was universally and deservedly esteemed. His natural history of birds will remain a monument of his knowledge.

---

[1] James Anderson, a native of Hermiston, near Edinburgh, a well known writer of agricultural, commercial and political essays. The University of Aberdeen conferred upon him the title of LL.D. In 1784 he was employed by the Government in investigating the North British fisheries, a subject on which he had previously written. In 1791 he commenced the publication of "The Bee," a weekly magazine, which had great success. About the year 1797 he removed to the neighbourhood of London and some time afterwards took a house near the church of West Ham, where he began publishing his "Recreations in Agriculture." During the latter part of his life he devoted himself almost entirely to the relaxation of a quiet life and particularly the cultivation of his garden, which was now become the miniature of his past labours, and here he died in 1808. His writings are very numerous; besides the agricultural articles contributed to the "Monthly Review" and some articles in the first edition of the "Eucyclopaedia Britannica," he published a "Practical Treatise on Chemistry," "Observations on Slavery," "Letters to General Washington," on an "Universal Character," etc.

[2] Mr. Edwards was born at Stratford in this parish in the year 1693. His "History of Birds" raised his name as the greatest ornithologist, who had ever appeared. After a long series of years, the most stupendous application and the most extensive correspondence, he completed in 1764 his "Gleanings of Natural History," a work, which contains engravings and descriptions of more than 600 subjects in natural history not before described or delineated. He also added a general index in French and English, which was afterwards completed with the Linnaean names by that great naturalist Linnaeus himself, who honoured him with his friendship and correspondence.

In the year 1769 he retired to a small house at Plaistow, where he died. His latter years were much embittered by a cancerous complaint, which deprived him of the sight of one of his eyes, but it was nevertheless remarked, that in the severest paroxysms of misery, he was scarcely known to utter a single complaint. Having completed his 80th year and become emaciated with age and sickness he died 1773 and was interred in the church yard of West Ham, his native parish, where his executors erected a stone with the above inscription to perpetuate his talents as artist and zoologist.

On the east side of the church-yard are ten alms-houses, built by the parish on the site of two cottages and gardens, left by John Newman, in 1636, and now inhabited by twenty poor women over sixty years old, each of whom receives three shillings and four pence weekly, and twenty shillings at Christmas. The vacancies are supplied by the different district boards, in rotation. There are also two alms-houses in Gift Lane, left by Roger Harris, in 1633, which have been rebuilt by subscription, and now provide homes for six more poor women.

Besides the alms-houses there are numerous bequests to the poor of West Ham, amounting in the aggregate to about £600 per annum, left from time to time by various benefactors, and vested in official Trustees, by whom they are now administered, pursuant to a decree of the Charity Commissioners, dated the 28th August, 1870.

The late Mr. Samuel Gurney, of Ham House, also left £1000 Consols, for a new clock at All Saints' Church, West Ham, and for maintaining several other clocks in the parish.

The Bonnell's School, at the north-east corner of the church-yard, was established and endowed, in 1769, with large sums of money, left by Sarah Bonnell, in 1761, for the education and clothing of poor girls; its income of £300 a year and upwards is derived from dividends on Stock. In consequence of the Elementary Education Act of 1870, and in conformity with the Endowed Schools Act of 1869, the old scheme, which was originally intended for the poor exclusively, was repealed and abrogated as far as relates to the management of the Foundation, and a new scheme was established, in 1873, to assist education for the middle classes. A governing body of 12 persons was thereupon appointed for the management of the Trust. A school for girls of the middle classes having in the meantime been erected in Ham Lane by funds realized from the sale of some of the Stock, the Governors of the Trust established a system of exhibitions tenable at the school, which entitled the holders to total or partial exemption from entrance or tuition fees. Forty exhibitions—the original number provided for in Mrs. Bonnell's will — were conferred upon poor girls, that is to say, one-third upon girls who were either orphans or children of necessitous parents, and two-thirds upon girls passing out of the elementary schools within the parish of West Ham.

Round the church, the village of West Ham is clustered. Many of the surrounding houses, which showed signs of great antiquity,

West Ham Church.

have in course of time been taken down; the "King's Head" public house, a low browed old-fashioned building, has within recent years also been removed and made room for a more modern and more fashionable edifice.

Between West Ham village and what is now called Upton Cross, is the "Lady-Well Field" (*see page* 126), which like most of the open spaces of this locality, is now well nigh covered with rows of dwellings. Nearly opposite the north-east corner of this field stands a large mansion, formerly known as "Upton Lane," now called "The Cedars," forming with its picturesque grounds of about 6 acres a distinct and as yet private part of West Ham Park. Of this house we shall have occasion to speak in the next chapter.

Before we, however, conclude this chapter, it may not be devoid of interest, to insert here a few extracts from a manuscript, which was found among the papers of the late Sir John Henry Pelly. The writer, who gives neither name nor date of his compilation, was by calling a farmer, and appears to have been a constitutional grumbler. The book contains extracts from the canons of the church, from the writings of divines, lawyers etc., and from the vestry books, besides other matters relating to the duties of the parochial clergy and officers. Amongst the memoranda several facts are stated, which are not only interesting in themselves, but also throw a great deal of light upon the state of affairs in this neighbourhood as well as on the customs and practices obtaining in this parish at the period, to which they refer.

The manuscript is headed:

Some general observations on the parrish of West Ham, in Essex, containing the villages of Stratford Langthorne, West Ham (proper), Upton and Plaistow, and then proceeds:

"The vicarage of West Ham is endowed with some glebe lands, but with no tithes, there being a 'modus' in lieu. Although the vicarages are generally endowed with some tithes, the tithes of the whole, and great part of the lands of the parish belonged to the Abbey, which maintained a vicar or curate to do the ministerial offices of the parish. His whole allowance was the 'modus,' which now subsists of four pence an acre on feeding lands; but he had his maintenance in the monastery. At the dissolution of the monastery the Court seized upon all its Temporals, and left to the vicar no more than the four pence an acre on feeding grounds. The tithes and lands were sold or granted on lease. So the whole great tithes fell into the hands of Lay Impropriators — I say, the great tithes, for there are no small tithes demandable, or payable of any person.

But as the parrish increased in buildings and inhabitants, and some lands have been bequeathed to the vicarage, the living is now valued at £250 or £300 a year, which arises from the offerings, the pewage, the glebe lands, house and premises, 'surplus' fees, and monies left for particular sermons, etc.

This large parrish is one among the poorest parrishes, I believe, within seven miles of the Bills of Mortality. The householders of the parrish, by the best information I can get, are in all about five hundred and seventy, of which only three hundred and sixty or thereabouts pay to the parochial taxes. Above two hundred of the householders are so very poor, that they are not able to pay any tax whatsoever.

There is but a very small trading. The shopkeepers for the most part can hardly subsist and yet they pay a very large proportion of the taxes; and they complain very much of the great market of London within three miles of them. And there are not many persons, considering the largeness of the parrish, that are possessed of estates, — and some of these provide themselves in great measure in London, or buy of the Country 'Higlars.'

I fear, the having upwards of sixty public Ale Houses in the parrish is no indication of riches among us;—I believe the contrary. I never yet heard of any one that gained any great matter by it. A bare subsistence, which very few can gain, without some other employment, as a labourer, gardener, coachman, etc. Certainly that parrish must be in an unhappy situation, and must show great Symptoms of Poverty, where much above one part in three of the Houses are Inhabited by Ale House people, or in the occupation of people unable to bear any of the Burthens or Taxes of the Parrish. But I should stop here, I have I fear offended too much already in mentioning the Poverty of the place; 'tis a Doctrine hardly to be suffered, and will be very ill relished.

I must say then little of my Brother Farmers. We see. We know. We feel. The planting of Potatoes, indeed, sometimes helps us to pay our Rents, and that perhaps not once in three years. But we have the pleasure of Employing and Maintaining numbers of the poor, tho' we cannot afford to pay the after Reckonings of our Parrish feasts. We know the Burthen of the Parrish Impositions lies heavy upon us. We, chiefly, pay the Reckonings of Parrish Treats, tho' not there. And yet what ungenerous treatment do we receive at our Vestrys, when we dare complain of Poverty, or the heavy Burthen imposed upon us. But for fear of offence I shall finish this Head."

Then follow a number of extracts from books of law, as well as extracts from vestry books with comments.

EXTRACTS FROM VESTRY BOOKS.

'At a Vestry held the 3d of Sept. 1656. At this vestry Richard Graves was chosen Parrish 'Register' in the place of Mr. Lawford, and ordered that Jeremiah Royston, Esq., one of the Justices, be desired to give him the oath and establishment in the said office.

'At a Vestry held the 3d of Sept. 1663. Upon consideration of the services of William Norrington (vestry clerk) upon the affairs of the Parrish at their Vestry Meetings and to the end, that all orders of the vestry may be Registered and kept on Record, we do order and agree, that the Head Churchwardens shall pay unto the said William Norrington the sum of three pounds for his attendance on this Vestry, and fairly entering into a Register Book all orders of the Vestry. And that he shall also have two shillings and six pence a day, for each day, that he shall spend in auditing the accounts of the Parrish, or for any other Publick Service for them besides the Vestry days.'

"This Vestry Clerk performed his Duties carefully and faithfully as the Books will shew, if they come to light again, and 'tis certain for this small 'Sallery' he did five times the Business the present clerk does. His capacity was good, his understanding clear, and his Integrity little disputed, and by examining the books, they shew he had the good of the parrish at heart."

'At a Vestry held the 24th of Sept. 1666. Ordered, that the order of Vestry of the 3d Sept. 1663 concerning the allowance of three pounds a year to William Norrington for Registering the Actions of the Vestry be continued.'

"Though it may now be thought, that these were small wages for a Vestry Clerk, yet I verily think that there are Honest, sober men at this time very capable of doing the business of the Vestry, that would gladly accept the place, at the same wages of Three Pounds a year.

This Vestry Clerk died about the year 1697, having been Vestry Clerk about 34 years, very well satisfied with his wages. He was a laborious, careful man, understood the Business, and did his duty to the satisfaction of all People. John Hodgekins succeeded him, to whom he had married his Daughter.

This Vestry Clerk was an attorney regularly bred, and performed his duty Fairly and Faithfully, and kept the fair Book duly filled up, and always willingly produced the said fair Book of Orders to any Parrishioner that desired to see it.

But this Book is now secreted and hid, as I am told, so that no one parrishioner can have recourse to it."

'1697. John Hodgekins had three pounds a year as Vestry Clerk, raised in 1700 to £4, provided he shall constantly and readily attend all Vestrys.'

Signed by John Smith, Vicar.

"This gentleman died in the year 1726, having been in that office near thirty years, well content and satisfied with his wages, and his son John Hodgekins succeeded him, and had the same wages of four pounds a year.

This gentleman died in the year 1736; the office had continued in his family about seventy three years, during most of which time the greatest Sallery allowed to the Vestry Clerk was not more than four pounds a year, if we may believe the orders of Vestry.

Never was any Parrish better served; they were men of knowledge and understanding, every way capable of doing the Parrish Business, and had capacity to perform it, and the Death of the last has been a Loss and Misfortune to the Parrish, who sensibly feel it.

They were not three half-witted sottish fellows, they were real gentlemen, they knew their business and were not the little low Scrub tools of any insignificant despicable Churchwarden.

William Norrington the grandfather was a man of Substance, of Real Estate. He married his daughter to Mr. John Hodgekins, an attorney, and Bequeathed his estate to him. Hodgekins had a large family, which he bred up in a genteel manner, and left the estate as he found it. The son, John Hodgekins, was bred a regular attorney, a very understanding Person, very ready at Business, of Quick and Solid parts, and of great Use and Service to the Parrish.

The present Clerk succeeded him, Hugh Wyat,[1] Vicar, at the yearly wages of ten pounds."

---

[1] As Hugh Wyat was appointed Vicar of West Ham, in 1727, we may assume that the manuscript was written about the beginning of the 18th century.

The following extracts refer to the Beadles.

OF THE BEADLES.

'At a Vestry held the 5th of March 1669: That Thomas Sutch do for these three years ensuing take care of all new Commers into the Parrish and Prosecute the Law against them, and that every Fortnight he do go about the whole Parrish to that purpose and shall receive forty shillings a year for his pains.'

Mr. Stanley, Vicar.

At a Vestry held the 23rd Septem. 1682.

'Ordered that John Clifford shall be Sexton of the Parrish for one year next ensuing, and as he behaveth, and to have three pounds a year allowed him for the looking after new Commers in, and to Prosecute the Law against them in the whole Parish.'

At a Vestry held the 22nd of April 1701.

'Mr. John Elkin, you are ordered to pay Goodman Purteen the sum of one pound, being for a year's Sallery for his Beadleship, due at Lady-day, last past.'

The following year an order is recorded of a 'payment of ten shillings to William Purteen, the Beadle, being half a year's Sallery.'

"This is the first person in the Books I find called a Beadle. By these three Vestry Orders, it seems he had but twenty shillings a year; certainly he did something for this small Sallery. He did something more than wait at Table at Parrish Feasts, or spending his time in Ale Houses. I am pretty sure that as much business was then done for the Parrish, when the whole charge of Beadles, as it appears was no more than twenty shillings a year, as was done by the three Beadles in the year 1738, 1739, 1740, who cost us in wages and clothes, above fifty pounds; but the poor people must pay it. So that in 36 years the expense for Beadles is raised near fifty pounds.

In the year 1712 I find Jonathan Waget was Beadle of Plaistow ward at the yearly Sallery of Twenty Shillings.

I find nothing else relating to Beadles' wages till the year 1732.

Yet Joshua Alexander, a Baker, was many years Beadle of the Parrish, and his Sallery at most was but four pounds a year, and I think that the man did his Duty and honestly earned his money."

At a Vestry held the 11th of April 1732.

'Joshua Alexander (the son) was chosen Beadle of the Parrish of Westham during pleasure, at the yearly Sallery of Twenty Six Pounds to commence from May Day; and that Mr. . . . . be desired to provide him a great Blew Coat or " Close " Trimmed with red and the Cape laced with gold lace, and Brass Buttons and a Gold Laced Hat.'

Hugh Wyat, Vicar.

"At this time another Beadle was at Westham, at four pounds a year, and a third at Plaistow (all in the same Parrish) at two pounds a year. A fine expense. It was supposed that Joshua Alexander was to Earn this Money by giving up his whole time to the Service of the Parrish.

In the year 1738 we had the Happiness to have a Churchwarden, who was pleased that year to Carry his Authority so far, as to make and provide three coats, and three hats trimm'd as before mentioned, for the three Beadles, without obtaining an order of the Vestry, or even consulting the Parrish. So that by the best Information to be got — since it is impossible to Obtain a Sight either in or out of Vestry of the Churchwardens' Account for that year — the charge the Parrish was at for Beadles was as follows, vizt.:

To Joshua Alexander, his Coat and hat ...	...	£6 10	0
His wages	...	26 0	0
To Church Street Beadle, his wages ...	...	4 0	0
His Coat & Hat	...	6 10	0
To Plaistow Beadle, his wages	...	2 0	0
His Coat & Hat	...	6 10	0
		£51 10	0

As no man can be supposed to know more, than the Editor does, of what service they all three were to the Parrish, so he declares and really believes, that all the three Beadles for three years have not been a real Benefit to the Parrish, to the Value of Five Shillings, without it was Serving some people by waiting at Table, when they were injuriously and Frandulently spending the Parrish Money. And what makes it the more grievous is, that the poor Tradesmen, the Graziers, the Farmers, the Gardeners pay the greatest part of the reekoning.

But certainly neither they nor their Landlords knew or dreamed, that Churchwardens had the power to spend, in one year only, at least sixty pounds in Taverns and Ale Houses, and to give above fifty pounds in one year to support three Lazy Fellows in gold 'close' and Hats and Wages, and who are of very little (if any) real service to the parrish."

The writer then proceeds to deplore the cupidity of the Vicar, the Rev. Charles Vernon, who had delivered in a bill of £3 2s 4d for burying the poor, and also concerning a pension of four pounds a year, that the vicar demands to be paid him.

Amongst other entries in this long chapter of grievances is:

'The following bill was lately sent in, the money demanded, and the money paid for the burial of a person not in the body of the Church, but near the Belfry.

The Parrish for the Bell and ground	...	£—	13	4
The Vicar for the Service in the Desk	...	—	7	6
The Clerk	...	...	...	...	—	4	0
The Sexton ringing the Bell	...	...	—	4	0
Making the Grave deep	...	...	...	—	5	0
The Trussels	...	...	...	...	—	1	0
The Bricklayer making good the Tyling	...	—	7	6
		£ 2	2	4
An overcharge deduct	...	...	...	—	6	2
		£ 1	16	2.'

The next grievances, stated in this remarkable record of parochial troubles, were the expenses incurred by the Church Wardens the day they were sworn in. The writer quotes from the Vestry Book orders on the subject. In 1707 they were not to spend more than £3, and in 1728, the expense was not to exceed £10, which he calls "an illegal Drunken order," and adds "that the same day

(23rd April 1728) the knavish illegal order of spending £20 on the Procession Day was pretended to be made."

He then proceeds:

Concerning the Charges of Procession Day.

"The Parrish of West Ham is computed to be about sixteen miles in circumference; but the Perambulation is supposed to be but five or six miles. Because all to the West is Bounded by the River Lee; all to the South by the River Thames. It is bounded to the North in great measure by Waltham Forest. So it may be reasonably supposed, the Procession of Five or Six Miles cannot be a great expence to the Poor Parrish; I can hardly forebear saying, perhaps the poorest Parrish within seven miles of London. Notwithstanding there are above sixty Public Houses in it."

Vestry Orders.

'1697. No Churchwarden to expend in going a Processioning any sum exceeding the sum of £3.'

'1707. Not to go a Processioning for the future, oftener than once in three years, and then not to bring to Parrish account more than Twenty Pounds for the same.'

"On Assention Day, 1738, they met at Mr. Snow's House at Plaistow (Thomas Snow, Ale House keeper, was Churchwarden in 1734), where the Honest Ale House man very Cheerfully drew what Drink the good Company desired, and the whole Cavalcade being there settled in due order and manner with Fasces before them, to the Terror of Children and Infants, Mr. . . . on Horseback, and the two Churchwardens at their ease in the Coach, having the fear of God before their eyes, and the good of the People in their Hearts, with great toil and labour marched about one mile and a half, and were then happily entertained with Hams, Drink, and Tobacco at the Eagle and Child on the Forest, and being then again new marshalled, Glorious Sight! They travelled again two or three more miles in a very grave and solemn Manner, partly over a dreadful barren Forest, Horrid Thought! The fatigue so great, that with difficulty their wearyed bodies and tired Horses got to George Burgesse's, (George Burgess victualler and Churchwarden 1734) Ale House at Stratford, who happily at that time had tapped a Special Tub of Brown Ale, which they say, was rare good, when topped with Brandy. They there began the last journey, and resolutely in great and Solemn State and in good health travelled a full half mile, and to the great satisfaction of the Cook Wench arrived at the King's Head Ale House in West Ham, where a Noble hot entertainment was provided, and the Day and Evening spent in studying the good of the Parrish, and in drinking Peace and Prosperity among the Fools, that were to pay the Reckoning, I suppose. Oh, Ale! Wine! Punch! and Tobacco, how great are thy Charms!"

"The Vicar can't pretend to claim any Tythe in the Parrish, either great or small; he claims a modus only of four pence an acre of those lands, that are fed. The feeding lands lye by the Rivers. The Uplands are poor, hungry; no profit comes from them to the Vicar. The Uplands are generally lett at about twenty shillings an acre, and the occupiers pay generally four shillings by the acre, and five shillings for the tythe of summer corn, and yet this cruel charge of Processioning falls altogether on the poor people."

With these interesting extracts from the above-mentioned manuscript, we conclude our chapter on West Ham, and proceed to give an account of the villages of Upton and Plaistow, which now are very considerable and important districts of the parish of West Ham.

CHAPTER XI.

(CONTENTS).

THE VILLAGES OF UPTON AND PLAISTOW.

I. UPTON.

T what time the village of Upton first started into being, and had its distinctive name of "Upton," has as yet not been ascertained. It consisted until recently, with the exception of the "Spotted Dog" public house, entirely of private residences more or less surrounded by pretty gardens and pleasure grounds. The village commences at Upton Cross and continues on either side of the road, called Upton Lane, as far as the great high-way leading from Stratford to Romford.

The hamlet situate beyond the highway, known as Forest Gate, and now an important district of the parish of West Ham, used in former years to consist of only two or three gentlemen's houses, and the little wooden hut occupied by the keeper of the "Gate of the Forest," which was generally shut to prevent cattle straying from the Wanstead Flats into the high road.

At the south-east corner of Upton Cross stood formerly two brick houses, one of which was pulled down in the beginning of this century; the other was the property and residence of Henry Hinde Pelly, Esq., an Elder Brother of the Trinity House, and a Captain in the Honourable East India Company's Navy, who owned here a considerable estate, extending on the south side to St. Mary's Church, Plaistow, and towards the east as far as Gipsy Lane, the ancient Green Street, which forms the boundary between the parishes of East and West Ham.

The Pelly family are traditionally said to have fled — in consequence of political troubles — from the Channel islands, where they then were and still are the feudal lords at Sark, to Poole in Dorsetshire. The branch which settled there, about 1582, owned both ships and houses. One of their descendants was Thomas Pelly, whose son John, born at Poole in 1684, was a Captain in the merchant service and an Elder Brother of the Trinity House, and had by Elizabeth Lagthorne a son, also named John, who was born in 1711. He married Elizabeth Hinde, daughter and heiress of Henry Hinde of Aveley and Upton, who possessed a large estate at Upton, in 1745.

To this estate the above-mentioned Henry Hinde Pelly succeeded, in the year 1780. He married Sally Hitchin, daughter and coheir of John Blake, of Westminster, and was High Sheriff of Essex in 1780—1. A singular circumstance occured in connexion with his death, in 1818. His widow wished, immediately after her husband's funeral, to occupy the room which they had used together, and in which she had nursed him in his illness, but she was at length dissuaded from doing so, as it was impossible to get it ready for her so soon. In the night a tremendous gale blew down a stack of chimneys, which fell upon the very bed she had so much wished to occupy, and which must have crushed her to death.

Mr. Henry Hinde Pelly was succeeded by his eldest son John Henry, who was created a baronet in 1840. He enlarged the house, removed the hedges and turned the grass lands into a Park. He died in the year 1852, aged 75, and was buried in the vault of St. Mary's Church, Plaistow, for which he had given the ground; here also repose the remains of Lady Pelly, his widow, who survived him four years. Lady Pelly who was the daughter of Henry Boulton, Esq., of Thorncroft in Surrey, and a most delightful person, resided during her widowhood at a house, on the opposite side of the road, called "The Farm," which has since become the vicarage house of West Ham.

On the death of Sir John Pelly the Upton Estate passed to his eldest son Sir John Henry, the 2nd baronet, who was High Sheriff of Cambridgeshire and Hunts. Having sold the estate, the park adjoining the family residence was, in 1856, partly cut up by making

the London and Tilbury Railway, and partly covered by rows of cottages, while the old mansion remained, until 1865, in the occupation of Mr. George D. Tyser. The garden and pleasure grounds were subsequently (1875) opened as a tea-garden, known as "The Shrubberies," but are now with the rest of the Upton Estate laid out for building purposes.

Although the family of Pelly have long ceased to reside in this locality, the present baronet, Sir Harold, eldest surviving son of the late Sir John Henry Pelly, by his second wife, who succeeded his half-brother Sir Henry Carstairs, in 1877, still possesses considerable property in this parish. (*See page* 144.)

HAM HOUSE.

This mansion, surrounded by a beautiful, well timbered park with fine spreading cedar trees and shrubberies, formerly known as Upton Park, but now called West Ham Park, was for many years the hospitable residence of Mr. Samuel Gurney, so well known in this parish for his philanthropy and benevolence, and has since his decease also temporarily been occupied by Lady Buxton and other members of his family.

There was a house on this site as early as 1566, called "Rooke Hall," from the name of its then possessor William Rooke, who by his will, dated March 5th, 1596, gave a rent charge of £5 yearly, "for bread for the poor of West Ham," which has continued to be paid by its subsequent owners down to the present day. On the death of William Rooke the property devolved on his son Robert, and remained in the possession of his family until the year 1666, when it was sold to Sir Robert Smyth, of Upton, whose name we have seen recorded in the West Ham Register, where he is styled "the worshipful Alderman and Justice of the Peace," before whom the marriages were at that time solemnized, and to whom a handsome monument is erected in the south aisle of the chancel.

The Smyth family sold the estate, after it had been in their possession nearly a century, to Admiral Elliot, who is said to have brought the cones of cedar trees from the Levant, and to have planted them in his garden. The fact, that he afterwards distributed a great number of the young trees among his friends and neighbours, may account for the two cedar trees, which fifty years ago were to be seen on nearly all the lawns of the gentlemen's residences in and near Upton.

In August 1762, Dr. Fothergill, a great botanist and eminent physician of his time, bought the estate. There were at that time growing in a part of the garden, called "the Wilderness," some very fine laurels, also five large Virginia Cedars, being no less than ten inches in diameter and supposed to be some of the first of the kind planted in England. The estate then consisted of the house and offices with about thirty acres of land, afterwards increased to sixty. The walls of the garden enclosed about five acres of land; a winding canal, in the figure of a crescent, divided the garden into two parts, occasionally opening on the sight through the branches of rare exotic shrubs, that lined the walks on its banks. A glass door from the house gave entrance into a suite of hot- and green-houses, nearly two hundred and sixty feet in extent, containing upwards of three thousand four hundred distinct species of exotics, whose foliage wore a perpetual verdure; and in the open ground, in summer, nearly three thousand distinct species of plants and shrubs vied in verdure with the natives of Asia and Africa. Dr. Fothergill spared no pains, in procuring a vast variety of plants and seeds from every part of the habitable globe, from China, the East and West Indies, from Siberia, North America, the new discovered islands, the Alps, and not a few from Africa. Not only did he introduce exotics into his garden at Upton, but thence he transported green Bohea teas

to South America. His garden, formed upon this extensive plan, and yearly improving by large supplies of the more rare indigenous plants and new exotics, arrived at length at that pitch of excellence, as in the opinion of the most competent judge—Sir Joseph Banks— to be esteemed the second in Europe, the Royal Gardens at Kew alone deserving pre-eminence; it was known all over Europe, and foreigners of all ranks asked permission to see it.

It was in this spot that a perpetual spring was realized, where the elegant proprietor sometimes retired for a few hours, to contemplate the vegetable productions of the four quarters of the globe, united within his domain.

When Dr. Fothergill purchased the estate, in 1762, there seems to have been little or nothing in the garden but a fine bay hedge, a larch, an acacia, the Virginia cedars before-mentioned, some large abeiles and fruit trees against the walls — not one other foreign plant or shrub in the whole garden. Whatever there is of this kind in the garden or adjoining fields — says his biographer, Dr. LETTSOM, from whom we have quoted above — was planted by Dr. Fothergill, soon after he came into possession. Some of the trees were fifteen feet high, when planted, and among them were many rare oaks brought out of the first great nursery of North American trees in England, at Fulham, belonging to Gray, an eminent gardener.

In 1764 Dr. Fothergill purchased of Peter Bigot, Esq., a parcel of land extending towards the Romford Road, and not long after he also agreed with the proprietor of the large field, called "Lady Margaret's Field," which adjoined this new purchase, to run a straight line between their respective grounds, the old fence being no other than a broad sandy bank and extremely crooked.

When this was settled and the fence made, a plantation was begun in the large field, called by the Gurney family the "Deer Park;" this plantation consisted principally of oaks of a very useful and durable kind, the acorns of which had been brought from the mountainous parts of Portugal.

Dr. Fothergill is said to have driven daily to London in his "Coach and four," and to have left his grounds by a drive, leading direct from his house to the Romford Road, where a simple but handsome gate between two octagonal lodges formed the entrance to the park. Although the drive had long been disused, the two lodges remained for a long time after, but falling into decay they were finally removed, about thirty years ago.

It appears that after the death of Dr. Fothergill, in 1780, the outlaying portions of the estate were sold, and that the name of the house, which until then had been called "Upton House," was changed into "Ham House."

About the year 1800 it became the property and residence of Mr. James Sheppard, by whom the grounds were carefully kept up. Although the conservatory was greatly diminished, enough remained to make it a marked feature of the place, forming a delightful

HH

addition to the suite of rooms with which it communicated by a glass door.

On the death of Mr. Sheppard, which occured in 1812, his son-in-law Mr. Samuel Gurney purchased the property. Mr. Gurney, the head partner in the firm of Overend Gurney & Co., Lombard Street, London, descended from an ancient family, who had settled in Norfolk at an early period in the history of our country. His father John Gurney, who married, in the year 1775, Catherine, daughter of John Bell, a London merchant, — and granddaughter of Robert Barclay, the well known apologist of the Quakers, and sister of the talented authoress Priscilla Wakefield, — lived at Earlham Hall, near Norwich. Here it was, at this old English mansion, that Samuel Gurney first saw light on the 18th of October, 1786. He was placed in London to learn a business, which resulted in his marriage with Elizabeth Sheppard. With her he lived at Ham

Ham House.

House, which afterwards became his settled residence, and the birth-place of his numerous family, and where, with the exception of one year, he passed his married life.

At this date, many of Dr. Fothergill's curious trees still survived, and although considerable alterations were made, the garden and grounds were carefully preserved. Mr. Gurney threw down the wall on the western side, thus laying the garden open to the park, and spent £500 in American shrubs which, planted in groups, still form a great ornament to the lawn.

The water supply of the canal, which divided the garden, gradually beginning to fail, the canal was partly filled up, but a picturesque little bridge still indicates the southern portion of the same.

On the death of Mr. Samuel Gurney, in 1856, the Ham House Estate came to his eldest son John, who residing at Earlham Hall, near Norwich, survived his father only about three months. The property then devolved upon his son John, grandson of Samuel Gurney, who -living at Sprowston Hall, near Norwich, and having no inclination to leave Norfolk, where his ancestors had been settled for many centuries, decided upon taking down the old mansion, in 1872, the site of which is still indicated by a "cairn," which now serves as a drinking fountain and bears the following inscription: "This fountain is erected on the site of Ham House, for many years the residence of Samuel and Elizabeth Gurney and their family. 1876."

Mr. John Gurney originated the idea of converting Ham House Park into a public recreation ground, and for this purpose he offered it for its estimated value of £25,000; but since he and the Gurney family had always felt a warm interest in the welfare of West Ham, they subscribed £10,000 towards it, provided the remaining £15,000 could be otherwise raised. A local Committee was at once formed and public meetings were held; — it was found, however, that though subscriptions in the district came in freely, £15,000 was a large sum to raise in a neighbourhood which was comparatively poor, and where the rates were high. After every persevering effort, there was still a deficiency of £10,000, and it was then that the local Committee through the late Alderman Sir Thomas White and Mr. Deputy Bedford made an appeal to the Corporation of the City of London, who after very careful consideration unanimously agreed to contribute £10,000, the balance required to complete the purchase. The Corporation also voluntarily agreed to keep the Park in order, so that not one shilling of expense, either directly or indirectly, is borne by the locality.

The Park is under the control of a Committee of fifteen, — eight of whom are nominated by the City Corporation, four by Mr. John Gurney (and since his death by his representatives), and three are elected by the local authorities.

The opening of West Ham Park which took place on July 18th, 1874, will ever be remembered by those who witnessed it. From Bow Bridge to the Park Gates the highway was decorated with thousands of flags of all existing nations, testifying to the universal feeling prevailing on the subject. A procession of 26 carriages, headed by the City Marshal, and including the Deputies, the Chairmen of Committees, the Sheriffs, the Aldermen, the principal officers of the Corporation, and lastly the Lord Mayor (Sir Andrew Lusk, Bart., M.P.) with the Sword and Mace bearers, went from the Guildhall to West Ham Park. The appearance of the Lord Mayor with the rest of the civic dignitaries within the Park was greeted by a tremendous outburst of cheering on the part of thousands of school children, who were ranged on both sides of the pathway from the entrance of the park to the pavilion, where the opening ceremony was held. The proceedings were opened by the City Solicitor, who addressing the Company said "that they were assembled that day to complete the transfer of that delightful spot, known as West Ham Park, from the ownership of a private gentleman to that of the people of the neighbourhood for ever. The Corporation had from time to time in its long history embarked on many matters for the public weal, but the ceremony of that day added for the first time to their care a public recreation ground for the people." After a suitable prayer offered by the Rev. Thomas Scott, vicar of the parish, Mr. John Gurney delivered the title deeds to the Lord Mayor, saying "that it had always been his wish and that of his family to see the park preserved as an open ground for the use of the people of West Ham and the surrounding district, and that he had great pleasure in carrying it out, hoping the people, who used it, would take care of these green fields and these beautiful trees, and that the park might be a lasting blessing to them and their children's children." The Lord Mayor accepted the title deeds amid great enthusiasm, and having expressed his great pleasure to be present on an occasion so full of interest to the inhabitants of the neighbourhood, he declared the park open, and the declaration, being conveyed by gunfire to the crowds outside, was received with the warmest enthusiasm.

After the ceremony, the guests, numbering about 700, were entertained at a sumptuous déjeûner in a pavilion in the grounds, at which the Lord Mayor presided, and various toasts appropriate to the occasion were given and heartily responded to. At 4 o'clock in the afternoon the park was thrown open to the people.

It is impossible to overrate the immense benefit, which by the preservation of this beautiful park has been conferred upon this populous district, where numerous factories send forth their noxious effluvia, and where the streets swarm with children. Every thoughtful and philanthropic man will heartily concur in the sentiment of the following sentence, extracted from a pamphlet, circulated amongst the visitors on the day of the opening "that it seems in the order of things that West Ham Park, so long the residence of two such people, as the late Samuel Gurney and Mrs. Katherine Fry, whose names were for a long period household words for deeds of pure and thoughtful philanthropy, should be dedicated for ever to the healthful enjoyment of all classes of the people and thus be preserved as a blessing at all times."

Mr. John Gurney was Mayor of Norwich in the year 1885—6, and though blind, an affliction which had latterly befallen him, and which he bore with great cheerfulness, he discharged the responsibilities resting upon him as the chief magistrate of that ancient city with great efficiency and zeal. After the expiration of his year of office he went with his family to Cannes, in the south of France, to recruit his health, and there he died rather suddenly on February 24th, 1887, in the prime of life, 41 years old, universally regretted and lamented. His mortal remains were brought over from Cannes and deposited in the little churchyard at Earlham, near Norwich, close by the family residence, where he had spent his youthful days.

"UPTON LANE HOUSE," NOW CALLED "THE CEDARS."

This house, which was for fifteen years, from 1829—1844, the home of Mr. Joseph and Mrs. Elizabeth Fry, stands in grounds of its own, adjoining the Ham House grounds, then the residence of her brother, Mr. Samuel Gurney. It was at that time a moderately sized though commodious dwelling, constructed out of a barn and farm buildings belonging to an ancient, handsome, red brick mansion, of Queen Anne's period, which stood close by, shaded by noble cedar trees, and formerly was the property of Thomas Staples, the tanner, whose memory is commemorated on a brass plate in West Ham Church, as leaving to the poor a rent-charge from land called " Rashetts, lying near Upton Cross." From Staples the property passed to Mr. Mildred, and subsequently to Mr. Spence, after whose death it was purchased by Mr. Samuel Gurney, who pulled down the old brick mansion and threw the new house, which had by him been considerably enlarged, with its beautiful terrace and garden into the Ham House grounds.

It was at this house that Mrs. Elizabeth Fry, the prison reformer and philanthropist of her day, had the honour of receiving Frederic William IV., King of Prussia, to a déjeûner, in the year 1842.

The king's visit to England was official since he was to stand sponsor to the Prince of Wales, the only other exception of the king remaining the exclusive guest of her Majesty Queen Victoria being an official state visit to St. Paul's, and afterwards luncheon at the Mansion House with the Lord Mayor of London.

It was on the 31st of January, 1842, that the king came down to "Upton Lane," after his visit to Newgate, where Mrs. Elizabeth Fry had met him. She describes the visit in her diary in the following words. "There were difficulties raised about his going to Upton, but he chose to persevere. I went with the Lady Mayoress and the sheriffs, the king with his own people. We arrived first. I had to hasten to take off my cloak, and then went down to meet him at his carriage-door with my husband and seven of our sons and sons-in-law. I then walked with him into the drawing room, where all was in beautiful order, neat and adorned with flowers. I presented to the king our eight daughters and daughters-in-law, our seven sons and eldest grandson, my brother and sister Buxton, Sir Henry and Lady Pelly—my brother and sister Gurney he had known before—and afterwards presented twenty-five of our grandchildren. We had a solemn silence before our meal, which was handsome and fit for a king, yet not extravagant. I sat by the king, who appeared to enjoy his dinner, perfectly at ease and happy with us. His Majesty accustomed to dine early, made a hearty meal and said it was the best meal he had eaten in England. He partook twice of oyster soup, a dish he had never heard of before, and which he highly commended. We went into the drawing room after solemn silence, and a few words which I uttered in prayer for the king and queen. We found a deputation of 'Friends' with an address to read to him — this was done — the king appeared to feel it much. We then had to part. The king expressed his desire that blessings might continue to rest on our house."

Although the visit was considered strictly private and every endeavour was made to keep it so, the road from West Ham to "Upton Lane" was crowded with people, and carriages were drawn up the whole length of it, so much so that mounted police were obliged to ride up and down to keep the road clear. The church bells were ringing, flags flying from the steeple, the charity school children drawn up along the church-yard, and the people shouting as the king passed by. The whole village was en fête and presented a scene which the quiet lane to Upton will probably never see again.

Upton House.

This handsome mansion with pretty pleasure grounds and two magnificent cedar trees, is situate in Upton Lane, opposite the east side of West Ham Park, of which it commands a fine view, and was in former years the residence of Sir Philip Hall who, in 1727, was appointed Sheriff of Essex, and then knighted. He bought the estate, in 1729, for the sum of £4947; it then contained 69 acres held free, but charged with the rate for the repairs of the bridges and causeway between Stratford and Bow, which shows it to have been Abbey land. Previous to his death, in 1745, he settled this property by a marriage settlement, dated Nov. 20th, 1741, upon Sarah Barrett Lennard.

In 1809 Upton House, with 6 acres of land attached to it, became the property of Mr. Joseph Bird, and was rented of him by Mr. (afterwards Sir) John Henry Pelly, whose second son Raymond was born there. Mr. Bird sold the estate to Mr. Thomas Aggs, and from him it passed by purchase into the possession of Mr. Joseph Jackson Lister.

In 1870 it was purchased by Mr. John Nutting, who resided there until the year 1882, when he sold it to the British Land Company. Since then the estate has been cut up for building purposes, but the dwelling house, with a small garden attached to it, still remains unchanged, and is now in the possession of Mr. Spedding Curwen.

Following the lane along West Ham Park we come to the ancient hostelry known as the "Spotted Dog." Here the parlour

is still shown in which the merchants of the City of London held their exchange during the time of the great plague (1665—1666), in commemoration of which a painting of the City Arms is still preserved on a wall in the entrance hall.

Bordering on the lane, which thence leads in a somewhat tortuous course towards the great highway, stood until recently a charming villa, shaded by magnificent elm-trees which, in 1631, was the property of William Fawcitt — who gave by will to the poor of West Ham, a rent-charge of his estate amounting to £2 10s annually — and subsequently became the property of the Cockfield family. In the middle of the last century, it was the residence of Zachariah Cockfield,

whose son Joseph married Elizabeth, daughter of Henry Gurney of
Norwich, by whom he had a son, Henry, who remained single, and a
daughter named Sarah who was married to Mr. Joseph Dimsdale. On
his death the property came to his son Mr. Joseph Cockfield Dimsdale.

This pleasant villa with a pretty lawn, shrubbery, and garden,
latterly known as " Elmhurst," was for many years, from 1866 to 1882,
the residence of Mr. Fred. Sewell who, having purchased the property
from the Dimsdale family, afterwards sold it to the British Land
Company. On his leaving, the house was taken down, and since
then the whole estate, comprising about 14 acres, has been well-nigh
covered with rows of dwellings.

The amiable and elegant, but little known poet, John Scott of
Amwell, seems to have been a frequent guest at this house, when
the Cockfields yet resided there. In one of his odes, addressed "To
a Friend," he gives a description of the neighbourhood, and also
alludes to Dr. Fothergill's garden at Ham House and its botanical
treasurers.

ODE XII. TO A FRIEND.

No Cockfield, no! I'll not disdain
Thy Upton's Elm-divided plain ;
Nor scorn the varied views it yields,
O'er Bromley's creeks and isles of reeds,
Or Ham's or Plaistow's level meads,
To Woolwich streets or Charlton fields.
Thy hedgerow paths I'll pleasant call
And praise the lonely lane, that leads
To that old tower upon the wall.

And there in happier hours the walk
Has frequent pleas'd with friendly talk,
From theme to theme that wander'd still—
The long detail of where we had been,
And what we had heard, and what we had seen,
And what the poet's tuneful skill,
And what the painter's graphic art,
Or antiquarians searches keen,
Of calm amusement could impart.

II

Then oft did Nature's works engage,
And oft we search'd Linnæus' page,
The Scanian Sage, whose wond'rous toil
Had classed the vegetable race:
And curious oft from place to place,
We rang'd and sought each different soil,
Each different plant intent to view,
And all the marks minute to trace,
Whence he his nice distinction drew."

It requires no great effort of the imagination to fancy the poet and his friend Cockfield wandering with Dr. Fothergill through the gardens, shrubberies, and hot-houses of Ham House, or strolling in friendly intercourse along the lonely green country lanes.

The two houses on the right hand side of the lane, which formerly were private residences, were, in 1862, converted into a convent, where the nuns of the Ursuline order are now carrying on a great educational work.

A little further on stood once an ancient wooden mansion of very picturesque appearance. The house has long since disappeared, but on its site two brick buildings have been erected, one of which was for several years the residence of Mr. James Sheppard, and, in 1882, the temporary asylum of Franciscan monks, who were exiled from France under a peremptory order of the French Government.

The other, now called "Lawn House," was for some time the residence of the late Col. Capper, and is now in the occupation of Mr. Benjamin Warner.

Proceeding towards the high road we pass on the left hand side a small mansion standing within its own grounds, with garden attached, which between the years 1765 and 1773 was the property of Peter Bigot, who gave a rent-charge to the poor of West Ham, issuing out of " a new erected messuage and field at the west corner of Upton Lane." Peter Bigot left this estate to James Godin Bigot, his grandnephew and heir-at-law. In 1794, part of the estate was purchased by Thomas Chant, whose granddaughter, Mary Ann Chant, sold it in the year 1882 to Mr. John Spencer Curwen, the present owner, who has considerably altered and enlarged the ancient dwelling house, which is now known by the name of "Herne House."

At the point, where the lane joins the Romford Road, used to stand a large old tree, from which the lane formerly took its name of "One Tree Lane." It was an oak of a rare species, said to have been planted by Dr. Fothergill, or, perhaps more probably, given by him from his large collection. At this corner now stands Emmanuel Church, built in 1852, to meet the necessities of the rapidly increasing population. The church which is of Gothic design and consists of chancel, nave, and aisles, and has a central bell turret, was designed by Sir Gilbert Scott, and has recently been much enlarged. The living is a vicarage, in the joint gift of the Vicars of East and West Ham, and is now held by the Rev. Robert Ross.

The whole aspect of this locality is completely changed. Building speculations have swallowed up the green fields and hedgerows; the magnificent trees, which once shaded the lonely lanes, are ruthlessly cut down, and the quiet rural little village of Upton is gradually being transformed into a town with rows of houses and tenements, chiefly to suit the working classes, who flock here from all parts of the metropolis, to find employment in the busy docks and the factories of the neighbourhood.

II. Plaistow.

The hamlet or ward of the parish of West Ham, known as Plaistow, derives its name from the family of de Plaiz, and signifies the "stow" *i.e.* the place or seat of de Plaiz. The reader will remember that Philippa, youngest sister of Richard de Montfichet and wife of Hugh de Plaiz, (*see page* 46), inherited as her third portion of the Montfichet estate the manor of Plaiz. The village of Plaistow, therefore, did not exist under its present name before 1267, the year in which Richard de Montfichet died.

On a map of the Pelly Estate at Upton is a rude sketch of the upper part of the village of Plaistow, in which a spot is marked as the site of the Manor House of Bretts, called "Brett's Bower."

It is represented as a tower with a gateway and buildings attached, but it is not easy to determine from the drawing, whether it is intended to represent a sort of castle, or a mansion approached

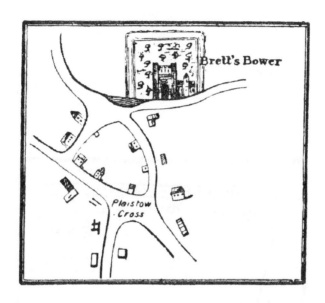

from the road under an archway. However, there is no doubt that it is a representation of the old manor house, where the feudal lords in ancient times resided.

Every vestige of it has long since dissappeared, but near the site of the present St. Mary's Schools, there was formerly a pond, over-shadowed by trees, which is supposed to have been the remains of a moat, by which the old manor house was surrounded. In the early ages the de Plaiz family were the feudal lords of the whole district, and as cottages began to cluster round or close to the manorial residence, a village gradually sprang into existence, which has since retained the name of Plaistow.

The earliest mention of Plaistow, as a distinct village, occurs in a lease granted by William Huddleston, the last Abbot of Stratford Langthorne, dated 1535, in which the highway leading from West Ham to "Plaistow" is mentioned, while in another lease, granted about the same time to Robert Wright, by the same abbot, Richard Parker of "Plaistow" is named.

It is, therefore, certain that early in the sixteenth century Plaistow was a distinct village. Tradition says that it was here, that the abbot and monks, after the noble house raised by their pious benefactors, where they and their predecessors had so long lived in holy retirement and alms-giving, had been ruthlessly destroyed, took refuge and lived out the remainder of their lives, subsisting on the allowance granted them by the Crown. An ancient mansion called Hyde House, which stood nearly opposite the Black Lion Inn, on

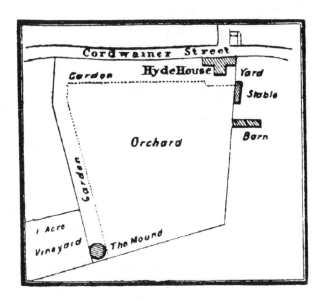

the south side of the road leading to West Ham, then known as Cordwainer Street—the place having in past years been famous for cordwainers—is supposed to have been their retreat. There still remain considerable portions of ancient brick walls, which appear to have surrounded an extensive enclosure, and on the premises to the south of the house there stood within recent years a large barn, in the occupation of Mr. Wm. Ireland, built over a buttressed door-arch of red brick, which is confidently asserted to have been the entrance into their premises from a lane, by which the monks used to pass into the village.

Over this gate, which is well remembered by many parishioners yet living, was the date 1579, and the following inscription: "This is the gate of everlasting life."

Hyde House is described in an ancient survey of the Manor of West Ham, as "a great mansion in Plaistow, with certain lands adjoining," among which is mentioned a parcel of ground, called "Le Hide," from which it probably took its name. In the early part of the 17th century (1605) it was in the occupation of Dr. Richard Tailor, and afterwards the seat of Sir Thomas Foot, who was Lord Mayor of London, in 1650. It subsequently passed into the hands of Sir Arthur Onslow, father of the first Lord Onslow, who married one of the coheirs of Sir Thomas Foot.

About 1738 it was the quiet rereat of Aaron Hill, a dramatic writer, whose tragedies and poems, though much neglected in later days, were well known and admired by his contemporaries. Here he devoted himself to his study and garden, and wrote a heroic poem, called the "Fanciad," and also adapted to the English stage Voltaire's tragedy of Merope, his last work, which he dedicated to

Lord Bolingbroke in the following lines, full of melancholy presage of his approaching end:[1]

"Cover'd in fortune's shade I rest reclin'd,
My griefs all silent, and and my joys resign'd,
With patient eye life's evening gleam survey:
Nor shake th' out hast'ning sands, nor bid them stay.

Yet while from life my setting prospects fly,
Fain would my mind's weak offspring shun to die;
Fain would their hope some light through time explore,
The name's kind passport—when the man's no more."

About the middle of the eighteenth century Hyde House became the property of Sir Jacob Des Bouverie, created Viscount Folkestone, in 1747, who sold it, in 1764, to John Alexander. It

was copyhold of the Manor of West Ham, and is described as "a large bordered house, fronted and backed with brick, in 1732. Over

---

[1] Aaron Hill died in 1749, after enduring a twelvemonth's torment with great fortitude and resignation. He was buried in the same grave with his wife—who was the only daughter of Edmnnd Morris of Stratford, Essex, and a lady of great merit and beauty—in the great cloister of Westminster Abbey, near Lord Godolphin's tomb

the mantlepiece in the best parlour was written in 'golding' letters: Prosperity and adversity. Life and death. Poverty and riches come all of the Lord."

Its last occupant was Mr. John James who, in 1753, was made by Francis Smart Esq., bailiff of his Manor of West Ham. In the beginning of this century the house was pulled down and the site covered with a row of cottages, which in their turn have again been replaced by modern houses, thus causing long breaches in the ancient brick wall which skirted the street.

On the north side of Cordwainer Street stood another large mansion called "Porch House," in former ages the seat of Jerome Rawstorne, whose daughter Dorothy was married to Sir Hugh Smithson, who was created a baronet in 1660. A descendant of theirs, Sir Hugh Smithson, of Stanwick, succeeded on the death of his father-in-law, Algernon, Duke of Somerset, to the Earldom of Northumberland, in 1750. The old house remained in the possession of the Rawstorne family for several generations, and came eventually to a Mrs. Rawstorne who, solely from the similarity of name, left it to a Colonel Rawstorne. The tittle deeds say, that in the time of Henry VIII. it was considered the oldest house in Plaistow. The large hall of this house was, about fifty years ago, used as a Lancasterian School, where many of the Plaistow inhabitants, yet living, received their education. The gardens and a carriage drive belonging to it communicated with the lane leading from Plaistow to Upton, now called Pelly Road, but Mr. McPherson, a nursery man, who occupied the site from 1840 to 1850, ploughed up the drive, and also removed the piers and stone balls from the old gateway. The whole property is now covered with houses, facing partly the present Plaistow Lane, and partly Church Street, which was taken out of the gardens adjoining the house.

At the corner, where the Black Lion Inn stands, a street branches off to the north, past Richmond House, which is said to have been so called from being the spot, where once an Earl of Richmond resided.

Beyond this stood until recent years another large mansion, which was at one time in the occupation of a grazier, named Giles, who had the notorious highwayman Dick Turpin as his servant.

Dick Turpin's career of vice is supposed to have commenced by gambling at the "Coach and Horses" public-house, whenever he could find an oppotunity of doing so. Giles, being a man of religious habits, discharged Turpin from his service, who thereupon married a woman at East Ham, where he afterwards lived for some time. His later career has already been described in a previous chapter.

At this point the road widens into an open space, where the ancient manor house once stood, on the site of which St. Mary's Church has been erected, in 1830, a small brick building of Gothic design, consisting of chancel, nave, and aisles. The living is a vicarage, in the gift of the Vicar of West Ham, and was held for a period of about 40 years by the Rev. R. W. B. Marsh, on whose resignation, in 1884, the present vicar, the Rev. T. Given-Wilson, entered on the incumbency.

It is a noteworthy, though somewhat humiliating fact that, before the erection of St. Mary's Church, there was in this hamlet no church nearer than that of West Ham on the one side, and that of East Ham on the other, the only places of worship being the "Independent Chapel," now adapted to business purposes, and the "Friends Meeting House," which has within recent years been converted into a Board School. Since then, however, great efforts have been made to meet the spiritual needs of the growing population, and besides St. Andrew's Church in the Barking Road, numerous chapels have been erected in connexion with the various bodies of Nonconformists, one of the most imposing being the Congregational Church in Balaam Street.

Near St. Mary's Schools the present Pelly Road branches off northwards, while another winding green lane—called Palsey Lane—whose recesses and grass-grown sides were for many ages the camping ground of gipsies, leads past the church eastward to the ancient "Green Street."

Another street — called North Street — leads past the abovementioned Independent Chapel and the old Friends Meeting House to another open space, whence Balaam Street and Greengate Street diverge in a southerly direction towards the Thames. This open space, which was covered with grass and in the beginning of the present century still called "the Green," where the men used to play at skittles and quoits, and the boys at trap and ball, gradually narrows

KK

up into what is called Greengate Street, until it reaches the "Green Gate" Tavern where, intersected by the new Barking Road, it leads into the marshes under the name of "Prince Regent's Lane."

On the western side of this street stood in former years the remains of an ancient mansion, said to have been the residence of the Duke of Somerset, who was appointed Protector during the minority of King Edward VI., and subsequently of an Earl of Essex, from whom it derived its name of "Essex House." Over the entrance gate may still be seen a ducal coronet wrought in iron.

It was a large and massive white mansion, with numerous Tudor windows and deep set stone mullions; the interior was of vast dimensions and great splendour, with wrought ceilings and pendent ornaments, and contained sixty rooms, besides a fine and spacious hall with a magnificent staircase and banisters of great beauty. In the year 1800 it was used as a school, the panelled parlour holding with ease sixty boys, seated at two long desks. The owner was at that date a Mr. Johnson, who cultivated the garden which, though considerably reduced from its original size, still comprised from eight to ten acres. From a school "Essex House" became a private madhouse, kept by a Mr. Cazey, who was a man of great cunning and, if judged by his actions, of rather doubtful principles, as the following anecdote, told of him, would imply.

At the time of the Spa Fields riots, in 1816, one of the leading rioters, Watson by name, escaped from justice and was, disguised as a female patient, brought down in a Hackney Coach to Cazey's madhouse, whence he escaped to America. Cazey got into trouble for harbouring a criminal; when brought before the magistrate he resorted to his accustomed trick of pretending deafness, whenever questions were put to him, by answering which he ran the risk of incriminating himself. At length the magistrate said that Mr. Cazey must be aware, that he had placed himself in a very serious position by harbouring this man Watson, and that the result could hardly be foreseen, nor would deafness screen him. Whereupon the madhouse-keeper added to his deafness a feigned idiotcy, and pulling some old nails out of his pocket and playing with them, said in reply to every question—"Old iron, old iron; my mother always taught me to take care of old iron."

The old mansion was pulled down, in 1836, by its then owner, Mr. Charles Curtis, who out of the old material erected a modern house, which under the name of "Essex Lodge" is now occupied by Mr. George C. Mackrow.

In the "Broadway" stood until recently an antiquated building known as the "Great House" or "Broadway House," which for many generations was the residence of the well-known family of Marten, its last occupant being Mr. Robert Humphrey Marten. In 1872 it was converted into a "Home for destitute children," supported by voluntary contributions, and providing a home for sixty outcasts under the superintendence of Miss Lee. The house was a few years ago taken down; its site and the grounds belonging to it have since been covered with dwellings.

Balaam Street, in ancient times called Balaam Lane, is a long narrow street, leading towards the Thames; the origin of the name is unknown, but it may possibly be a corruption of Baalun, several members of the Baalun family having held property in "Ham," as far back as the twelfth century. The street once boasted of a number of family residences, many of which were occupied by wealthy citizens and merchants of London, but they have one by one been demolished, the day being long past, when Plaistow was a fashionable village.

The first house, worthy of notice, is immediately at its entrance on the right hand side, and is now divided into two, one of which is used as a private school, while the other is in the occupation of Mr. John Jackson. It was in this house, that Dr. Dodd, (*see page* 189), resided—between the years 1752 and 1772—with his pupils, one of whom was the Hon. Philip Stanhope, afterwards Lord Chesterfield. This fact is confirmed by the circumstance, that the family of Pigrome, who for generations have lived at Plaistow, carrying on the trade of a shoemaker, still keep in their possession a relic carefully wrapped up in brown paper, consisting in the quarter pattern for a pair of shoes with buckles, and marked "The Hon. Philip Stanhope," which had evidently been used in making shoes for him.

The late Mr. Pigrome, who died about 1850 at a great age, also positively asserted, that Dr. Dodd left this neighbourhood in 1772, when the living of Hockliffe in Bedfordshire was given to him—some years, therefore, before his apprehension and execution.

Further down Balaam Street stood an old-fashioned dwelling,[1] where the great statesman Edmund Burke, who was very fond of the country, for some time resided, and where he wrote his well-known work on the "Sublime and Beautiful." When he left Plaistow, an old portrait was left in the house, and fell into the possession of Mrs. Adams, the next occupant who, attaching no value to the same, gave it to an old servant, in whose cottage it was often seen by Mr. Beal, her medical attendant. Observing that it excited his admiration, she begged him to accept it, as she should die happier, if she knew it was in his possession. Mr. Beal, in whose family the portrait is still preserved, considered it to be the likeness of Samuel Pepys, whose celebrated "Diary," one of the most delightful books in the English language, forms his best claims to our remembrance.

At the bottom of Balaam Street, beyond the Barking Road, still stands a mansion, called "Cumberland House" from having been in the possession of Henry, Duke of Cumberland, brother of King George III., who kept a racing stud, and frequently used to pass the night there, attended by only one servant. Mrs. Skelton, wife of his head-groom, who resided in the house, used to prepare the meals for his Royal Highness. The Royal Duke being also an amateur agriculturist, his farm carts used in those days to be frequently seen about Plaistow, with the city arms and his name upon them. Being a citizen of London, he had the right to use the city arms, which freed them from certain tolls. After the death of the duke the farm was carried on by his bailiff, Mr. Galloway, who was succeeded by Mr. Hudson; latterly the farm was in the occupation of the late Mr. Joseph Ireland, and is now in the tenancy of Mr. Al. Mills.

Nor is this the only instance of Royal horses being kept on Plaistow marshes. King George IV., when Prince of Wales, used to turn out his colts to grass there, while the grooms in charge of them took up their quarters at the public house, known as the "Abbey Arms," which in former years had a sign post standing in front of the house with the arms of the Abbey of Stratford painted upon it, viz.: the three golden chevrons of Montfichet on their field of gules, with the Abbot's crosier across.

---

[1] A portion of this house, which is still standing, has been new fronted, and is now in the occupation of Mrs. Fisher.

There is also near this spot, in the farm-yard belonging to Cumberland House, a very ancient tithing barn, the interior of which is arched after the manner of a cathedral; both the barn and the sign of the above-named Inn, are obviously traces of abbey lands and influence.

In concluding this account of Plaistow, it should not be left unnoticed that, though flat and unattractive, this locality has inspired the poets. There is still extant a poem by JEREMIAH DUMMER, who died 1739 and lies buried in West Ham Church, from which we quote the following lines:

Thy meadows Plaistow and thy fleecy care,
Thy yellow harvest and thy healthy air,
Invite my lays. Attend ye sylvan maids,
Lay by your work and seek the cooling shades.
Arcadia's fields or Candia's lovely plains,
Or Tyber's meads describ'd in softest strains,
Can equal thee in anything but song,
'Tis from their poets they exist so long.
And were my heart inspir'd with equal flame,
Our village justly should excel their fame.
What tho' our hills no azure summits crown,
With bearded grain and fertile plains abound.
Houses thick interspers'd and trees appear,
Whose lofty tops ascend the ambient air.
A chequer'd land-skip each parterre displays,
Admitting all the genial sun's bright rays.
Here flowers rise, in gayest dress the rose,
Opening each morn doth sweet perfumes disclose,
With white the snowdrop, hyacinth with blue,
Junquil with yellow. Iris' varied hue

Kind nature decks. Why should I more? the field
Unask'd a thousand different beauties yield,
Pomona here her richest blessing pours,
And from each tree descend th' empurpl'd show'rs;
Kind Ceres here repays the farmer's toils,
With plenteous harvest every farrow smiles;
Pan here his flocks 'to flow'ry herbage leads,
And while they're feeding, tunes his sevenfold reeds.

But since the days, that Dummer lived in this vicinity, nay, within the last twenty years, the aspect of this once small and quiet village of "genteel houses," has undergone a great change. The rural village of Plaistow is no more, it has been swallowed up in the town of Plaistow. The wealthy citizens and merchants, who used to live here, and nearly all kept their carriages, have left; most of the interesting old mansions have been demolished and their sites covered with rows of houses for the working classes, while the once solitary marsh lands, used for grazing purposes only, have been converted into mighty docks, or covered with work-shops and factories. The whole district has become a busy place of industry and commerce, and the population, which at the beginning of the century amounted to but 1069, and even as late as 1841, curiously enough to exactly 1841 souls, may now be reckoned by tens of thousands, the combining districts of Plaistow (proper), Canning Town, and Silver Town containing rather more than 70,000 inhabitants.

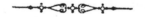

CHAPTER XII.

EAST HAM.

AST HAM—as its name implies—is situate to the east of West Ham, and was until recently a long and straggling village, extending from the Wanstead Flats to the Thames at North Woolwich, and apparently of little or no interest except to market gardeners. But uninteresting as the village may appear, it possesses one of the most remarkable ecclesiastical edifices, which for antiquity and interest ranks before many others, and there is probably no church in the vicinity of the metropolis, which can be compared with this little church, or which possesses architectural features of such unusual interest. Surrounded by the tombs of whole generations that have passed away, and full of tender and pious associations, it stands upon the very fringe of an extensive track of marshland, an object well worthy of the study of the antiquary and the ecclesiologist.

It is at first difficult to conceive, why a church should have been built in such an undesirable locality, but there is little doubt, that there was even in those remote times a rural population, tilling those broad arable lands, and requiring their spiritual welfare to be provided for, as well as those living in some more favoured localities. Moreover, there can be no doubt, that an old Roman road, passed very close to the spot, where the church stands, thus rendering it easy of access.

The church, dedicated to St. Mary Magdalene, is built of flint and stone, and presents externally a rural appearance from its low and massive tower, the lower part of which is of Norman workmanship while the upper portion is of comparatively recent date. There

East Ham Church.

is a western porch, also embattled, and like the tower plastered over with stucco, which now is the only entrance into the church, the south porch having been converted into a vestry.

The church is a perfect Norman structure of a very simple, though somewhat unusual plan. A nave without aisles, a chancel, and beyond, an apsidal sacrarium, sometimes described as a double chancel. The arch from the tower into the nave is not very lofty, and has more the appearance of a doorway than of a tower arch, but looking from this arch into the church one cannot help being impressed by the dignity of its proportions and the solemnity of its appearance even now.

The walls of the nave—which was originally lighted by small narrow circular-headed windows, two of which still remain in the north wall partly blocked by a monument—are very massive, being three feet thick.

The chancel, that is to say the first or outer chancel, rises one step from the nave. From the rough and unequal state of the wall there can be no doubt of the former existence of a chancel arch, now hacked and cut away. Mr. KING, in his description of the church in the Essex Archaeological Transactions (Vol. 2, p. 102) remarks that "by this act of Vandalism a grand religious and architectural effect has been entirely destroyed, as the distant adytum, where the christian mysteries were celebrated and the august sacrifice was offered, when seen through the arched opening of the chancel under a more subdued light than it can now be viewed—recess beyond recess—sanctum and sanctum sanctorum—must have invested the rite with more solemn and awful significance, and inspired the worshipper with greater awe and reverence."

The most striking architectural feature of the edifice is contained in the chancel, in that curious Norman arcade of intersecting arches, enriched with chevron mouldings, carried continuously round both jambs and arches. On the south side, this arcade has been shaved off to make way, partly for the erection of a monument, and partly for extra convenience to a huge pew, a modern fire place with ordinary grate having been inserted in the wall. On the north side a larger portion remains, which is, however, partially concealed by pews. This part of the edifice is lighted by an ugly modern window immediately over the fire place, but on the north side an original Norman window still remains.

The chancel opens by a plain Norman arch into the sanctuary, which is lighted by three little Norman windows. On the south side of the apse is constructed a very beautiful piscina with a double drain, divided by a column forming two plain Gothic arches, between which is a beautiful corbel bracket, supported by a projecting human head, probably intended for carrying a lamp.

In the south wall is a blocked doorway in the usual position of a priest's door, which occupies the entire space between the piscina and the abutment of the arch of the sanctuary.

LL

The font, now at the west end of the church, is a portable marble basin, set upon a wooden pedestal; an inscription round the bowl informs us, that it was the gift of Sir Richard Heigham, in 1634, whose arms and quarterings are rudely incised upon it.

On the walls of the chancel and sanctuary may be discerned the beautiful, but much faded remains of early English painting, the discovery of which, in 1858, was due to Mr. Harris, the sexton, by whom they were carefully uncovered under the superintendence of Mr. Streatfeild, then vicar of the parish. It is very probable, that the whole interior of the edifice was at one time richly decorated, but there are now no remains except in the chancel and sacrarium.

In each spandrel over the arch of the sacrarium a faint outline may still be discerned of a large figure, nearly life size; the one on the left is a female, crowned, holding in her right hand a sceptre or staff, while the left hand is elevated, holding a pair of scales; the other corresponding figure has been nearly destroyed by the insertion of a mural tablet. Faded and obliterated as all this fresco-painting now is, it is sufficient to give an idea of how richly even a small country church was adorned in those days.

Of the tower of the church little need be said, except that it contains an ancient bell with this inscription of a jingling Latin rhyme:

Dulcis sisto melis, vocor campana Gabrielis.

Mr. George Buckler, the architect, and author of a valuable volume on the "Churches of Essex" says, that, it is quite possible, that the lower chancel, may have been built in Saxon times. If this be so, it is not improbable, that Edwin, the free priest, (*see pages* 8 *and* 13), mentioned in Domesday-Book as owning a little estate in East Ham, may have built or served in it.

We have stated in a former chapter, (*see page* 47), that John of Lancaster, who was heir to the manor of East Ham, gave, in 1307, the rectory and advowson of the church to the Abbot and Convent of Stratford Langthorne. But there was no vicarage endowed, till Ralph de Baldock, Bishop of London, in 1309, upon the complaint of the Abbot and Convent "that they were much depressed for want, by reason their lands were frequently overflown and their cattle often perished, and besides their charge in hospitality, by which they were so pressed, that they could not keep up the reputation of Religion, as they ought"—did with the counsel of his chapter appropriate this rectory to the said monastery, and at the same time endow a perpetual vicarage with a pension of 5 marks per annum, a house, and all the tithes, except those of corn, hay, and windmills. So that from this time the Abbot and Convent became proprietaries of the rectory, and so continued till the suppression of the monastery, while the vicarage was vested in the Bishop of London and his successors, in whose patronage it continued until the year 1864, when, by way of exchange, the living became vested in Brasenose College, Oxford.

It may not be out of place to mention here, that since the year 1868, when the Bishop of London, the late Dr. Tait, was translated to the Archbishopric of Canterbury, both parishes of East and West Ham, as well as the other parishes in Essex, which still belonged to the diocese of London, were then transferred, first to the diocese of Rochester, and subsequently to that of St. Albans, which was formed in the year 1877.

The following list of Vicars of East Ham is taken from Newcourt's Repertorium, and begins with the year 1328.

	PATRONI.
Sewallus Sharp, pr. 2 Kal. Feb. 1328.	Episc. London:
Ric. de Bourn, pr. Id. Sept., 1330, per resig. Sharp.	,,
Sim. Ridesdale.	,,
Joh. Sadeler, 15 Feb., 1387, per resig. Ridesdale. ..	,,
Thos. Isaac.	,,
Joh. Bette, 11 Aug., 1391, per resig. Isaac.	,,
Joh. Forster, 27 Oct., 1393, per resig. Bette. ...	,,
Tho. Capon.	,,
Will. Gay, pr., 14 Oct., 1395, per mort. Capon. ...	,,
Joh. Coke.	,,
Ric. William, pr., 21 Aug. 1439, per mort. Coke. ...	,,
Joh. Pentelen, 13 Apr. 1441, per resig. William. ...	,,
Joh. Episc. Olen, 17 Sept., 1444, per mort. Pentelen.	,,
Rob. Byrton, pr., 12 June, 1446, per mort. Olen. ...	,,
Tho. Episc. Dunen et Connoren, 18 January, 1459. ...	,,

	Episc. London:
Will. Hebbenge, pr., 7 Maii, 1460.	
Joh. Croxby, S.T.P., 12 June, per resig. Hebbenge. ...	,,
Rob. Hope.	,,
Rob. Walleis, cap., 13 Sep., 1473, per resig. Hope.' ...	,,
Ric. Lothes, D.B., 24 Nov. 1486, per mort. Walleis. ...	,,
Will. Smith.	,,
Jac. Gilbert, A.M., 17 Jul., 1511, per mort. Smith ...	,,
Tho. Wolf, Lacedaemon Ep., 2 Maii, 1514, per res. Gilbert.	,,
Joh. Wagott, cap., 6 Nov., 1518, per mort. Wolf. ...	,,
Tho. Sudbury, 21 Nov., 1544.	,,
Ric. Finch, cl., 12 Feb., 1545, per mort. Sudbury. ...	,,
Will. Harwood, cap., 8 Nov., 1553, per resig. Finch. ...	,,
Joh. Plowghe, cl., 18 Feb., 1559.	,,
Will. Margets, 18 Nov., 1562, per mort. ult. Vic. ...	,,
Ric. Smith, cl., 7 Jul., 1569, per mort. Margets. ...	,,
Tob. Chalfont, cl., 13 Oct., 1589, per mort. Smith. ...	,,
Joh. Leese, pr., Apr., 1600, per resig. Chalfont. ...	,,
Owen Gwyn, S.T.B., 5 Oct., 1605, per mort. Leese. ...	,,
Joh. Whiteing, A.M., 28 Sept., 1611, per resig. Gwyn...	,,
W. Fairfax, S.T.P.	,,
Edw. Rust, cl., 16 Aug., 1660, per mort. Fairfax. ...	,,
Steph. Robins, A.M., 9 Jul., 1690, legit. vacan. ...	,,
Richard Welton, D.D., 13 Sept., 1710, upon Robins' cess.	,,
Henry Topping, 25 Oct., 1716, upon Welton's depr. on account of seditious practices.	,,
Lewes Desbordes (Debord), M.A., 4 Oct., 1728, upon Topping's cess.	,,
John Nade, M.A. 2 Nov., 1733, upon Desbordes' d. ...	,,
Jos. Sims, M.A., 9 Jan., 1756, upon Nade's d. ...	,,
Francis Haultain, 14 Aug., 1776, on the desease of Sims.	,,
William Streatfeild, 19 Oct., 1827, on the decease of Haultain.	,,
Edw. Fitzmaurice Boyle, 24 Jul. 1860, on the decease of Streatfeild.	,,

John William Knott, 13 July, 1866, by presentment of Brasenose College, Oxford.	Brasenose College, Oxford.
Thomas Henry Rodie Shand, 1869.	,,
S. H. Reynolds, M.A., the present Vicar, 1871. ...	,,

Little is known of the ancient vicars, as a rule, but we are told, that John Plowghe fled beyond the sea in Queen Mary's reign, and returned unto England upon Queen Elizabeth coming to the throne—when he was instituted to this vicarage by Bishop Grindall, then newly advanced to the See of London, upon the deprivation of Bonner. Bishop Grindall was likewise a voluntary exile in Germany for the sake of the Protestant religion, but returned upon the accession of Elizabeth, and was ultimately (1575) made Archbishop of Canterbury.

Owen Gwyn, Dr. of Divinity, became, after having resigned the living of East Ham, Archdeacon of Huntington, and ultimately Master of St. John's College, Cambridge, where he died, in 1633.

Dr. W. Fairfax was ejected from the vicarage of East Ham, during the civil wars, by the committee for plundered ministers. When the Commissioners, appointed by Parliament, in 1650, examined into the state of ecclesiastical benefices, they found that there was no settled minister at East Ham; the rectory was valued at £70 per annum, the vicarage at £65, a fifth part of which was allowed to the widow of Dr. Fairfax.

In 1651 a pension of £50 per annum was voted to John Horne, then minister of East Ham.

In 1655, John Page was presented by Cromwell, and in 1656, John Clarke.

Richard Welton, who was collated to this vicarage, in 1710, was a non-juror and distinguished himself as a politician. He was deprived of this benefice, in 1716, and having rendered himself obnoxious to the Government by seditious practices, he was obliged to flee to Lisbon, where he died in 1726. A volume of his sermons and several of his discourses are still extant.

Henry Topping, who succeeded Welton, in 1716, has published several sermons.

Joseph Sims, who was appointed vicar in 1756, had been chaplain to the English factory at Lisbon. He printed a sermon on the rebellion, in 1745, and a volume of his discourses was published after his death. During the time he was vicar of East Ham, his friend Dr. Stukeley, the great antiquarian, seems to have been a frequent guest at his house.

Passing on to more recent years, we come to the name of the Rev. Will. Streatfeild, who was Vicar of East Ham for 32 years, and to whom his affectionate parishioners have dedicated a marble tablet in the church, in testimony of their high esteem of his eminently christian character. During his incumbency, Forest Gate was formed an ecclesiastical district, and Emmanuel Church erected at the corner of Upton Lane, in the Ilford Road.

The Rev. E. F. Boyle was instrumental in the erection of the new church of St. John the Baptist, 1866, and the Rev. J. W. Knott, in that of St. John's Church, at North Woolwich.

During the incumbency of the present vicar, the Rev. S. H. Reynolds, two more churches have been built, to meet the spiritual requirements of the increasing population, viz: All Saints' in the Ilford Road, in 1886, and St. Stephen's at Plashet, in 1887, while the church of St. Michael's at Beckton, which, in 1887, was destroyed by fire, has been restored.

EXTRACTS FROM THE PARISH REGISTER.

Sir Wm. Coryton, of West Newton, in Cornwall, married to Sarah William, widow, May 26th, 1698.

The Hon. Elizabeth Graham, buried 25th July, 1761.

The Rev. Dr. Stukeley, late rector of St. George's, Queen Square, London, buried March 9th, 1765.

Lady Dick, from Harley Str., buried Feb. 7th, 1781.

Sir Robert Ralph Foley, Bart., from London, buried March 11th, 1782.

Thomas Mathews, aged 91, buried Oct. 12, 1782.

John Emmott, aged 92, buried Jan. 13th, 1793.

The alms-houses in the parish were originally founded by Giles Bream, who died 1621, for three poor men of East Ham and three of Bottisham, Cambridgeshire, and endowed by him with an estate in Braintree and Felstead, now producing £120 per annum. The profits of the estate are divided between the two parishes, but the tenements are all inhabited by parishioners—at present 3 married couples and 6 widows—a certain rent being paid for three of them to the parish of Bottisham.

There are also various charitable bequests to the poor:

1585. Robert Rampston, of Chingford, rent charge of £1.
1604. Sir John Hart, Knt., rent charge of £4.
1620. W. Heigham, the rent of two acres and half of marsh land in the parish of Barking.
1653. Sir Jacob Garrard, £3 annually, to apprentice a boy.
1661. The Countess Dowager of Westmoreland, 2 acres and a half in Middlemarsh, West Ham, out of the rent of which 20s was to be paid for a sermon, 5s to the clerk, 5s for repairing the tomb of her husband Nevill, Earl of Westmoreland, in the chancel, and the rest to the poor.
1833. Daniel Holt, the interest of £19 19s.
1838. The Countess Poulet, the dividends of £50 stock.

MONUMENTS AND INSCRIPTIONS.

We now give a list of the various monuments and inscriptions, commencing with those inside the church.

In the Apse.

That, which is of most historical interest, is a sumptuous monument of black and white marble behind the communion table, with the following inscription: In memoria sacrum.

In memory of the Right Honorable Edmond Nevill, Lord Lattimer, Earle of Westmorland[1] and Dame Jane his wife with the memoryalls

---

[1] The particulars of Edmond Nevill's claim to the Earldom—of which he always assumed the style and title—may be briefly stated as follows: Charles Nevill, the 6th Earl of Westmoreland, was implicated in an attempt to place Mary Queen of Scots on the throne, in 1570. He fled to the Netherlands and on his attainder all his honours were forfeited. In the reign of James the first, Edmond Nevill, whom this monument

of thire 7 children, which Edmond was lineally descended from the Honorable blood of Kings and Princes and the 7th Earle of Westmorland of the name of Nevills.

> By God's great power, (who doth command all powers)
> To us thise seaven children were for blessings given,
> Some do survive, as images of owers
> And some are gone, from whence they came, to Heaven,
> Birth, Blood and Beutie like to flowers still fade,
> Death turns each living substance to a shad.

> From Princly and from Honorable blood
> By true succession was my high descent
> Malignant crosses oft oppos'de my good
> And adverse chance my stat did circumvent,
> Yet howsoe're my will was counterchekt
> By faith my earthly hopes in heaven were laid.
> Assured that God the same would not reject
> Through Christ my Saviour and Redeemer's ayd,
> In joy, griefe, weale, woe, I my life did spend
> In hoop to gaine that life that nere shall end.
> Let honor life or fortune sink or swimm
> Thogh God shold kill me I will hoop in him.

> Amidst a world of crosses and cares
> I past my transitory pilgrimage
> By God's great mercie guarded from the snares
> Of world and and flesh and Satan's cruell rage.

---

commemorates, claimed the Earldom, but James I. could never be got to properly acknowledge it, on the ground that the attainder had caused all the honours, possessed by the said Charles, to be forfeited to the crown as an estate of inheritance. It could not, however, have applied to this Edmond Nevill, who was descended from the first Earl Ralph Nevill, by his second wife Joan Plantagenet, a daughter of John of Gaunt, Duke of Lancaster. It appears from a letter, preserved in the Lansdown MSS., that James actually promised this Edmond that he would reinstate him, as it was in his mother's cause, that the family had suffered.

The gratious vertue (Prudence) was my guide
Throgh all the wavering waves of tottering stat
Sweet prudence told me honor hence wold slid,
And earthly glorie must have ending date
Which made me lay all hoop, all faith, all trust
In Christ, to live in heaven amongst the just.
My soule doth magnify the Lord, my spirit
Rejoyceth in my God and Saviour's merrit.

The Earl and Countess—as they are styled—are sculptured in marble, each kneeling within a niche; their seven children likewise in devotional attitudes. He is accoutred in the armour of his time, and both himself and his wife are habited in robes lined and trimmed with ermine. The monument is profusely adorned with escutcheons.

Beneath the monument, enclosed with iron railings, is an altar tomb with the following epitaph to a daughter:

Upon the death of the right Vertuous faire and Noble Ladie Katherin Nevill, first daughter of Edmond, Earle of Westmorland and Jane his wife, who died a Virgine, the fifth of December 1613, being of the age of xx3 years.

Surviving marble choysly keepe
This noble Virgine layde to sleepe,
A branch untymely fal'n away
From Nevill's Royallized tree;
Great Westmorland too deere a pray
For death, if she could ransom'd bee.

Hir name was Katherin, not in vaine,
Hir nature held true reference
Hir Beutie and hir parts againe
Were all compos'd of Excellence.

Blud, Beutie, Vertue did contend
All thies advanc'd in Eminence—
Which of them could her most commend
When death enamord tooke her hence.

Yet marble tell the tyme to come
What earst she was when I am dumbe.

MM

Beneath the centre window are two brass plates with the following inscriptions:

Robert Rampston of Chingford, in the County of Essex, gent. deceased, as he was careful in his lyfe tyme to releive the poore, soe att his ende by his Testament he gave xxii *l.* yerely for ever to the poore of divers parishes whereof to the poore of this parishe of Est Ham he hath given yerely for ever xxs to be paid in the moneth of November. He departed this mortall lyfe the thirde daye of August 1585.

The other is in memory of William Johnson, the sonne of William Johnson, of East Ham, in the County of Essex, Esq., who came into the world the 18th of June, 1631, and went out the 24th of the same.

Dominus dedit, Dominus abstulit
Sit nomen domini benedictum.

A mural monument bears the following inscription:
In full assurance of a most joyfull resurrection at the second cominge of Christ Jesus in glory.

Here under rest the bodies of William Heigham late of Est-Ham in the County of Essex, Esq., and of Anne his wife (he was the third son of Sir Clement Heigham of Barrow Hail in the County of Suffolke, Knight, some tymes Lord Cheife Baron of the Exchequer and one of the Privie Councell to Queene Mary) and the said Anne his wife was one of the daughters and coheirs of Richard Stonely, Esq. They had issue five sonnes, Richard, Clement, Daniell, William and Joseph, and three daughters, Anne, Dorothie, and Dorothie, they lived lovingly, honestly and peaceably with all, and died most christianly and much bewayled.

Ipse obiit 10 Julii anno salutis 1620 aetatis suae 73, ipsa obiit IV. Novembris 1612 aetatis suae, 54.

In piam memoriam utriusque parentis Richardus Heigham, Esq., amatus filius et haeres ejusdem Willielmi et Annae hoc monumentum posuit.

In the Chancel.

There is a small mural monument on the south reveal of the chancel arch, which has the following inscription:
Phoenix Maria jacet.

Marie Heigham, a rare and hopefull childe not fully 8 yeares of age yealded her soule to God, her body to the earth the 30th day of Januarie An. Do. 1621, to whose memorie Sir Richard Heigham, Knight, her sorrowful father hath consecrated this small monument.

> Short was thy life
> Yet livest thou ever,
> Death hath his due
> Yet diest thou never.

———

A mural monument on the south spandrel of the chancel arch facing the nave has the following inscription:

Memoriae aeternae

Of Elizabeth Heigham, wife of Sir Richard Heigham, who died 1622.

On the south wall is a mural tablet in memory of Heigham Bendish, Senior, of East Ham, who died 1723, aged 49 years. He married Audry, third daughter of Richard Harrison, of Balls, in the county of Hertford, by whom he had twelve children.

Here also lieth the body of Heigham Bendish, Junior, of East Ham, who died 1746, aged 40 years.

On the North wall is a large monument, with two effigies in stained alabaster, of the family of Breame, adorned with 5 escutcheons of their arms and alliances. It bears the following inscription:

Giles Breame the sonne of Arthur Breame of Est Ham in the county of Essex and Anne Alington, the daughter of Robert Alington, of Horsheath in the county of Cambridge, married the daughter of Thomas Edwards of Sofham in the county of Cambridge aforesaid, which Giles Breame did dispose of the greatest parte of his estate to the buildinge of one Almeshouse, endowinge the same with fortye pounds a yeare for six poor men for ever and for other good and charitable uses to his kindred and servants.

For the performance whereof he made Sir Giles Alington of Horsheath aforesaid, Knight, and his kinsman his sole executor and died the 31st of March, An. Dom. 1621.

Also a small tablet in memory of Charles Hitch, Esq., of Plashet, in this parish and citizen of London, who died 1781, aged 42 years.

In the Nave.

On the south wall is a mural tablet to the memory of Ynyr Burges, Esq., of East Ham, in Essex, for which county he was in the Commission of the Peace for many years.

He died on the 23rd December, 1792, aged 69 years. Universally respected and lamented, his remains lie interred in a vault in this churchyard. He was in the service of the Honorable East India Company 56 years, during 30 of which he filled the office of Paymaster with the strictest honor and integrity; as a Magistrate he ever worked to prevent litigation; his benificence as a patron will ever excite a grateful remembrance of his virtues; as a man, the best testimonials are the regrets of his numerous friends and the heartfelt sorrow of the many, who to his benevolence owed their success in life; the loss of such a father will ever be deplored by his affectionate daughter and sole heiress, Dame Margaret Smith Burges, of Havering Bower, in Essex, who erected this tribute to the memory of her beloved parent on the 21st of Jan. 1794.

Also are interred in the stone vault in this churchyard the remains of Sir John Smith Burges, Bart., who departed this life April 24th, 1803, aged 69 years. A tablet to his respected memory is erected at Havering Bower Chapel by his widow, Dame Margaret Smith Burges, only child of the above Ynyr Burges, Esq., of East Ham.

Also a tablet with the following inscription:

George Samuel Collyer, Esq., who died 1858, aged 94.

Mary Collyer, his wife, who died 1850, aged 79.

Keep innocency and take heed unto the thing that is right, for that shall bring a man peace at last. Psalm 37, v. 38.

———

On the north wall is a mural monument to the memory of George Higginson, Esq., who died 1763, aged 56, also Martha Higginson, relict of the above, who died 1763, aged 52.

Also a mural monument in memory of Margaret, Dowager Countess of Poulett, daughter and sole heiress of Ynyr Burges, Esq., of this place. She was married 1771 to Sir John Smith, Bart., of Havering Bower, who took the name of Burges. Secondly, 1816, to John, fourth Earl of Poulett, and departed this life May 28th, 1838.

Also a small white marble tablet to the memory of Mr. Samuel Moates of Woodhouse in this parish, who died 1832, aged 47 years. Also Mrs. Sylvia Moates, wife of the above, who died at New Cross, 1846, aged 66 years.

Also a marble tablet in memory of the Rev. William Streatfeild, M.A., formerly Fellow of Trinity College, Oxford, and 32 years vicar of this parish, who died whilst preaching on the evening of Sunday, May 27th, 1860, aged 69 years.

"Blessed is that servant whom his Lord when he cometh shall find so doing." Matthew xxiv. 46.

This tablet is erected by his affectionate parishioners in testimony of their high esteem of his eminently christian character, and the faithfulness and love with which he proclaimed to them the saving truths of the Gospel of Christ.

On the floor are several slabs with the following inscriptions:

Mr. Samuel Hunton, who died 175—, aged 90.

George Maxwell, Esq., who died 1763, age 64.

Warwood Johnson, daughter of Thomas Johnson and Anne his wife, aged 11 months, died 1678, the youngest aged 10 months died 1680.

Memento mori.

Here lieth the body of Mr. John Simpson, late of Tower Hill, who died 175—. He left two sons.

Cecilia Bendish, youngest daughter of Heigham Bendish, Esq., of East Ham, died 1766, aged 66.

John Knapp, Esq., who died 1746, in the 58th year of his age.

There are also two monumental brass effigies:

One in memory of Elisabeth, the eldest daughter of James Harvey, of Dagenham, in the county of Essex, and late the vertuous loving and most beloved wife of Richard Heigham, of East Ham, by whom she had issue one sonne and two daughters, that is to say James, Marie and Elisabeth, and departed this life right godly and christianly the —— day of July the yeare after the incarnation of our Saviour Christ, 1622.

The other, a very interesting example of the costume of the period, is in memory of Hester Neve, the vartuous, loveinge, and obedyent wife of Francis Neve, citizen and marchant taylor of London. Shee departed this life the eyght daye of July, An. Dom. 1610, in or abowght the 58 yeare of her age.

———

In the Churchyard.

The tombs of Alexander Henderson, clerk, 1702.

Thomas Hinchliff, citizen of the Salters Company, London, 1741.

Sir John Dick, Bart., of Mount Clare, Roehampton, Surrey, 1804, aged 84 years.

Sir John Smith Burges, Bart., 1803, aged 69 years. A monument erected by his widow, Dame Margaret Smith Burges, of Havering Bower, in this county.

Ynyr Burges, Esq., of East Ham, 1792, aged 69. This monument is erected to his respected and beloved memory by his affectionate daughter and sole heiress, Dame Margaret, Lady of Sir John Smith Burges, Bart., of Havering Bower.

George Wheeler, citizen and baker of London, 1719,—aged 55.

> As you are now, so once was I,
> Reader, prepare therefore to die,
> As I am now, so must you be
> Therefore, prepare to follow me.

———

Susannah Hall, wife of Edward Hall, of Norton Folgate, citizen and weaver of London, 1727, aged 59. Edward Hall, 1730, aged 78. Elizabeth Hall, daughter of the above, 1771, aged 73.

Jane Ward, 1781, aged 42. William Ward, Esq., late of Rickmansworth, Herts, son of the above, 1790, aged 24.

John Wickham, late of the East India House, Gent., 1789, aged 38.

William White of this parish, yeoman 1799, aged 42.

Mrs. Sarah Morley, late wife of William Morley, of Green Street House in this parish 1805, aged 69. Universally beloved and lamented. Also William Morley, Esq., 1832, aged 91. Also Sarah Morley, relict of the above William Morley, 1852, aged 79.

Nathaniel Collyer, Esq., 1819 aged 83.

Mr. John Dennison, late of this parish, wheelwright, 1820, aged 52.

Also Mrs. Mary Hannah Dennison, late wife of Mr. William Dennison, 1828, aged 26. Besides several other members of their family.

Mrs. Winifred Sims, the wife of the Rev. Joseph Sims, vicar of this parish, rector of St. John's, Westminster, 1768, aged 63, also the said Rev. Joseph Sims, 1776, aged 83.

Close by lie the remains of the Rev. Dr. Stukeley [1] in a spot which he had long fixed on, when on a visit to the Rev. Sims, the Vicar. By his own request "the turf was laid smoothly over his grave without any monument."

In the north Churchyard beneath the hedge is an armorial stone with the following inscription:

Here lieth the body of Dame Cecilia Garrard, widow of Sir Nicholas Garrard, Bart., who dyed the 8th day of July, 1753, in the eighty-first year of her age, and by her desire was buried in this place.

———————

The parish of East Ham comprises several hamlets, viz: Wall-End, Manor Park, and Plashet. The latter, which until recently was a small rural village, has grown into a busy little town, since the London Tilbury and Southend Railway have established a station there, under the name of Upton Park.

A short distance from the station is a large mansion of great antiquity, formerly called Green Street House. This house locally

---

[1] Dr. Stukeley, " the Archdruid of his age," as he was called, was born at Holbeach in Lincolnshire, in 1687. He received his education at Bennet Col., Cambridge, where he took his doctor's degree. He first began to practise at Boston, in his native country, but in 1717 he removed to London where he became a fellow of the College of Physicians of the Royal Society, and also of the Society of Antiquarians, to which he was secretary for many years In 1726 he left London and retired to Grantham, where he practised with great success. In 1729, by the encouragement of Archbishop Wake he entered into holy orders and the same year was presented with the living of All Saints in Stamford. In 1747 the Duke of Montague gave him the rectory of St. George, Queen Square, London, which he held till his death in 1765. His principal works are "Itinerarium Curiosum, Palaeographia Sacra or Discourses on the Monuments of Antiquity, that relate to sacred history." "History of Carausius," "Dissertation on the Spleen," etc. He died in London, 1765.

known as "Anne Boleyn's Castle," is a fine old red brick building, with brick gables facing the north, and a long gallery, fronting the ancient Green Street, at the north end of which stood a red brick Tudor archway. Inside the house there are, with the exception of some panel work and a black and white marble paved banquet-room, scarcely any features of interest; the adjoining grounds are

well laid out and shaded by some fine cedar trees of considerable antiquity. The most conspicuous feature is an old embattled octagon tower, standing a short distance from the house, at the end of a wall skirting the lane, and surmounted by a turret, which until recently bore a short flagstaff with a curious vane. The room in the third storey of this tower was at one time hung with leather, richly embossed with gold, but an avaricious owner of the property burnt these costly hangings in order to collect the precious metal, which was sold for £30. The lead having been also removed from the roof, the subsequent owner, Mr. Morley, had the upper part of the tower which had fallen into decay repaired (about the year 1800) and the roof—from which an extensive view is obtained over the Thames valley, of Greenwich Hospital, Shooter's Hill, and other places in Kent—recovered with copper.

There is a peculiar interest attached to this tower from a tradition that it was built for Anne Boleyn by her royal lover, Henry VIII., in the days of his courtship, and "that the beautiful Anne—to use the words of COLLER in his history of Essex—sat there listening to the wooing of a king, with the parting sigh of the cast off Catherine still fresh in his ears." The tale which may be read in the Gentleman's Magazine of the year 1833 is, that Anne Boleyn was betrothed to a young nobleman, who was deceased but ten months since, and the custom being, that she should complete the twelve-month of mourning for her lover, Henry built for her amusement this tower, from which she had "a view of the Thames from Greenwich to Gravesend."

Another tradition still lingering about the neighbourhood and religiously believed in is that, when the fickle passion of Henry VIII. had been quelled, the fair victim was for a time confined in this tower, whence she was taken to Greenwich, and so on to the Tower of London; and it is said, that the king was waiting there on the day that she was beheaded, until the Tower guns were fired as a signal of the completion of the sanguinary deed, on hearing which he started off with his attendants on a hunting party to Haynault Forest.

These traditions, however, are not supported by the statements of authentic history; the sceptic has also pointed to marks about the building of later date than that of Henry VIII.

As the early registers of East Ham, up to the year 1696, are entirely missing, it is impossible to trace the earlier occupants of this mansion, which is supposed to have been the seat of the Nevilles, whose monument we have seen in East Ham Church. We find, however, that in the middle of the 17th century it belonged to

NN

Sir Francis Holcroft, Kt., who afterwards conveyed it to Sir Thomas Garrard. Sir Thomas had two sons, Jacob and Nicolas; on the death of the former without male issue, his brother, Sir Nicolas, succeeded him in title and estate. He married Cecilia, daughter of Sir Edwin Steed, of Kent, but he also dying without issue, this seat and the chief of his estates descended, in 1727, to Sir Jacob Garrard Downing, Bart. Afterwards it became the property of a Mr. Barnes, who resided there for more than 50 years, and from him it was conveyed to William Morley, Esq. The Morleys sold it to the Archbishop, now Cardinal Manning, in 1869, when the red brick Tudor gateway was taken down and substantial buildings were erected which, in 1870, were opened as a Roman Catholic Reformatory School for boys, under the management of the "Brothers of Mercy," who teach the boys various useful trades and occupations, as shoemaking, tailoring, and baking, and also instruct them in the cultivation of the land, of which there are altogether about 14 acres.

Another mansion, noticeable for its having been for many years the home of Mrs. Elizabeth Fry, is:

Plashet House.

This pleasant country house with pretty gardens and a small park, well stocked with trees, was about the middle of the last century the property of Charles Hitch, a citizen of London, who purchased it of the heirs of Bendish and Heigham, and is said to have added to it two wings, in one of which was a large and beautiful drawing-room. In 1787, it passed into the hands of Mr. William Storrs Fry, whose son Joseph resided here with his wife Elizabeth, the prison philanthropist, from 1809 to 1829, in which year they removed to "Upton Lane." In recent years it was in the occupation of Mr. Raymond Pelly—second son of Sir John Henry Pelly—who lived here from 1860—1870. It then became the residence and property of Mr. Thomas Mathews, who, on his removal to Warley Elms, sold the estate, in 1883, to a building company, reserving, however, a small plot of land for the site of a church. Every trace of the old mansion having been swept away, and the beautiful park and gardens having been parcelled out for building, a movement was set on foot to perpetuate the memory of

Mrs. Elizabeth Fry's former connexion with the district by a memorial church.

To take this subject into further consideration an influential meeting was held, by the permission of his Grace the Duke of Westminster, at Grosvenor House, on June 20th, 1884, when it was resolved, that a place of worship would be a most appropriate memorial of her noble and self-denying work. Her Majesty the Queen readily approved the proposal, and since Mr. Thomas Mathews had kindly given a portion of the grounds for the site of a church, and large and small donations had been liberally subscribed, the foundation stone of St. Stephen's Church was laid by the Princess Louisa on the 7th of June, 1886. The royal visit created much interest in the neighbourhood, and the loyalty of the residents was evidenced by the gay appearance of the main thoroughfares and the hearty welcome which her Royal Highness received from those who were assembled to witness her arrival. The Princess was received at Upton Park Station by the High Sheriff, Mr. Henry Ford Barclay, and a guard of honour, formed by the 1st Essex Artillery Volunteers, under the command of Col. Howard. In an address to her Royal Highness, read by the Rev. Canon Procter, it was stated, "that although Mrs. Fry did not belong to the Church of England, it was felt that that church in her national character might fittingly commemorate one of the greatest female servants of England, and the first to lead the way in the noble work of women, which was so effectual in rescuing the out-cast and in seeking the lost."

The present incumbent of St. Stephen's Church is the Rev. W. G. Trousdale.

Besides the above-named houses there may yet be seen the remains of several other ancient mansions. One of them, which stood opposite the White Horse public house, is said to have been the seat of Sir Thomas Hart, who was Lord Mayor of London in 1589, and M.P. for the city. The stabling belonging to it, which is still standing, has been converted into cottages.

Another mansion, known by the familiar name of the " Clock House," and situate in the old Roman Road, now called High Street, was in past times the property and occasional residence of the ancestors of Mr. Ynyr Burges, who at the present time is the principal land-owner in the parish or East Ham. An old dilapidated iron gate still indicates the site of the old house, but most of the ground attached to it has within recent years been utilized for building purposes.

East Ham Hall — the old Manor House which with lands belonging to it was, after the dissolution of the Abbey of Stratford Langthorne, given by Henry VIII. to Richard Bream—stands near the old church, and is now a farm house.

About midway between the Church and the Beckton Road, the Metropolitan High Level Sewer in the form of a huge grass-covered embankment traverses, after having passed the marshes of West Ham and Plaistow, the broad track of marsh-land known as East Ham Level, which until the construction of the River wall was a portion of the estuary of the Thames. During the excavations for getting the ballast to make the embankment, about a quarter of a mile west of the Church, several leaden coffins and a stone coffin with a coped lid were disinterred (as has been already mentioned, page 3) besides cinerary urns with other Roman fictilia, whence it has been suggested, that the spot had been used as a place of sepulture by the force stationed at Uphall Camp, whilst the adjacent marsh was in course of reclamation from the river by captive Britons. Mr. YNYR BURGES in his remarks on Roman vestiges, found at East Ham, which were published in the 22nd vol. of the Archaelogical Journal, points out "that the Anglo-Saxons could scarcely have had the ability to carry out so gigantic an operation as the drainage of the marsh, and adds, that we may, therefore, reasonably conclude that the work was achieved by the Romans, who were skilled alike in the arts of peace as in those of war."

A large portion of East Ham Level is occupied by the Beckton Gas Works, which belong to the Gas Light and Coke Company and are among the most extensive yet constructed, covering about 150 acres of land. They were laid out in the year 1869, and give employment to no less than 3000 hands. Numerous dwellings having also been erected in close proximity to the works, for the accommodation of the workmen and officers, the lately dreary marsh has been converted into a busy thriving colony.

The parish of East Ham is much improved by a very excellent road, sixty feet wide, which was made in the year 1812. Joining the Commercial Road from the East India Docks, it crosses the river Lea by an iron bridge, and then passes through the village over two smaller bridges over the river Roding to Barking. Before this road was made, there existed only a narrow lane, called Wall-End Lane, which led from the point, where the road from Plashet intersects the Barking Road, to the little hamlet of Wall-End, and thence over two narrow bridges to the town of Barking. One of these bridges, the remains of which may still be seen within a short distance from the high road, close to the windmill, was called "Cow Bridge," and is said to have been so narrow, that no vehicle could pass it, unless the wheels on one side were first removed.

During the last ten years the parish of East Ham has almost entirely lost its rural character; while a few years ago it was still looked upon as a village of market gardens for the production of cabbages and onions, it is now fast becoming a manufacturing and residential town. It is marvellous to see the rapid manner in which building estates are being developed, and rows of dwellings are everywhere springing up at the shortest notice. Nowhere, perhaps, is this rapid growth more noticeable than in Gipsy Lane, the ancient Green Street, and at Manor Park, a rising locality situate to the north of the Ilford Road, with a station on the Great Eastern Railway. The wide area of arable lands, over which the plough passed not many years ago, has been gradually converted into streets of crowded dwellings, almost entirely inhabited by artizans and the humble city clerks, who are attracted by the low rents of the houses. It is worth mentioning here that, while in the time of Edward III. the whole parish of East Ham consisted of only 18 houses with 43 inhabitants, its population had in the beginning of the present century risen to 1165, and may now be estimated at about 20,000 souls.

Nor has the parish improved in point of numbers only, for since the year 1874 it has its own School Board, and there is no room for doubt, that the Board has done excellent work, the several schools, which have been erected within the last ten years, being a living testimony of its untiring energy and devotion to the welfare of the rapidly increasing population.

The Local Board of Health too, which was established in the year 1879, is exerting all its power to keep pace with the growth of the parish, as may be seen from the many improvements which have of late been effected.   The Board is now also about to embark on a most important and complete system of drainage, which cannot fail materially to assist in adding to the health and general well-being of the parishioners.

CONCLUSION.

HAVING traced the history of the parishes of East and West Ham, and the various changes they have undergone from the earliest period down to the present day, there remains but little to add. From small rural villages, which in past times abounded with pleasant villas and delightful residences of the nobility as well as of the wealthy and industrious citizens of London, who found here in the calm tranquillity of the country a quiet retreat from the cares of business and the din of a crowded city, they have in course of time been transformed into large and busy towns. The green pastures and smiling fields, which skirted the various roadsides, the shady walks and pleasant country lanes have gradually disappeared. No longer do the rich and noble turn to the east, and instead of the handsome mansions once inhabited by them, tall chimneys and busy factories, modern shops and inns, and dwellings of all shapes and sizes for the accomodation of Greater London meet the eye in every direction.

Until the middle of the century the great bulk of the population was settled along either side of the main street of Stratford, and at the more rural village of Plaistow, but since the construction of the Great Eastern Railway with its extensive Works at Stratford, and the establishment of the Thames Ironworks at Canning Town, followed by the formation of the Victoria and Albert Docks, the Beckton Gas Works, the London and Tilbury Company's Works at Plaistow, and many other factories, fresh districts have sprung up, and the whole neighbourhood is now a mass of bricks and mortar.

There are, perhaps, few towns, if any in England, that have with such miraculous rapidity increased in respect to population, as the parish of West Ham. In the beginning of the century its population was about 6000, in 1850 it had risen to 18,000 but at the present time it falls scarcely short of 200,000, so that, with the exception of the vast metropolis, it now stands tenth in the list of the great towns and cities in England and Wales. Thus, teeming with numbers, alive with industry, and steadily extending its trade and commerce, it is now not only the most populous town of the southern division of Essex, but also a commercial and manufacturing centre of the first importance.

The parish, which with reference to secular matters is divided into three wards, respectively designated, Stratford, Church Street, and Plaistow, includes 13 ecclesiastical districts. Not many years ago there were, besides the mother church of All Saints, but few places of worship; within recent years, however, great efforts have been made to supply the spiritual wants of the ever-growing population, and the numerous Churches, Chapels, and Mission Halls of all creeds and confessions, that have been erected throughout the whole parish, bear witness, that there has been great activity in religious matters.

Much has also been effected in the way of education by the West Ham School Board, which was formed in 1871; during the 17 years of its existence no less than 23 Board Schools have been established, providing education for nearly 25,000 scholars. There can be little doubt that the Board has ample work on hand, to keep pace with the requirements of a population which increases at the rate of many thousands a year.

By the Redistribution scheme, which came into operation in 1885, West Ham has obtained direct Parliamentary representation, the Borough being divided into North and South; the present members are Mr. J. F. Fulton for the northern, and Major G. E. Banes for the southern division.

In 1886, West Ham was accorded a Royal Charter of Incorporation, by which the new corporate body took over the duties and responsibilities of the Local Board of Health, which had governed the town under the Public Health Acts since the year 1856. The Corporation is composed of a Mayor, 12 Aldermen, and 36 Councillors, who are elected by the Burgesses of the four wards of Stratford, Forest Gate, Plaistow, and Canning Town, into which the borough is divided for municipal purposes. The first election took place on the 1st of November of the same year, and on the 9th of November following, Mr. John Meeson was unanimously chosen the first Mayor.

John Meeson, Esq., J.P., the first Mayor of West Ham.

Bearing in mind that Mr. Meeson entered upon a quite new office, with no traditions to follow, the responsibilities resting upon him as the first mayor were by no means light; but being possessed of an intimate knowledge of the borough and of an unsurpassed command over matters of local government, he was equal ⁑ to the task imposed upon him, and it is only fair to

oo

acknowledge that with the cordial assistance of an energetic council he performed his various and onerous duties with great tact and skill, as well as with great credit to himself and to the general satisfaction of the burgesses.

On the 9th of November, 1887, Mr. Meeson retired from his office, full of honours, and Mr. Alderman Hay was elected his successor without a dissentient voice, and was at once invested by the out-going mayor with the chain of office. Since his election Mr. Hay has most earnestly devoted himself to the important duties devolving upon him, and has by his ardour and zeal in the discharge of his multifarious functions and engagements proved himself well qualified for the office of Mayor.

There is no doubt of the fact that, during the short time of its existence, the Town Council has exercised great energy and watchfulness in its endeavours to amend the condition of this extensive and densely peopled district, and looking forward to the future, we may confidently hope that every effort will be used to make further sanitary improvements and local reforms, which will materially assist in fortifying the health and in promoting the prosperity of the Borough of West Ham.

INDEX.

ILLUSTRATIONS.

MAPS.

LIST OF SUBSCRIBERS.

Adams, W., Loxford, Barking.
Angell, Lewis, Town Hall, Stratford.
Atkins, Samuel Elliot, East Ham House, East Ham, E.
Banes, Geo. E., M.P., Chestnut House, Plaistow, E.
Barclay, J. G., Leyton, Essex, E.
Barclay, Henry Ford, Monkhams, Woodford, Essex.
Bawtree, John, Colchester.
Boardman, C., Grove House, Stratford, E.
Breeze, Louis, Broadway, Stratford, E.
Bunsen, Madame de, Abbey Lodge, Regent's Park, N.W.
Burges, Ynyr H., Colonel, Parkanaur, Castle Caulfield, Tyrone, Ireland.
Burges, J. Y., Parkanaur, Castle Caulfield, Tyrone, Ireland.
Buxton, Dowager Lady, Colne House, Cromer, Norwich.
Buxton, T. F., Sir, Bart., Brewery, Spitalfields.
Buxton, T. F., Easneye, Ware.
Buxton, E. N., Knighton, Buckhurst Hill.
Buxton, C. L., Bolwick, Marsham, Norwich. Esq.,
Buxton, A. F., 5, Hyde Park Street, W.
Buxton, Gerald, Knighton, Buckhurst Hill.
Casselton, E., 55, Romford Road, Stratford, E.
Cockett, John, Wanstead, E.
Cohu, Thomas, Black Lion, Plaistow, E.
Courtney, G. H., Rutland House, The Grove, Stratford, E.
Creswell, Mrs., Bank House, King's Lynn, Norfolk.
Crouch, Walter, F.Z.S., Grafton House, Wanstead, E.
Crow, William, 140, The Grove, Stratford, E.
Cunnington, A., Braintree.
Curtis, Miss Mary, The Hall, Plaistow, E.

Curtis, Edward Charles, Mortimer Lodge, Romford Road, Forest Gate, E.
Curtis, Robert Leabon, The Broadway, Plaistow, E.
Curwen, John S., Herne House, Upton Lane, Forest Gate, E.
Curwen, Spedding, Upton House, Upton Lane, Forest Gate, E.
Dennison, Thomas, High Street North, East Ham, E.
Dennison, John W., East Ham, Essex, E.
Dorton, John, Macgregor Hall, Maryland Point, Stratford, E.
Dowling, James L., Romford Road, Upton, Forest Gate, E.
Drake, Arthur, Stratford, E.
Durrant, Edmund, 90, High Street, Chelmsford.
East, J. T., The Limes, North End, East Ham, E.
Edwards, George Canning, 178, Romford Road, Stratford, E.
Fairchild, The Rev. J., Training College, Carnarvon, Wales.
Freeman, Joseph, The Green, Stratford, E.
Fry, Mrs., The Cleeve, Ore, Hastings.
Fry, Joseph, Fairkytes, Hornchurch.
Fry, Walter J. 38, Duke Street, St. James, S.W.
Fry, Wendover, 3, Crosby Square, E.C.
Fry, H. W., Dashwood House, London, E.C.
Fry, Gurney S., Silverhill, St. Leonards.
Fry, Henry D., Colchester.
Garrett, Edmund, Lieut.-Col. Shrewsbury House, East Ham, E.
Gingell, Miss, Highfield House, Southampton,
Govier, Albert, 125, The Grove, Stratford.
Green, Joseph J., Tayspill House, Stansted Montfichet, Essex.
Guildhall Library, City.
Gurney, J. H. Northrepps Hall, Norwich.
Gurney, Mrs., Sprowston Hall, Norwich.
Gurney, Mrs. Samuel, 42, Sussex Square, Brighton.
Harrison, Mrs. Smith, Woodford, Essex.
Hay, George, Mayor of West Ham, 17, Broadway, Stratford, E.
Heward, S Barclay, 28, Threadneedle Street, E.C.
Hilleary, G. E., Fernbank, Stratford, E.
Hilleary, Mrs., Fernbank, Stratford, E.
Hoare, Samuel, M.P Cromer, Norfolk.
Hoare, E. Brodie, M.P., St. Bernards, Caterham.
Hogg, Mrs., The Cottage, West Ham Park, West Ham, E.
Howard, David, City Mills, Stratford, E.
Howard, Wm. D., City Mills, Stratford, E.

Hubbard, C. E., The Rev., St. Michael's Rectory, Lichfield.
Jackson, Jesse, Leyton, E.
Jackson, John, Balaam Str., Plaistow, E.
Kennedy, J. B., Stratford Hall, Stratford, E.
Kidd, John, Wine Office Court, Fleet Street, E.C.
Lawford, Godfrey, Loughton, Essex.
Lawrence, J., The Lodge, West Ham Park, West Ham, E.
Linington, G. E., East Ham, E.
Luckin, J., 70, Amity Road, West Ham, E.
Martin, Fred. S., High Meads Manor, Stratford, E.
Mathews, Thomas, Warley Elms, Brentwood, Essex.
Matthey, Rich. D., 97, Belgrave Road, S.W.
Maw, James, Blenheim House, Margery Park, Forest Gate, E.
Meeson, John, J.P., Witham Lodge, Stratford, E.
Morley, John, Heathlands, Chadwell Heath.
Noble, C. A., White House, East Ham, E.
Nevill, James, British Lion, West Ham Lane, West Ham, E.
Nutting, H. W. W., 106, Southwark Street, S.E.
Pelly, Richard, Capt., R.N., Forest Rise, Walthamstow, E.
Pelly, Mrs., Hollington, Sussex.
Pelly, R. P., The Rev., St. John's Vicarage, Stratford, E.
Pelly, D., St. John's Vicarage, Stratford, E.
Pelly, John Gurney, Goldings, Loughton, Essex.
Poole, F. 51, Hamfrith Road, Stratford, E.
Powell, Nath., Buckhurst Hill, Essex.
Price, Ralph, Marshalls, Romford.
Ram, Geo. S., The Rev., St. Peter's Vicarage, Bournemouth.
Ram, A. J., 3, Chester Square, S.W.
Ram, R. Digby, The Rev., Hampton, Middlesex.
Ripley, Mrs., Earlham Hall, Norwich.
Sant, Edward, The Rev., Portway, West Ham, E.
Savage, W. H. Local, Board, East Ham, E.
Scott, Th., The Rev. Canon, The Vicarage, West Ham, E.
Seale, Joshua B., Plaistow Lodge, Balaam Street, Plaistow, E.
Sedgwick, G. A., Linton, Upton Lane, Forest Gate, E.
Self, Jer., 69, The Grove, Stratford, E.
Sewell, Fr., 38, Redcliffe Square, W.
Sewell, H. Balaam Street, Plaistow, E.
Shand, Alex. F., Oakdale, Eden Bridge, Kent.

Sheppard, Sam. G., 28, Threadneedle Street, E.C.
Smith, Fred., 84, Romford Road, Stratford, E.
Squiers, S. W. Horndon-on-Hill.
Streatfield, Mrs., Charts Edge, Westerham.
Streatfeild, W. C., The Rev., Kingsworthy Rectory, Winchester.
Tanner, Howard, The Elms, Stratford, E.
Thornber, J. H., 37, Hamfrith Road, Stratford, E.
Tricker, Reuben, 10, Crescent Road, Upton Manor, Plaistow, E.
Ursula Convent, Upton Lane, Forest Gate, E.
Wentworth, Steph. T., The Ferns, Cecil Road, Upton, West Ham, E.
Whitworth, J. C., Broadway, Stratford, E.

Lightning Source UK Ltd.
Milton Keynes UK
UKOW062037090713

213518UK00010B/620/P

9 781241 604943